The Essential Guide to VMS Utilities and Commands

The Essential Guide to VMS Utilities and Commands

VMS Version 5

Paula Sharick

VAN NOSTRAND REINHOLD
New York

Copyright © 1990 by Van Nostrand Reinhold

Library of Congress Catalog Card Number   90-32256
ISBN 0-442-00266-1

Printed in the United States of America

Van Nostrand Reinhold
115 Fifth Avenue
New York, New York 10003

Van Nostrand Reinhold International Company Limited
11 New Fetter Lane
London EC4P 4EE, England

Van Nostrand Reinhold
480 La Trobe Street
Melbourne, Victoria 3000, Australia

Nelson Canada
1120 Birchmount Road
Scarborough, Ontario M1K 5G4, Canada

16 15 14 13 12 11 10 9 8 7 6 5 4 3 2 1

Library of Congress Cataloging-in-Publication Data

Sharick, Paula, 1947–
The essential guide to VMS utilities and commands : VMS version 5
/ Paula Sharick.
p.   cm.
ISBN 0-442-00266-1
1. VAX/VMS (Computer operating system)   I. Title.
QA76.76.063S54   1990
005.4'44--dc20   90-32256
                                                                          CIP

Contents

Preface

The Essential Guide to VMS Utilities and Commands is the result of repeated requests I have received over the last several years from friends, associates, and clients. Given the length, depth, and breadth of the VMS documentation set, there is clearly a need for a single guide that introduces the material needed by beginning and intermediate users.

Within these pages, you will find an explanation of many important VMS concepts, but only as much as needed to get you up and running smoothly. Purposely, many fine points of the operating system and unnecessary command details have been omitted. If you have the stamina to go through the book from cover to cover, you can expect to be fairly skilled by the time you complete Chapter 16. Information not included here can be easily collected from the master VAX/VMS documentation set, from the online HELP utility, or from DEC's Bookreader product which reads the VMS documentation set on a CD.

As there is no replacement for hands-on practice, I encourage you to try the examples as you work through the material. Also, try the exercises and compare your answers with those included with each exercise. Be advised that under normal circumstances, there is absolutely no way you can break or destroy VMS, regardless of the mistakes that you make. Although you may find the error messages cryptic, as is the case with most operating systems, patience and perseverance will carry you through.

I do have a few words to say about the title of this book. The use of "Utilities and Commands" is based on common folklore rather than fact. There are many more commands than utilities in VMS — but the accepted description of the base information set required for a working knowledge of VMS is "Utilities and Commands," rather than vice versa.

Acknowledgments

I want to thank my extended network of friends and professional acquaintances, without whose encouragement and support I probably never would have finished this book. In particular, I would like to recognize the technical contributions of Gina Boice and Don Huffman and to thank Tom Warren and Kata McCarville for their editorial expertise. Finally, I would like to thank Auto-Trol Corporation for access to the corporate VAXcluster during preparation of this book.

1

Introduction

THE VMS OPERATING SYSTEM

Digital Equipment Corporation (DEC) celebrated the tenth anniversary of the VMS operating system in 1987 with fireworks and a birthday cake. From a small single-processor operating system, VMS has grown to support multiple processors in a single cabinet and many configurations, including the desktop VAX, local area networks, VAXclusters, and wide area networks. VMS installations circle the globe, at tens of thousands of locations worldwide.

The sophistication and flexibility required to support these extended configurations create ever increasing demands on the sophistication of VMS users. First-time users can feel overwhelmed when faced with the task of becoming proficient using the VMS operating system. The first instinct of new users is to refer directly to the master documentation set.

THE DOCUMENTATION JUNGLE

In fact, intimidation is a common reaction from anyone who has stood in front of the VAX/VMS documentation set for the first time. I have two bookcases in my office. One has 34 bright orange three-inch binders documenting Version 4 of VMS, the other 34 corporate grey three-inch binders for Version 5 of VMS. Together, these technical reference manuals consume 22 feet of shelf space, packed tight.

The full documentation set is large and very expensive. Few installations have more than one or two master sets, which makes finding the correct reference manual a difficult task. At some sites, you may have to check out the manuals or use them in a library. We all learn better if we have reference material at our fingertips.

Even if you have ready access to the documentation set, as a novice in the VMS world you can search in vain through the titles to find a primer or beginner's guide. Surprise! The General User documentation consists of ten gigantic grey binders. The master list of VMS commands, the *DCL Dictionary*, has 679 pages for Version 5.0. It's hard to get started when the task looks so overwhelming.

This book will help you acquire a basic working knowledge of VMS without having to wade through the documentation jungle. You can get started without covering your desk and part of the floor with a multitude of binders, all open to different pages related to the same command or topic. In a reduced form, the material in this book has been used for several years by thousands of users, from undergraduate and graduate students to clerical and administrative users, to experienced application programmers, operators and new system managers.

INTENDED AUDIENCE

Technically, this text assumes you are "computer literate," which means you understand a little about how a computer works, what a file is and how files are used, and have a basic understanding of file manipulation. For example, you know an editor is used to create a text file, you are familiar with copy, rename, and delete file operations, and you understand how to move files from one location to another. You know that files are stored on a disk, hardcopy comes from a line printer, and can find the on/off switch on your terminal.

You are a member of the target audience if you have used a micro, mini or mainframe computer for more than six months. If your experience is mostly with menu-driven applications, I encourage you to take a computer literacy class. There is no replacement for basic concepts, and familiarity with basic concepts will make a huge difference in how quickly you acquire new skills.

BOOK OVERVIEW

This book begins by discussing VAX hardware and configurations and the VMS operating system. Then we learn how to use a terminal server, how to log in, and how to look at the user environment. This is followed by a review of the rules for entering valid VMS commands and an in-depth lesson on the VMS HELP utility.

The bulk of commands are organized into five chapters (Chapters 9-13): files and directories, file manipulation, file protection, the EVE text editor, and printing. A chapter is devoted to electronic MAIL, followed by a chapter that reviews several of the most popular VMS utilities. Chapter 16 covers the commands and techniques you can use to personalize your VMS environment.

This organization reflects my personal philosophy that users gain a better under-standing of a new computing environment if they first understand how the en-vironment is constructed. Then as commands are explained, each fits nicely like a puzzle piece into the big picture.

For example, when you understand the configurations in which a VAX can be found, the SHOW commands make a lot of sense. Likewise, understanding con-figurations helps explain why there are six parts in a complete VMS file specifica-tion and when and where each part is necessary.

VAX Hardware and VMS Software

After teaching this material for several years, I have found that a few basic con-cepts about the VAX (the hardware) and VMS (the operating system) help you un-derstand how the world works according to DEC. Chapter 2 starts off with a quick review of VAX hardware from the standpoint of interconnectivity and com-patibility. The components of the VMS operating system are examined, along with the functions they perform, and how they relate to users.

Terminal Servers

If you are in a standalone VAX environment, you can skip Chapter 3. However, your installation probably has several networked VAX systems that provide user access via DEC terminal servers. Before you can log in to the VAX, you must first log in to a terminal server.

This chapter discusses the function of terminal servers and the commands used to connect to a specific node or application. Although Ethernet terminal servers are available from many vendors, this book is dedicated to VMS, so only the com-mands used with DEC terminal servers are covered. All the examples in this chap-ter were created on a DECserver 200 — commands and output from other server models may vary slightly.

Logging In and Logging Out

Once you have passed the terminal server barrier, you are ready to log in to a VMS system. Chapter 4 covers logging in, login messages, the system prompt, passwords and security considerations, the password generator, and logging out. The exercises at the end of this chapter integrate information from the terminal server lesson and demonstrate some of the features of multiple server sessions.

The User Environment

Chapter 5 presents an overview of the user environment, which consists of terminals and terminal setup mode, an electronic mail file, printers, and a login file. Next we introduce VMS concepts that are central to the user environment: username, account, user authorization parameters, User Identification Code (UIC), and the use of standard input, output, and error devices. Finally, several pages are devoted to a discussion of the VMS process, process privileges, process quotas, and process priority.

In Chapter 6, we explore several versions of the SHOW command that allow you to examine the user environment and the system environment. You learn how to identify other users logged in to your system, how to examine process characteristics and terminal characteristics, and how to display cluster and network configuration information.

Digital Command Language

Chapter 7 starts with a review of the rules for entering correct commands using the Digital Command Language (DCL). Next is a quick lesson on command line editing, which involves using control characters to correct mistakes rather than retyping the entire command line. A built-in VMS feature allows you to recall your last 20 commands using the UP arrow key, CTRL/B, or the RECALL command. Becoming proficient with command line editing saves many keystrokes and improves your efficiency on the system.

Online HELP

Chapter 8 is an in-depth lesson on the HELP utility, which provides extensive information on all the utilities and commands supported by VMS. We discuss HELP information organization, HELP prompts, and the various ways in which you can request information. If you learn the HELP utility well, you will probably never need one of those three-inch binders unless you plan to become a software developer.

Files, Directories and File Manipulation

Chapter 9 begins by reviewing the complete VMS file specification, including the remote file specification used to access files across a network. Then we delve into directories, your "home" directory, and creating new directories under your home directory.

We learn how to examine the current directory location, and how to move from one location to another. We explore using the DIRECTORY command to search for files located anywhere in a directory tree, along with the use of wildcards, the ellipsis, and absolute and relative file specifications. Last, this chapter examines the four dates the system stores in each file header, and how these dates are used with the DIRECTORY command.

Once we understand how to create directories and move around in a directory tree structure, we learn how to manipulate files and structures using the base set of VMS file manipulation commands. Chapter 10 covers CREATE, TYPE, COPY, RENAME, APPEND, DELETE, PURGE, RUN, and SPAWN. Each command is accompanied by several examples, which you are encouraged to try as you read through the material. Finally, we examine several file attributes, including file ownership, version limits, and the backup attribute, and the commands used to examine and modify them.

File Protection

Chapter 11 contains a lesson on the basics of VMS file security, including volume, directory, and file protection. We review the file protection code and the commands used to examine and change protection (SET and SHOW PROTECTION). This ensures that you understand the levels of file security and are able to properly delete files, directories and complex directory structures.

EVE Text Editor

Chapter 12 covers EVE, the most popular text editor provided with VMS. EVE has a large set of programmed functions and is easily customized to suit individual editing styles. When you define new functions, they can be automatically loaded each time you start the editor. Additional EVE features support multiple windows and allow you to edit multiple text files during a single editing session. EVE also provides a direct interface to VMS so you can read your mail or perform nearly any other DCL command without terminating your edit session.

Printing and Print Queues

Now that you can create and manipulate files, you are ready for print queues and the PRINT command in Chapter 13. VMS allows you to control many aspects of a print job, including the time it is started, the number of copies, and which pages to print. We discuss queue concepts and terminology, learn how to identify the printers on your system, and learn how to identify and use predefined forms on the printer of your choice.

Electronic MAIL

Chapter 14 covers electronic MAIL which is the most popular VMS utility. We review commands for sending, receiving and printing messages to a single user, several users, and to a distribution list. Then we cover the more sophisticated commands used to extract messages to an external text file, and to create and manage folders in which messages are stored. MAIL has an excellent HELP utility and a predefined keypad with 35 MAIL commands.

Utilities

Chapter 15 reviews some of the more popular utilities: PHONE, SEARCH, DIF-FERENCES, and SORT/MERGE. PHONE is an excellent tool for communicating with any user logged in to the system and provides most of the features of a real telephone. The SEARCH utility locates a word, string, or phrase in one or more files and DIFFERENCES compares files and highlights where they are different.

The SORT and MERGE utilities are handy for ordering and combining files. Any file can be organized using one or more alphabetic or numeric fields in ascending or descending order. The exercises at the end of this chapter should make you comfortable with all these utilities.

Personalizing Your Environment

Chapter 16 explains personalizing your environment with several SET commands and custom key definitions. This chapter also covers creating abbreviations for commands (symbols), a shorthand notation for file specifications (logical names), and an introductory lesson on command procedures. Last, this chapter shows you how to create, test, and use a login file.

EXAMPLES

All the examples in this book were created using Version 5.2 of VMS. If you are running an earlier version of the operating system, some of the commands may not be available and some may not work exactly as shown here. You can expect everything you learn in this book to translate directly to any future release of VMS. As always, VMS commands remain upwardly compatible from one release to the next.

EXERCISES

I encourage you to try all the commands included in each chapter. We have worked very hard to make sure every single example is accurate and correct. Nothing is more frustrating than an example that doesn't work, and I have encountered more than my fair share after 20 years in the computing business. The answers to each exercise can be found following the exercises themselves. As with most things, there is frequently more than one correct answer to each problem. Well, take a deep breath and plunge in. Believe it or not, this is going to be fun!

CONVENTIONS

This book follows Digital Equipment Corporation conventions with respect to command format, syntax, and notation and all key names are shown in uppercase. Once familiar with these conventions, you will be able to read the master VMS documentation set with no additional instruction. All prompts and system messages are displayed exactly as they appear in VMS.

RETURN key

All terminal server commands, VMS commands, and utilities are completed with the RETURN key. This key is referenced in the text, but is not shown when the commands are illustrated or used.

ENTER Key

The ENTER key is in the lower right corner on the numeric keypad of a DEC or DEC compatible terminal. This key is used with terminal setup mode and with the EVE text editor. In the EVE editor, ENTER and RETURN are interchangeable.

CTRL Key

On a DEC keyboard, the control key is located on the lower left side of the keyboard next to the SHIFT key. VMS understands many two-key control functions. These combination keys are represented as CTRL/key, which indicates that you press and hold CTRL, then press the other key. For example, enter CTRL/Y by pressing CTRL and Y at the same time.

Command Description and Output

All commands are presented in uppercase. In each command description, formal parameters are represented in lowercase and usually hyphenated to indicate that no blanks are allowed in a parameter. Parameters are represented in uppercase when used in examples. Wherever you see commands and parameters in uppercase and boldface, you can assume that you are looking at a legal VMS command. Command output is shown exactly as it is generated by VMS.

Square Brackets

In each command description, square brackets indicate the enclosed item is optional. However, square brackets are mandatory when you specify a directory name alone or as part of a file specification.

Lists

The horizontal ellipsis (,...) indicates that one or more parameters may be entered on the command line, as long as each is separated from the previous one by a comma.

Double Quotes

A string is composed of letters, numbers, special punctuation and blanks. When you are to provide a string as a parameter, it is noted as "string" in the command format. If the string you use contains blanks or special punctuation or you want to preserve the case, enclose it in double quotes.

Parentheses

When special characters are referenced, the name of the character is given, followed by the actual character in parentheses. For example, there are many references to the asterisk character (*). Use only the special character, not the parentheses, in a VMS command.

OTHER INFORMATION SOURCES

The master VMS documentation consists of 34 volumes organized into three categories: System Management, Programmer, and General User. The General User documentation contains ten volumes, several of which augment the material in this book.

- Volume 2B, *Using VMS* (Mail, Phone, Sort/Merge)
- Volume 4, *The DCL Dictionary* (DCL commands)
- Volumes 6A and 6B, *System Messages and Recovery Procedures*

The *Digital Dictionary*, available from Digital Press, contains a master glossary of all terms referenced in the VMS documentation set. You may find this an excellent addition to your VMS reference material.

Digital Equipment Corporation supports some 50,000 DEC users through free membership in DECUS, the Digital Equipment Corporation Users Society, which sponsors both national and local activities. Contact the National DECUS office in Marlboro, Massachusetts (508-480-3259) for more information.

VMS General User Documentation Set

- Volume 1: *General Information*. Master Index, General User Master Index, and Glossary

- Volume 2A: *Using VMS*. Using VMS, Guide to Using VMS, Guide to Files and Directories

- Volume 2B: *Using VMS*. Mail, Phone, Sort/Merge

- Volume 3: *Using DCL*. DCL Concepts, Guide to Using Command Procedures

- Volume 4: *DCL Dictionary*

- Volume 5A: *Processing Text*. Guide to Text Processing, EDT Reference

- Volume 5B: *Processing Text*. VAX TPU Reference

- Volume 5C: *Processing Text*. Digital Standard Runoff (DSR)

- Volume 6A: *System Messages*. System Messages and Recovery Procedures, Part I, (A-L)

- Volume 6B: *System Messages*. System Messages and Recovery Procedures, Part II, (M-Z)

Volumes 6A and 6B contain an exhaustive list of VMS messages, a possible cause of the problem, and corrective action. The messages are ordered alphabetically by the facility within VMS that generated the error.

VMS System Management Documentation Set

- Volume 1A: *Setup*. System Management Master Index, Introduction to System Management, Guide to Setting Up a System, SYSMAN

- Volume 1B: *Setup*, VAXcluster Manual, EXCHANGE, Install, LAT Control Program (LAT), SYSGEN, Terminal Fallback

- Volume 2: *Maintenance*. Guide to Maintaining a System, Analyze/Disk_Structure, Backup, BAD, Error Log, Mount

- Volume 3: *Security*. Guide to System Security, Access Control List (ACL) Editor, Authorize

- Volume 4: *Performance*. Guide to Performance Management, Accounting, Monitor, Show Cluster

- Volume 5A: *Networking*. Guide to DECNET-VAX Networking, Networking Manual

- Volume 5B: *Networking*. Networking Control Program (NCP), DTS/DTR

VMS Programming Documentation Set

- Volume 1: *Introduction.* Programming Master Index, Guide to Programming Resources, Guide to Creating Modular Procedures

- Volume 2A: *Utilities.* Debugger

- Volume 2B: *Utilities.* Command Definition, Librarian, Linker, Message, Patch, SUMSLP

- Volume 3: *System Routines.* Introduction to System Routines, Utility Routines

- Volume 4A: *System Services.* Introduction to System Services

- Volume 4B: *System Services.* System Services Reference Manual

- Volume 5A: *Run-Time Library.* Introduction to Run-Time Library, DECtalk (DTK$), Mathematics (MTH$), General Purpose (OTS$), Parallel Processing (PPL$)

- Volume 5B: *Run-Time Library.* Library (LIB$)

- Volume 5C: *Run-TIme Library.* Screen Management (SMG$), String Manipulation (STR$)

- Volume 6A: *File System.* Guide to File Applications. Analyze/RMS_FILE, Convert and Convert/Reclaim, File Definition Language (FDL), National Character Set (NCS)

- Volume 6B: *File System.* Record Management Services (RMS)

- Volume 7A: *System Programming.* I/O Users: Part I, I/O Users: Part II

- Volume 7B: *System Programming.* Delta/Xdelta, System Dump Analyzer (SDA)

- Volume 8: *Device Support Manual.*

- Volume 9: *VAX MACRO.* VAX MACRO and Instruction Set

The first volume in each set contains a very complete index. If you are searching for specific information check the index first— you can normally find the exact subject you are looking for.

## 2

VAX Hardware and VMS Software

INTRODUCTION

After teaching this material for several years, I have found that a few basic concepts about the VAX (the hardware) and VMS (the operating system) help you understand how the world works according to DEC. This chapter starts off with a review of VAX hardware and the most common VAX configurations. Then we examine the main components of the operating system from a user persepctive, the functions they perform and how they interrelate.

VAX ARCHITECTURE OVERVIEW

Digital Equipment Corporation has been making computers for more than 25 years. In the mid-1960s, DEC introduced the PDP-11 16-bit minicomputer, which has been one of the most popular small computer systems ever built. There are tens of thousands of these PDPs still in use today worldwide. In the early 1970s, DEC started development of the VAX 32-bit system that has provided users with adequate computing power for more than a decade.

The VAX architecture includes both the hardware (VAX) and the operating system (VMS). The VAX is based on a 32-bit CPU (Central Processing Unit) chip which, when first introduced, greatly extended the power of the minicomputer class of machines. The 32-bit CPU supports a program address space of over four gigabytes, compared with the 64K limit of 16-bit CPUs. This four-gigabyte address space is called virtual memory because it greatly exceeds the physical memory capacity of the computer system. When the VAX was introduced, no system could support four gigabytes of main memory, or four gigabytes of disk space, for that matter.

The VAX architecture allows developers to easily create and run programs much larger than the physical memory installed in the machine. In earlier systems, a program larger than physical memory had to be segmented by the programmer and loaded in pieces. The VAX architecture manages this process transparently with a special set of hardware registers that translate a 32-bit virtual address into an address within the bounds of the installed memory. The virtual memory management of the original design was on the cutting edge of operating system technology in the 1970s. In keeping with this state-of-the-art technology, the developers selected the hardware term VAX for Virtual Address eXtension, and the software term VMS for Virtual Memory System.

The early VAX chip was so successful that Digital Equipment Corporation poured millions of research dollars into making the chip more compact and faster. During the last 12 years, the VAX chip has been continually refined. The first two-board VAX now fits on a single card and runs from 3-40 times faster than the original version.

In 1977 DEC introduced the original VAX family, consisting of the 11/780, 11/750, and 11/730 systems and there are still many of these workhorses running today, albeit much more slowly than any of the newer processors. You may even have one of these systems at your site. Since then, DEC has introduced many new VAX product lines, including the MicroVAX 3000 series, the 8000 series, and more recently, the 6000 and 9000 product lines.

Until recently, DEC used only the VMS operating system on all versions of the VAX hardware. You use the same commands and utilities on the 780 that you use on a VAXstation 3100, an 8800, and a 6440. The skills you acquire from this book will transfer to any VMS system from the desktop VAX to the multi-CPU configurations that are so popular today.

VAX HARDWARE COMPONENTS

You may have a standalone VAX at your site, in which case terminals and other peripherals (including line printers, laser printers, and tape drives) are directly connected to the computer. The basic hardware components of any VAX are illustrated in Figure 2-1. Each system contains four basic components: a console, a CPU, memory, and an Input/Output subsystem.

Console

The console is "command central" for the computer. Operators and system managers use the console to boot (start) or shut down the machine, run diagnostics, and perform maintenance activities. Although the actual hardware components vary from one VAX product line to the next, each console contains a terminal and keyboard, a boot medium (floppy disk, hard disk, or tape) and a minicomputer that understands and executes the low-level instructions necessary for startup, shutdown, and performing hardware diagnostics.

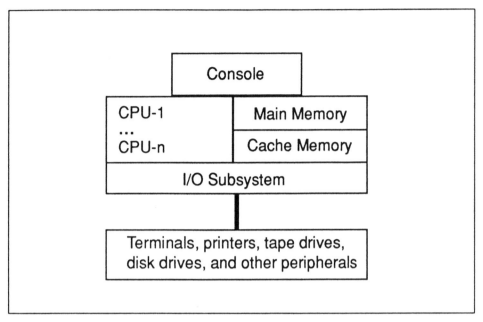

Figure 2-1. VAX Hardware Components

Main Memory

Main memory provides high-speed access to data. When programs are not in use they are stored on slow peripherals (*e.g.*, hard disk or tape drives). When a program is activated, it is moved to main memory so it can be accessed quickly by the CPU. Data moves from main memory to the CPU and back again on a special path called a memory bus. Each of the VAX product lines has a memory bus that accurately matches the computing power of the available CPUs — a fast processor or several processors must have a correspondingly fast memory bus to ensure data is available to each processor in a timely fashion.

Cache Memory

Cache memory is faster than regular memory and temporarily holds data being manipulated by the CPU. The data stored in cache memory can be moved to the CPU 20 percent faster than data located in main memory. The size and speed of cache memory varies from one product line to the next, but in all cases, cache significantly enhance the performance of a VAX system.

Central Processing Unit (CPU)

The 32-bit CPU performs all the work done by the system. Data moves from cache memory or main memory to the CPU, is manipulated in one of 16 hardware registers, and moves back to cache or main memory until it is needed again. In multiprocessor systems, each CPU works independently and special code in the operating system coordinates and manages shared processor resources.

Input/Output Subsystem

Every computer system has a special path used for moving data from main memory to a disk drive, tape drive, line printer, terminal, or other external storage device. This Input and Output (I/O) subsystem consists of an electrical path that connects the external devices and special programs called device drivers that understand how each device works. The devices that comprise the I/O subsystem vary from one installation to the next and each VAX product line has different I/O subsystem characteristics which are designed to balance the availability of externally stored data with the speed of the CPU(s).

MULTIPROCESSOR CONFIGURATIONS

In response to the ever-increasing demands for computing power, DEC began exploring systems with multiple CPUs in the early 1980s. The first dual-processor system introduced was the 11/782. Adding a second processor required modification to the operating system to make use of the second CPU. This resulted in a version of VMS that could use two processors — one CPU did all the computation, the other managed input and output.

This implementation of the operating system (Version 4 of VMS) was termed "asymmetric processing," because the work was not evenly shared by both processors. Asymmetric processing enhanced the ability of a VAX to perform work, but the increase provided only a 20-30 percent improvement over the single-CPU configuration. The performance gain did not justify the additional cost associated with the second processor. Since the original dual-processor configuration, VMS has undergone several incarnations aimed at efficiently managing multiple processors. Under Version 5 of VMS, adding another CPU results in a gain of up to 90-95 percent of the new processor capacity. This version of VMS is called SMP for "symmetric multiprocessing," a term that describes sharing work evenly among all available processors.

Version 5 of VMS also introduced a parallel processing library that allows software developers to implement applications with parallel processing techniques. Parallel processing involves breaking a program into several independent tasks, which allows all available CPUs to work on parts of the same problem concurrently. For heavy computational programs, parallel processing techniques at best provide a linear increase in execution speed (double for a dual-processor system, quadruple for a four-processor system, and so on). Parallel processing should be an area of rapid growth for DEC and third-party software developers in the next several years. We can expect large modeling programs and transaction processing systems to take advantage of parallel processing techniques during the early 1990s.

LOCAL AREA NETWORKS

Several years after the VAX was introduced, increased demands resulted in two, three, and four systems being installed in many computer rooms — Digital Equipment Corporation itself experienced this growth in its corporate computing systems. And, with multiple systems, the need arose for sharing data among systems. DEC introduced DECnet, a networking package of hardware and software to allow a user on one system to access data on other networked systems.

A network consists of both physical and logical connections among computer systems. In a local network, a communication link — a cable — physically connects each system and networking software provides the logical connection by uniquely identifying each system and passing messages among them. In an extended network that connects sites in geographically distant locations, connectivity is achieved through a combination of cables, modems, telephone lines, and an occasional satellite link. Each system on a network, whether local or extended, is referred to as a node. Each node has a unique name and address which is used by the networking software to manage and control the delivery of messages.

Current network systems are based on a networking standard called Ethernet, which has all but replaced older versions of communication technology. DECnet has been continually modified and refined to keep pace with improvements in communications technology and the international Open Systems Interconnect (OSI) standards. DECnet now supports many protocols and several types of networking hardware which allows DEC installations to successfully build local and extended networks with computers from a variety of vendors.

Digital Equipment Corporation itself supports one of the largest networks in the world — there are just under 40,000 nodes on a network that spans the globe. As one of the biggest consumers of its own products, DEC has a vested interest in their quality and flexibility. Users benefit significantly from the resulting depth and breadth of DEC's networking expertise.

Figure 2-2 is a diagram of a simple two-node network, called a Local Area Network or LAN. We will add to this diagram in the next several pages to give you an idea of the ways in which VAX systems interconnect and how networks can grow. From a network node, you can communicate with other systems and share data in a variety of ways. You can access another node in a network by a remote login, which makes all files on that node immediately available. You can also access data on another node by providing a network file specification to a command, utility, or application program. The remote login procedure is discussed in Chapter 4 (Logging In and Logging Out) and remote access initiated by a network file specification is covered in Chapter 9 (Files and Directories).

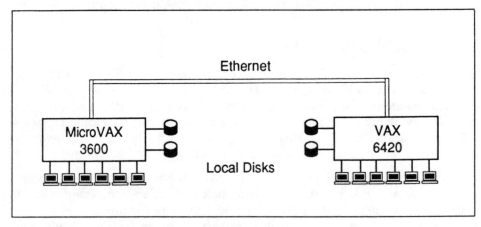

Figure 2-2. Simple Local Area Network (LAN)

TERMINAL SERVERS

With the proliferation of networks, DEC greatly improved user access to systems and applications by introducing the terminal server. Terminal servers are Ethernet devices that allow users access to services (specific computers or applications) defined by the system or network manager. Currently, servers support between 8 and 128 ports — each port can be dedicated to a single terminal or shared by several users.

Terminal server concepts and server commands are covered in Chapter 3. Server based terminals have advantages over direct-connect terminals:

- users can access any system or application on a network or cluster
- printers, plotters, modems, and other output devices connected to a server can be shared by all users
- users are allowed multiple interactive sessions
- servers can balance user activity across all available systems

In Figure 2-3, two terminal servers have been added to the simple network in the previous figure. There are terminals connected to each server, as well as terminals connected directly to the individual computer systems. Users on direct-connect terminals have easy access only to that system, but server users have ready access to any network node or application.

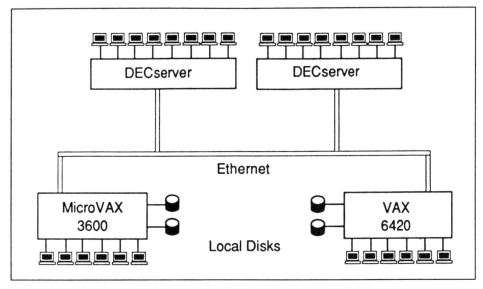

Figure 2-3. Local Area Network (LAN) with Terminal Servers

THE PC/VAX CONNECTION

About the same time that networks became well established, personal computers appeared in the office environment. With networks in place as a convenient means of sharing data, users demanded that DEC support personal computers in the VAX/VMS network environment.

The first attempt to integrate PCs into the computing environment was the appearance of DEC terminal emulators which allowed a PC to function as a terminal on a standalone or networked VAX. Today, there are many communication packages available for personal computers that provide DEC terminal emulation and file transfer capability.

While this solution is acceptable for many installations, a truly integrated solution allows PCs to participate as real nodes in the VMS network environment. Digital Equipment Corporation responded to these demands with a new network architecture called the Personal Computer System Architecture (PCSA). PCSA allows a variety of PC models to become fully functioning nodes on a VAX network, in addition to serving as DEC terminals.

To make your PC a network node, you must install an Ethernet communication board and PCSA networking software. PCSA software must also be installed on the VAX. Then as a PC user, you can transparently access data on VAX disks, transfer files between the PC and the VAX, and transfer files from your PC to any other PC. Figure 2-4 adds three personal computer nodes to the local area network and conveys the speed with which network links grow in the office environment.

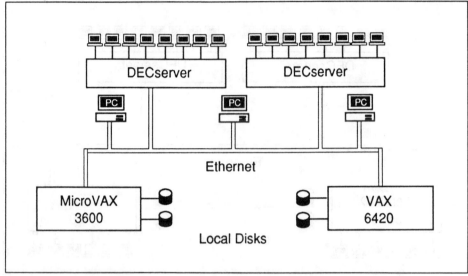

Figure 2-4. Local Area Network (LAN) with PC Nodes

LOCAL AREA VAXCLUSTER

A network solution works well if data sharing requirements are moderate. When users move data frequently from one system to another, the transfers consume significant amounts of resources. Also, as the data center adds applications the need for sharing increases, which makes further demands on the network. The Local Area VAXcluster configuration (LAVC) shown in Figure 2-5 allows networked VAX users to share applications and data on disks located on any network node. A Local Area VAXcluster adds three important features to the network configuration, significantly reducing the complexity of the user environment and system management and maintenance activities:

- users can access specially mounted disks anywhere in the network

- the system manager can manage all users from a central location

- all nodes may boot from common system files on shared disks

The Local Area VAXcluster avoids some of the cost and provides all the flexibility of the Computer Interconnect (CI) VAXcluster configuration discussed next. Current LAVC implementations provide slightly less performance than the large cluster configuration for two reasons. First, the central control needed for management of shared resources is located primarily in software, which is always slower than a hardware implementation. Second, Ethernet communication speed, at 10 Megabits per second, is currently slower than the communication medium used in large VAXclusters, although the 100 Megabits per second Fiber Distributed Data Interface (FDDI) promises to remove this restriction in the near future.

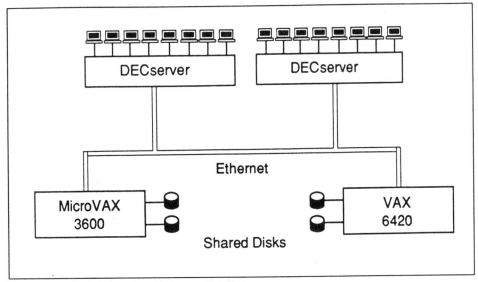

Figure 2-5. Local Area VAXcluster (LAVC)

THE VAXCLUSTER

The VAXcluster configuration accommodates large data sharing demands in a performance intensive environment. A VAXcluster consists of multiple systems with one or more processors, one or more disk servers, and many disks connected in a "star" configuration, as shown in Figure 2-6. Each CPU and each disk server is called a node in the cluster and current cluster technology supports up to 96 nodes in a single configuration.

The VAXcluster incorporates two hardware components that are found in no other VAX configuration: the star coupler and the hierarchical storage controller (HSC). The star coupler is a passive switching device that routes signals from one node to another and provides a dual-path connection to each node for redundancy purposes. The hardware connection between the star coupler and each node is called a Computer Interconnect and is noted as a CI in Figure 2-6. The HSC is a small but sophisticated computer that efficiently manages input and output requests from all CPU nodes to all disks connected to that HSC.

Hierarchical Storage Controller (HSC)

The hierarchical storage controller (HSC), also referred to as a disk server, is an important part of a VAXcluster. An HSC can manage up to 32 disks or 96 tapes (depending upon the model) or an appropriate combination of both. The HSC manages requests for data on all devices connected to it, which makes data from all HSC-served disks and tape drives available to all users on a VAXcluster.

DEC continues to invest manpower and resources in improving the HSC. The latest model contains 19 processors and uses sophisticated parallel processing techniques to achieve excellent throughput on busy systems. The latest model also runs twice as fast as the original version, and no doubt more improvements are waiting in the wings.

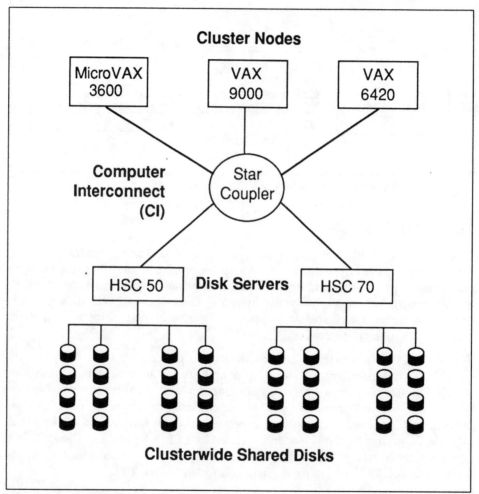

Figure 2-6. VAXcluster Configuration

VAXcluster Benefits

A VAXcluster shares the same two advantages of the Local Area VAXcluster over network configurations — centralized management and data sharing — and introduces a third, hardware redundancy to maximize system availability.

Central Management

System and user management is centralized, benefitting data center administrators and users alike. On a network, a user may have several different username/password combinations, while on a cluster a user can access any CPU with a single username/password combination. On a network, a user must contend with several different disks and possibly duplicate files, but on a VAXcluster the same user has one home disk and directory and only one copy of all files.

Data Sharing

Efficient data sharing is inherent in the design of the CI-based VAXcluster. Users on any node in the cluster can access data on any disk managed by an HSC, which accomplishes most of the data sharing with hardware. Because hardware is more efficient than software, the VAXcluster is a better solution than the LAVC when large amounts of data are shared by many users.

Hardware Redundancy

The star coupler provides a dual-path connection to each node. If one path fails, the other is automatically used. A new node can be added to a running system without impacting users in any way (except for a short pause while the existing nodes recognize the newcomer). A CPU failure does not impact users on other nodes. If there are at least two HSCs, and the storage devices are dual ported, an HSC failure is transparent to cluster users. When one HSC fails, its devices are automatically switched to the other HSC. Dual-porting of disks and HSC failover work so well that you can walk into the computer room and power off an HSC at any time. As long as the devices are also connected to another HSC, users experience no interruption in service. In a well designed VAXcluster, there is seldom a single point of failure, which results in increased reliability and uptime.

VAXCLUSTER/NETWORK CONFIGURATION

To illustrate the flexibility of VAX configurations, Figure 2-7 combines the previously described network with a VAXcluster. We have terminal servers, PCs, and VAX nodes on the network and three VAX nodes and an HSC in the VAXcluster. Ethernet is the common communication link between the network nodes and the VAXcluster 9000 node. From a terminal server, a user can access any network node or log in to the VAX 9000 and access data on any disk in the cluster. VAXcluster users can log in to any cluster node and transfer files to and from the cluster to network nodes. Because of its flexibility, this configuration is one of the most popular at mid- to large-scale VAX installations.

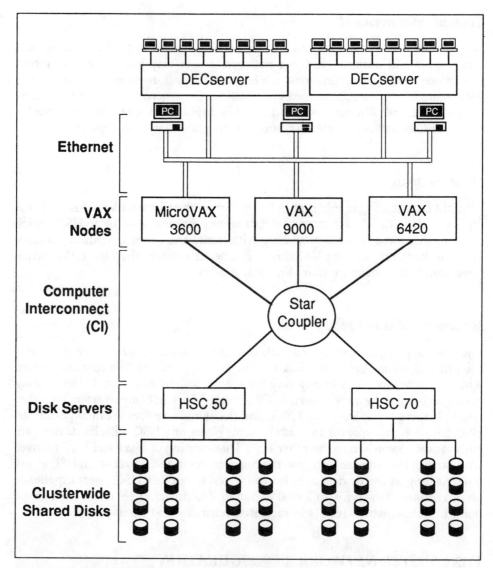

Figure 2-7. Mixed VAXcluster/Network Configuration

CONFIGURATION FLEXIBILITY

VAX/VMS supports standalone systems, many varieties of network configurations, Local Area VAXclusters based on Ethernet and hardware emulation in software, and large clusters based on Computer Interconnect hardware and software. We can mix and match processors on a network or cluster, mix large and Local Area

VAXclusters, and use either local or HSC-served disks, tapes and other peripherals. Each node on a network or in a cluster can exchange information with any other node (security considerations permitting). There are many additional configuration options available based on site specific needs — high security, uptime requirements, and distributed processing goals, to name a few.

In the multiprocessor world, the trend toward ever-increasing numbers of CPUs is well established and should continue for many years. The robust and flexible VAX/VMS architecture easily adapts to this challenge. DEC users find comfort in the availability of upward migration paths and benefit from the consistency of VMS from version to version across the VAX product line.

VMS SOFTWARE COMPONENTS

The VMS software environment is fairly complex and completely described in 34 fat volumes of documentation. To make it more understandable, the software environment is built in layers as shown in Figure 2-8. You use the Digital Command Language to perform file manipulation and operating system functions at the user level. Programmers have access to more sophisticated features through the callable interface provided with each category. The I/O interface contains low-level code that communicates with each device supported by VMS.

Digital Command Language (DCL)			User Interface
FILES	UTILITIES	EXECUTIVE	
Record Management System	Help Mail/Phone Sort/Merge TPU and EVE	System Services	Programmer Interface
CLUSTER	DEVICES	NETWORK	
Cluster Control Services	QIO Logical/Physical Input/Output	Network Control Services	I/O Interface

Figure 2-8. VMS Software Components

Digital Command Language

Users interface with VMS through the Digital Command Language (DCL). DCL is the collection of commands you use to create, manipulate, and print files, to examine and modify your personal environment, and to invoke VMS utilities. Commands fall into several natural groupings:

- commands that display and modify your personal environment
- file creation and manipulation commands
- commands to examine and change file protection
- commands to print using a special form and printer
- text editing
- utilities

Each command is implemented using the lower level functions in the Record Management System, operating system, and modules in the I/O interface. This design purposely hides operating system internals from users and results in a very friendly user interface.

Utilities

Utilities are most frequently distinguished from commands by the fact that they present a special prompt and understand several internal commands. This does not hold true for all utilities and the grouping of utilities versus commands is, at times, arbitrary and not consistent from one DEC publication to the next. For example, although HELP has its own prompts and usage conventions, the VMS documentation refers to it as a facility.

The most popular VMS utilities include HELP, EVE, PHONE, SEARCH, DIFFERENCES, and SORT/MERGE. HELP provides extensive online documentation and EVE is a sophisticated and easily customized text editor. PHONE is an excellent tool for communicating with any user logged in to the system. SEARCH locates a word, string, or phrase in one or more files, DIFFERENCES compares files and highlights where they are different, and SORT and MERGE are handy for ordering and combining files.

There are many other utilities available in VMS that are not covered in this book because they are targeted at experienced users and programmers. The File Definition Language (FDL) utility supports custom file design and file tuning and Convert modifies the record format or organization of any VMS file. The Librarian routines create and manipulate special file structures called libraries that implement application specific HELP documentation and support the development of large application packages. Other utilities compress and expand data (DCX), implement site-specific print job handling (PSM and SMB), and modify the standard command table to implement application or site-specific commands (CLI).

Record Management System

The Record Management System (RMS) provides file creation and manipulation functions. RMS supports three standard file organizations — sequential, direct, and multi-key Indexed Sequential Access Method (ISAM). If you are a first-time user, you need not be concerned with file organizations, as the details of file organization and management are handled directly by the command, utility, or application package.

RMS also supports both exclusive and shared file access. The controls necessary for managing simultaneous access to a file by several users are inherent in the design of the file management system. Files, directories, file manipulation commands, and file protection are covered in Chapters 9 and 10. Mastery of these commands will allow you to accomplish most routine tasks with ease.

System Services

System services provide access to executive operating system functions needed by commands and utilities. There are several functions in each of several categories: time and date manipulation, I/O management, process control, memory management, and logical name creation and translation. The lexical functions used in command procedures provide a direct user interface to system services. If you are not developing comand procedures, you will be unaware that system services are being used, as this occurs transparently while each command, utility, or application runs.

Input/Output Interface

The Input/Output interface contains modules used to control low-level cluster and network services and the I/O functions used to communicate with VAX peripherals (*e.g.*, terminals, printers, disks, tape drives, CD readers). All commands used at the DCL level to create, manipulate, and move files and data are eventually processed by VMS routines at this level. These functions should not concern you unless you plan to become a software developer.

## 3

Using a Terminal Server

INTRODUCTION

This chapter discusses the function of terminal servers and the commands used to initiate and control interactive VMS sessions. If you are in a standalone VAX environment, you can skip this chapter. However, your installation probably has several networked VAX systems that provide user access via terminal servers. Before you can log in to the VAX, you must first log in to the terminal server. Although Ethernet terminal servers are available from many vendors, this book covers only the commands used with DEC terminal servers.

TERMINAL SERVER OVERVIEW

Terminal servers provide up to 128 Ethernet terminal connections per unit, depending upon the model. Servers provide access to systems and applications on a network or cluster, allow users to conduct multiple interactive sessions, and provide shared access to devices connected to a server anywhere in the configuration. Shared devices might include laser printers, plotters, dialout modems, and personal computers.

Server usage is based on the concept of a "service." Each server has a list of available services, which may be composed of computer node names or applications or both. At your site, each server may offer the same services or the services might be different from one server to the next. Occasionally, security considerations restrict services to certain classes of users.

There are several models of terminal servers, called DECservers, available from Digital Equipment Corporation. All the server examples were created on a DECserver 200, and unfortunately, the displays are not identical from one model to the next. However, service, session, and session manipulation concepts are the same, regardless of the model, and all provide the same functionality from a user perspective.

LOGGING IN

Terminal servers frequently provide both local and dialup access. When your terminal is connected directly to a server port, you have local access to the server. A modem may also be connected to a server to allow users in other locations to call the system. Modem access may have security controls that are not required for a local connection.

Dialup Access

If you are calling a modem on a terminal server, you may be required to enter a server password before initiating an interactive session. Press the RETURN key two or three times. When a server password is required, you will see a pound sign (#) and hear a beep. You normally have three chances to type the server password correctly. However, the system manager can control the number of allowable failures on an individual server basis.

If you make a mistake, the # and beep are repeated. After several illegal passwords, the connection is terminated. Assuming the server password is entered correctly (or the server does not require one), each server presents an identification line, followed by either an Enter username> or a Local> prompt (Fig. 3-1).

```
#
DECserver 200 Terminal Server V2.0 (BL29) - LAT V5.1
Local Dial-in Modem use Only
Please type HELP if you need assistance
Enter username>
```

Figure 3-1. Server Prompt Screen

Local Access

If your terminal is directly connected to a server, press RETURN twice for the server prompt (Fig. 3-2). Most users will see the Enter username> prompt, so respond with your authorized VAX username. This username identifies users on each server and aids in diagnosing port problems. Username is only entered once, regardless of the number of server sessions you initiate. If a permanent username has been defined for your port, the server skips the Enter username> prompt and responds with Local>.

```
Enter username> VMSWIZ          Enter your VAX username
Local>                          Enter a server command
```

Figure 3-2. Terminal Server Prompts

SERVER HELP

Terminal servers have an excellent HELP utility which contains extensive documentation on server usage and server commands. The main DECserver 200 HELP screen is shown in Figure 3-3. For information on any subject listed on the screen, enter the topic as shown at the Topic? prompt and complete the command with RETURN.

For example, to see information on the SHOW command, enter SHOW at the Topic? prompt. HELP responds with the main SHOW screen which describes the various SHOW options and a SHOW Subtopic? prompt. At this prompt, you can enter SESSIONS, USERS, or any other legal option to see a description of how that option is used.

RETURN exits one level of HELP. Pressing RETURN at a Subtopic? prompt returns you to the Topic? prompt. Pressing RETURN at the Topic? prompt exits the utility and returns you to the server Local> prompt.

```
Local> HELP
HELP
The online HELP facility allows you to access reference and tutorial
information about the DECserver 200. Choose one of the following
options:

o Enter TUTORIAL to see a succession of HELP frames with "getting
  started" information on basic DECserver functions (for beginners)
o Enter HELP for full information on how to use the HELP facility
o Choose a HELP topic from the following list:

   BACKWARDS            FORWARDS             RESUME
   BROADCAST            HELP                 SET
   CONNECT              LIST                 SHOW
   DEFINE               LOCK                 TEST
   DISCONNECT           LOGOUT

Topic?
```

Figure 3-3. Terminal Server HELP Display

EXAMINING THE SERVER ENVIRONMENT

The server SHOW command has several options you use to examine the server environment. Of the available options, SHOW SERVICES, SHOW USERS, and SHOW SESSIONS are most popular. Use SHOW SERVICES to see which applications and systems are available — and select a service name from the list. You then use this service name with CONNECT to establish a server session. In Figure 3-4, this command lists nine services. The last service, W11, has a status of "Connected" preceded by the digit four, which indicates four users are using the WORD-11 application.

```
Local> SHOW SERVICES
    Service Name        Status         Identification
    ACC                 Available      AP/GL/FA
    CC                  Available      C-CALC/Budget
    DIALOUT             Available
    GRAPH               Available      Business graphics
    MM                  Available      MANMAN/OMAR
    PHONEMAIL           Available
    SUN                 Available
    SERVICEMAN          Available      Serviceman inventory system
    W11               4 Connected      WORD-11
```

Figure 3-4. SHOW SERVICES Display

SHOW USERS displays a list of users on this server (Fig. 3-5). It lists the preassigned username or the text entered at the Enter username> prompt for each port. In this display, a status of "Connected" indicates an active server session. A status of "Local" indicates the user is at the server prompt. The last column of this display lists the service to which each user is connected.

```
Local> SHOW USERS

    Port    Username          Status
     1      geowat            Connected      JECKYL
     3      marbru            Connected      DIALOUT
     5      ginabo            Connected      W11
     6      robsta            Connected      DTR
     7      jimgre            Local
```

Figure 3-5. SHOW USERS Display

SHOW SESSIONS displays server sessions on your port by number, username, and service name (Fig. 3-6). Your current session is identified by number on the first line of the display. If you have more than one active session, use this command to identify session numbers for the RESUME and DISCONNECT commands.

```
Local> SHOW SESSIONS

    Port 5:  VMSWIZ        Local Mode      Current Session 2
    - Session 1: Connected    Interactive     SYBIL
    - Session 2: Connected    Interactive     JECKYL
```

Figure 3-6. SHOW SESSIONS Display

ESTABLISHING A SESSION

CONNECT, which can be abbreviated C, initiates a session. If your port has been configured for an automatic connection to a preferred service, all you need to type is C. If you do not have a preferred service or you want to use another service, you specify a service name after CONNECT on the same line. When the connection is established, a welcome message and the VMS Username: prompt appear on your screen (Fig. 3-7).

```
Local> CONNECT W11
Local -010- Session 1 to W11 on node SYBIL established

        Welcome to the Corporate Data Center

Username:
```

Figure 3-7. CONNECT Command

Each time you connect to a service, the connection is called a session. Although some sites restrict users to a single session, more commonly you are allowed to have between three and five concurrent sessions. The connection you are using at any one time is called the "current session."

MULTIPLE SESSIONS

Multiple sessions aid immensely in user productivity. When your terminal is tied up during a long master file update, you can break out and start a new session or continue a previous session, returning to the first session to check status every so often. The BREAK key returns you to the server Local> prompt. If multiple sessions are active on your port, you are allowed to establish additional sessions, up to a server-specific maximum. A limit of between three and five is very common.

Using the BREAK key

On DEC terminals, the BREAK key is in the top row of function keys, the fifth key from the left. If you can use multiple sessions, the BREAK key interrupts the current session and places you at the Local> prompt, at which point you can enter any server command. Pressing BREAK at the Local> prompt causes the Local> prompt to be repeated. Some sites may disable BREAK or redefine the server control character to another key. If BREAK doesn't work, talk to your system manager.

Session Management Commands

There are three server commands used to manage multiple server sessions: RESUME, FORWARD, and BACKWARD. Use SHOW SESSIONS to find your session numbers. RESUME restarts the current session, which may be your only session, and RESUME n continues the nth session. FORWARD continues the next higher session and BACKWARD continues the previous session (Fig. 3-8).

```
Local> SHOW SESSIONS

  Port 5:  VMSWIZ            Local Mode    Current Session 2
  - Session 1: Connected     Interactive   QUERY
  - Session 2: Connected     Interactive   PLATO

Local> RESUME 1
Local -012- QUERY     session 1 resumed

QUERY$
Local> FORWARD
Local -012- PLATO     session 2 resumed

PLATO$
Local> BACKWARD
Local -012- QUERY     session 1 resumed

QUERY$
```

Figure 3-8. RESUME, FORWARD, and BACKWARD Commands

When you resume a session, you will not see the standard system prompt, which is confusing the first few times. There is a good reason for suppressing the prompt. If you break out of editing a document and resume editing later on, you do not want a system prompt to overwrite text on the screen. The same is true if you are using an application package — the system prompt could be incorrectly interpreted as input to the application. If you are using an editor or application, use CTRL/W to repaint the screen after you RESUME the session. If you are not running a utility or application, press RETURN to redisplay the system prompt.

Terminating a Session

The DISCONNECT command terminates one or all server sessions. If you are logged into the VAX, this command logs you out and deletes the session you specify. This command is not a substitute for logging out of the VAX because it interrupts your VAX session — if you are working with an editor or an application when you DISCONNECT, you will lose all your work.

SECURING YOUR TERMINAL

The LOCK command secures your terminal and prevents unauthorized access to the server and your server sessions (Fig. 3-9). LOCK requests a password and disables your terminal until the same password is entered again. Enter the password twice, once at the Lock Password> prompt and again at the Verification> prompt.

Password is a string of one to six characters and is never echoed on the screen. After the password is entered, no further terminal activity is allowed until the same password is entered at the Unlock Password> prompt. If you change your mind and decide not to lock your terminal, press RETURN at the Lock Password> prompt. The server responds with the message "Illegal password" and returns you to the Local> prompt.

```
Local> LOCK
Lock Password>
Verification>
Local -019- Port 6 locked

Unlock Password>
Local>
```

Figure 3-9. LOCK Command

INACTIVITY DISCONNECT

An inactivity timer may be enabled on server ports. When this is the case and you have no active sessions, you are automatically logged off the terminal server when the inactivity period expires.

LOGGING OUT

When all sessions are complete, you should log off the terminal server with the LOGOUT command, which can be abbreviated LO on most servers. If server ports are shared among users, this frees the port for someone else to use. If the system manager has scheduled terminal server maintenance, a shutdown cannot be performed until users log off and all ports are inactive.

SUMMARY

This chapter has convered the most important server commands. There are many other commands available to display and set your port characteristics for the current session (SHOW PORT and SET PORT), display server characteristics (SHOW SERVER), list the nodes reachable from the server (SHOW NODE), and so on. Consult server HELP for information on these more sophisticated commands.

SERVER EXERCISES

You can access a server even if you do not have a VAX username and password. These exercises familiarize you with server HELP information and several of the server SHOW commands. Multiple session examples are located in the exercises at the end of the next chapter (Chapter 4, Logging In and Logging Out).

If you enter the HELP command before you provide a username, you see only introductory information about the server. This information is different that the information displayed after you respond to the Enter username> prompt. In these exercises, text displayed by the HELP commands has been abbreviated with a dotted line.

1. Press RETURN twice. If you see a # and hear a beep, enter the server password.

```
#
DECserver 200 Terminal Server V2.0 (BL29) - LAT V5.1
Please type HELP if you need assistance
Enter username> VMSWIZ
```

2. At the Local> prompt enter the HELP command.

    Local> **HELP**

    HELP

    The online HELP facility allows you to access reference and tutorial infor-
    mation about the DECserver 200.
    ....
    Topic?

3. Read the TUTORIAL information and press RETURN when prompted.

    Topic? **TUTORIAL**

    TUTORIAL HELP

    LOGGING INTO THE DECSERVER
    To login to the DECserver you may be required by your server manager to enter
    a login password. If you are not required to do so, go on to the next screen
    Enter <CTRL/Z> to exit HELP or press <RET> to continue...

4. Ask for help on SHOW, SHOW SESSIONS, and SHOW USERS. When you are
   finished, press RETURN for the Topic? prompt.

    Local> **HELP SHOW**

    SHOW

    Use SHOW commands to display current status or information from the
    server's operationa database.
    ....
    SHOW Subtopic? **SESSIONS**
    SHOW SESSIONS

    Use the SHOW SESSIONS command to display information about the current ses-
    sions at a port..........
    SHOW SESSIONS Subtopic?   [Press RETURN]
    SHOW Subtopic? **USERS**

    SHOW USERS

    SHOW USERS displays information about active port users. Port number, user-
    name and current service are displayed.
    ....
    SHOW Subtopic?   [Press RETURN]

5. At the Topic? prompt request information on CONNECT and RESUME.

```
Topic? CONNECT

CONNECT

Use this command to establish sessions with services offered by service
..........
CONNECT Subtopic?                        [Press RETURN ]
Topic? RESUME

RESUME

Use this command to resume a session when you are in local mode. If you do
..........
RESUME Subtopic? SESSION

RESUME SESSION

SESSION session-number lets you specify the session to resume
..........
RESUME Subtopic?                         [Press RETURN]
Topic?                                   [Press RETURN]
```

6. Return to the Local> prompt and enter SHOW SERVICES. How many services are available at your site?

```
Local> SHOW SERVICES
Service Name       Status        Identification
ACC                Available     AP/GL/FA
CC                 Available     C-CALC/Budget
DTR                Available     Datatrieve
MAILER             Available     ULTRIX LAT SERVICE
SUN                Available     Graphics
W11                Available     WORD-11        ,
```

7. Enter the SHOW SESSIONS command. Because you have not connected to a service, you should not see any active sessions.

```
Local> SHOW SESSIONS
Port 5:  VMSWIZ     Local Mode     Current Session:  None
```

8. Enter SHOW USERS. Are there any other users on this server?

```
Local> SHOW USERS
Port    Username           Status        Service
2       jimgre             Connected     JECKYL
3       ginabo             Connected     SYBIL
5       VMSWIZ             Local
6       marbru             Connected     SUN
```

9. Ask for HELP on the LOGOUT command.
   Local> **HELP LOGOUT**

   LOGOUT

   Use LOGOUT to log out of the DECserver. LOGOUT disconnects all your sessions
   ....
   LOGOUT Subtopic?   [Press RETURN]

10. Exit HELP and LOG off the server.

    Topic?   [Press RETURN]
    Local> **LOGOUT**
    Logged out port 5

## 4

Logging In and Logging Out

INTRODUCTION

Once you have passed the terminal server barrier, you are ready to log in to a VMS system. This chapter covers logging in, login messages, the system prompt, passwords, the password generator, security considerations, and logging out. The exercises at the end of this chapter integrate information from the terminal server lesson in the previous chapter and demonstrate some of the most useful features of multiple server sessions.

DELETE Key

You may make a typing mistake when responding to server or VAX prompts. The DELETE key, labeled ⟨x⟩ on a DEC keyboard, erases the character to the left of the cursor. Press this key once for every character you want to delete.

LOGIN PROCEDURE

To log in to a VAX, you may need to go through three or four steps, depending upon site-specific controls.

- If your terminal is connected to a terminal server, you may have to provide a server password and a username to get the server Local> prompt.

- At the Local> prompt, use CONNECT to establish a session with a specific computer or service.

- If you are working at a high-security terminal, you may have to enter a system password before the username prompt is displayed. Otherwise, this step is not necessary.

- Respond to the VAX Username: and Password: prompts with your authorized username and password. Again, at a high-security site, you may have to enter a secondary password to complete the login sequence.

Logging In

To log in, make sure the terminal is on and press RETURN. Respond to the server prompts as discussed in the previous chapter. If a Username: prompt is not displayed, enter the system password. If you have the correct password, a system information message may be displayed, followed by a Username: prompt. Enter your username and respond with your password to the Password: prompt as shown in Figure 4-1. For security reasons, your password is purposely not echoed on the screen. Complete each response with RETURN.

```
              Welcome to the Corporate Data Center

Username:VMSWIZ
Password:


     Welcome to VAX/VMS version V5.2 on node SYBIL
Last interactive login on Friday,  9-DEC-1989 11:19
Last non-interactive login on Friday, 10-OCT-1989 20:33
   1 failure since last successful login


     You have 1 new Mail message.

$
```

Figure 4-1. VMS Login Sequence

Login Failure

You have from one to several chances to enter your username and password correctly, depending upon site-specific controls. If you enter either one incorrectly, the message "User Authorization Failure" appears. After the maximum number of allowed login failures, you are returned to the Local> prompt if logging in from a server, or to the Username: prompt on a direct-connect terminal. When logging in remotely via a modem or SET HOST command, you will be disconnected after the login failure maximum is reached.

After a login failure, VMS disables login from the same terminal for a variable amount of time. When the waiting period expires, begin the login sequence again.

Login File

After validating your username and password, VMS executes your login file. If a file with the name LOGIN.COM exists in your home directory, VMS performs each command in the file before you see the system prompt. You use a login file to personalize your environment with shorthand commands, custom key definitions, and other tailoring functions. Refer to Chapter 16, Personalizing Your Environment, for a description of the function and purpose of a login file and instructions on how to create your own personal login file.

Login Messages

Most sites have a welcome message that appears before the Username: prompt. After you successfully log in, several other messages appear which help you monitor your account use. The first message reports the date and time of the last interactive login for this account. A second message reports the same information for the most recent batch (*i.e.*, non-interactive) login.

The third message, reporting the number of login failures, is an important one to watch. If there have been several login failures and you did not have trouble entering your password, someone else may be trying to access the system using your account. Each time someone enters a password incorrectly, the login failure count is incremented. Report any suspicious activity to the system manager or security manager immediately.

A fourth message, reporting new MAIL messages, appears if new mail has arrived since you last logged in. Any or all of these messages can be disabled by the system manager on a user-by-user basis.

SYSTEM PROMPT

The "$" is the standard system prompt. It indicates that the VAX is ready for a command. However, the system manager may redefine the system prompt at cluster and network sites to be the node name. If you work on many systems, having the prompt reflect the system makes life much simpler. Your site may use the $, or may have redefined it to some other string. The $ is used throughout this book as the system prompt.

PASSWORDS

The system manager usually assigns a temporary password that you are expected to change the first time you log in. If this is the case at your site, you will probably see the message "Your password has expired; you must set a new password to log in" after a successful login. In this case, the SET PASSWORD command is automatically invoked and you will not be allowed to use any commands until you change your password.

Passwords may expire as often as once a week or they may never expire. The system manager controls both password length and expiration time. Most system managers require users to change their passwords once per quarter, or, at a minimum, twice a year. At some sites, users may select their own password and at others users may be required to select a password from a list created by the password generator.

Changing Your Password

Use SET PASSWORD to change your password (Fig. 4-2). Before you can change it, you must enter your current password. This prevents someone else from changing your password while you are logged in. Next you are asked for a new password. Enter your new password and type it again for verification. For security purposes neither the old or new password is echoed on the screen.

```
$ SET PASSWORD
Old password:
New password:
Verification:
```

Figure 4-2. Changing Your Password

If you make a mistake entering the old password, you are returned to the system prompt. If you make a mistake on the verification, your password is not changed. When the new password and the verification are identical, the system permanently changes your password. The next time you log in, use the new password.

Also, there is no command to display your password. If you forget your password, you must contact the system manager and ask for a new one before you can log in again.

The Password Generator

If you are required to select a system generated password, SET PASSWORD may be automatically started with the password generator. You can also start the password generator explicitly with the SET PASSWORD/GENERATE command (Fig. 4-3). The generator presents you with five password choices. If you don't like any of the choices, press RETURN for another set. If you change your mind, you can abort this command or any other VMS command with CTRL/Y.

```
$ SET PASSWORD/GENERATE

Old password:
  ruepekby     rue-pek-by
  wabnep       wab-nep
  thorykew     tho-ry-kew
  shuakas      shu-a-kas
  synkom       syn-kom


Choose a password from this list, or press RETURN to get a new list


New password:
Verification:
$
```

Figure 4-3. The Password Generator

Passwords can be up to 31 characters long. Valid characters include underscore (_), asterisk (*) and dollar sign ($). Blanks are not allowed. Most system managers set the minimum length of a password at six to ten characters. When length controls are in force, the system will not accept a shorter password.

Password Security Considerations

Never share your password. When you share your password, you can no longer guarantee the integrity and privacy of your files. When you share, you provide an opportunity for someone else to access your files and read your mail. And, in the worst case, the person you share with may accidentally or purposely delete or corrupt your files. You can pay a large price for doing another person a favor by granting him or her access to the system with your username and password.

It is wise to select a password that has at least eight characters and is not easily guessed. Do not choose your username, first or last name, department name, and so on. If security is a serious consideration, you should not select a word commonly found in a spell-checker type dictionary. Passwords that are a combination of several words or misspelled words are much harder to decipher. Some people use a keyboard pattern, rather than a real word, for example a horizontal or vertical sequence of keys. Such passwords are very difficult to break using standard dictionary matching techniques.

Stories of system breakins accomplished by using a password that matches a username are common, so do not make this obvious mistake. You have a good incentive for protecting your work, considering the hours it takes to restore valuable data and the additional hours it may take to find and correct an error. Remember, that the security of your data is ultimately your responsibility.

REMOTE LOGIN

Once you are logged in to a VAX, you may want to log in to another node in the network to check your mail or access a file. Find out which network nodes are reachable from your current node with the SHOW NETWORK command (see Chapter 6, Looking at the System.) Then, assuming you are an authorized user on one of the nodes, you can initiate a "remote login" using the SET HOST command (Fig. 4-4). The node name used with this command is a network node name, not a service. Do not confuse the node name with the service name you provide to the server CONNECT command.

Respond to the Username: and Password: prompts with the ones you use on this node. You may have the same username, but more often, you will have a different username and password, because network nodes maintain their own copy of the user authorization file. The rules for logging in remotely are identical to those for a local interactive session. When the session is complete, enter LOGOUT to log off the remote node and return to the system from which you started.

```
$ SET HOST node-name                 Command Format

$ SET HOST JECKYL

          Welcome to the R&D Node

Username: VMSWIZ
Password:
...
$ LO
VMSWIZ        logged out at 24-JAN-1990 08:57:52.31
%REM-S-END, Control returned to node _SYBIL::
$
```

Figure 4-4. Remote Login

You use a remote login to initiate an interactive session on a network node. If you only need to access a file on a remote system, you can use a network file specification with any VMS command. The remote login is handled transparently and the file transferred to your local system. Chapter 9, Files and Directories, discusses the network file specification and the particulars of remote file access.

LOGGING OUT

When your interactive session is finished, terminate it with LOGOUT (Fig. 4-5). If you leave your terminal or turn it off without logging out, you provide a wide-open opportunity for illegal system use. Another person can use the system with your account and copy or alter important data.

```
$ LOGOUT                        Command Format

$ LOGOUT/FULL

VMSWIZ        logged out at  8-SEP-1989 11:19:17.32
Accounting information:
Buffered I/O count:           80    Peak working set size:  442
Direct I/O count:             36    Peak page file size:   2697
Page faults:                 558    Mounted volumes:          0
Charged CPU time:  0 00:00:01.86   Elapsed time: 0 00:04:29.11

Local -011- Session 1 disconnected from XMI
Local> LOGOUT
```

Figure 4-5. LOGOUT Command

The LOGOUT command can be abbreviated LO. Some system managers redefine this command to do a full logout, which provides statistics on system use as part of the logout process. The display in Figure 4-5 summarizes all resources consumed during the current session. Peak working set size reflects the maximum amount of memory used; CPU time, the number of hours, minutes, and seconds of CPU used; and elapsed time, the number of hours, minutes, and seconds you were logged in. This resource summary is also posted in the system resource accounting file.

When you log out from a session you initiated from a server, you are returned to the server Local> prompt. If you are finished for the day, remember to log off the server as well.

LOGIN EXERCISES

In the examples below, PLATO$ and QUERY$ are system prompts. These prompts help illustrate the use of multiple server sessions.

1. If you are not on a terminal server, skip to number 3. Press RETURN twice. If you see a # and hear a beep, enter the server password. Enter your username at the prompt.

```
#
DECserver 200 Terminal Server V2.0 (BL29) - LAT V5.1
Please type HELP if you need assistance
Enter username> RSTATZ
Local>
```

2. Enter SHOW SERVICES and CONNECT to a service.

```
Local> SHOW SERVICES
Service Name        Status        Identification
HOBBES              Available     MICRO_MACHINE_II
OPUS                Available     Iceberg CASE VAXcluster V5.1
PLATO               Available     PLATO a place for great minds
QUERY               Reachable     CAM VAX 6310
Local> CONNECT PLATO
Local -010- Session 1 to PLATO established
        Internal Use Only - Unauthorized Access Prohibited
Username:
```

3. Log in to your VAX system with your username and password. If you are successful, you will see the $ or your site default system prompt. If you are not on a terminal server, skip to number 9.

```
        Internal Use Only - Unauthorized Access Prohibited
Username: RSTATZ
Password:
    Welcome to VAX/VMS version V5.2 on node PLATO
Last interactive login on Wednesday, 7-JAN-1990 11:25

PLATO$                                  [System Prompt]
```

4. After you are logged in, press the BREAK key. You should see the Local> prompt on the next line. If BREAK does not work, ask the system manager to enable the BREAK key or give you the equivalent character.

```
PLATO$                                  [Press BREAK]
Local>
```

5. Enter SHOW SESSIONS at the Local> prompt and RESUME the current session. When you have only one session, RESUME continues that session.

```
Local> SHOW SESSIONS
 Port 5:  RSTATZ           Local Mode    Current Session 1
 - Session 1: Connected    Interactive   PLATO
Local> RESUME
Local -012- PLATO session 1 resumed
```

6. Press BREAK a second time and CONNECT to either the same service or a different service.

```
PLATO$                                  [Press BREAK]
```

```
Local> CONNECT QUERY
Local -101- 1 other session(s) active
Local -010- Session 2 to QUERY established
                        DBMS VAXcluster
Username: RSTATZ
Password:
     Welcome to VAX/VMS version V5.1 on node QUERY
Last interactive login on Wednesday, 8-JAN-1990 10:55

QUERY$                                  [System prompt]
```

7. Return to the server a third time and use the SHOW SESSIONS command. You should see two sessions, with session number and service name.

```
QUERY$                                  [Press BREAK]
Local> SHOW SESSIONS
  Port 5:  RSTATZ          Local Mode      Current Session 2
  - Session 1: Connected   Interactive     PLATO
  - Session 2: Connected   Interactive     QUERY

Local>
```

8. Resume the second session. Because you have two sessions, you must specify a session number with the RESUME command.

```
Local> RESUME 2
Local -012- QUERY session 2 resumed
                                        [Press RETURN]
QUERY$                                  [System prompt]
```

9. Log off the VAX. If you are not on a terminal server, ignore the server messages shown in this example and continue with the next chapter.

```
QUERY$ LOGOUT
  RSTATZ  logged out at 8-JAN-1990 10:46:56.36
Local -011- Session 2 disconnected from QUERY[Server messages]
Local -101- 1 other session(s) active
Local>
```

10. At the Local> prompt, resume the first session, terminate the VAX session with the LOGOUT command, and log off the server.

```
Local> RESUME 1
Local -012- PLATO session 1 resumed
                                        [Press RETURN]
PLATO$ LOGOUT                           [System prompt]
  RSTATZ   logged out at 8-JAN-1990 10:51:53.79
Local -011- Session 1 disconnected from PLATO
Local> LOGOUT
Local -020- Logged out port 5
```

## 5

The User Environment

INTRODUCTION

In this chapter, we discuss several important components of your computing environment. First we discuss DEC terminals, the DEC keyboard, and using terminal "Setup" mode to control terminal characteristics. Then we briefly review login files, your personal mail file, and printers. The remainder of this chapter introduces several VMS concepts that are central to the user environment: user authorization parameters, the User Identification Code (UIC), and the VMS process. Several pages are devoted to a discussion of process types, process devices, process privileges, quotas, priority, and process resource accounting.

DEC TERMINALS

A VAX terminal may be one of a variety of DEC and third-party VT200 or VT300 clones, a microcomputer, or a terminal used with other systems (*e.g.*, IBM, HP, Prime). Non-DEC terminals rely on a software package called a terminal emulator to make the terminal look and act like a real DEC terminal. The system manager may predefine terminal characteristics at system startup to insure the terminals are properly identified and use the correct communication protocol. You also have control over many aspects of terminal operation and can change characteristics using setup mode on DEC-style terminals. Emulator packages typically implement most of the standard DEC setup functions in software.

The DEC Keyboard (LK201)

VT200 and VT300 keyboards have the normal typewriter keys, a row of 12 function keys across the top, a special 12-key grey editing keypad which includes the arrow keys, and a numeric keypad of 18 keys on the right side. You use function keys, the grey editing keypad, and the numeric keypad with VMS text editors. The numeric keypad also functions like a calculator for data entry purposes.

VMS uses several special purpose keys. As you read the key descriptions below, locate each one on your keyboard.

- **HOLD SCREEN**, the leftmost key in the top row of function keys, stops and starts terminal output. When this key is pressed once to disable terminal output, the LED labeled HOLD SCREEN on the upper right of the keyboard is illuminated. When you press HOLD SCREEN a second time to enable terminal output, the HOLD SCREEN LED indicator is turned off.

- **PRINT SCREEN**, second from the left in the top row, directs a locally connected printer to produce a hardcopy of the terminal screen. If you do not have a local printer, this key is ignored.

- **SET UP**, third key from the left in the top row, displays a menu of terminal characteristics. Press SET UP once for the menu and a second time to return to normal terminal operation.

- **BREAK** is the fifth key from the left in the top row of function keys. If you are on a terminal server, BREAK returns you to the server Local> prompt.

- **HELP**, in the top row above the grey editing keys, displays keypad diagrams when you are using one of the text editors.

- **DO**, next to the HELP key, causes the EVE editor to issue a Command: prompt at the bottom of the screen.

- **DELETE**, labeled $\boxed{\langle\text{x}}$ above the RETURN key, erases the character to the left of the cursor.

- **CTRL** (the control key), above the SHIFT key on the left side, is combined with other keys for special functions.

- **ENTER**, the lower right key on the numeric keypad, selects terminal characteristics in setup mode.

Terminal Setup Mode

DEC and DEC-compatible terminals have a local setup mode used to control terminal characteristics like 80- or 132-column screen width, uppercase or lowercase display, and local modem and printer definitions. If you have a DEC-compatible terminal, the SET UP key is in the top row of function keys, third from the left.

You can enter setup mode at any time without affecting your interactive session. When you press SET UP the first time, you are presented with a menu similar to the one in Figure 5-1. Press SET UP a second time to return to normal terminal operation. To change terminal characteristics, use the arrow keys to move the cursor from one option to the next on the main menu. To access the menu for a particular subject, position the cursor on that item and press ENTER on the numeric keypad.

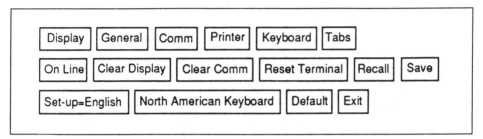

Figure 5-1. VT200 Set-up Directory

In each category menu, the first choice is **Next Set-Up.** After you change the menu settings, place the cursor on this box and press ENTER to go to the next menu. The **To Directory** selection places you back in the main menu where you started.

Most of the options are self explanatory. The **Display** category controls normal or reverse-video screen display, 80 or 132 column screen width, and block or underline cursor style. The **General** option defines terminal type (*e.g.*, VT100, VT200, VT300) and the **Comm** and **Printer** menus control characteristics for a modem or printer attached to auxiliary ports on the back of the terminal.

The **Keyboard** menu controls the margin bell and key click, whether a key autorepeats when it is held down, and enables or disables the BREAK key. Use **Tabs** to define terminal tab stops and **Clear Display** to clear the screen. The **Reset** function on the main menu clears the terminal and restores predefined parameters. **Save** permanently stores changed settings so they are loaded each time the terminal is powered on, **Default** sets the terminal back to factory default settings, and **Exit** leaves setup mode.

Once in a specific menu, place the cursor on the desired option and press the ENTER key on the keypad to modify a setting. If there are preprogrammed settings, another legal choice will appear each time you press ENTER. Stop when the desired option is displayed. If you pass up the correct selection, continue pressing ENTER until it shows up again.

Your selections are now active and will remain so until the terminal is powered off. To permanently save the setting, move the cursor to the **To Directory** box and press ENTER, which returns you to the main screen. Select the **Save** option on the main menu and press ENTER again. The current settings are now permanently stored and will load each time you turn on the terminal.

To leave the Set-Up Directory, move the cursor to the box labeled **Exit** and press ENTER or press the SET UP key. Following either action, the terminal returns to normal operation.

LOGIN FILES

Most sites have a site-specific environment created by the system manager. Each time you log in, the systemwide login file defines shorthand commands for frequently used utilities and applications at your site. If you are part of a group, you may have a group login file that creates custom commands for functions specific to your group. You can also personalize your environment with a private login file that defines custom keys, custom commands, and logical names. Thus, tiered login files may define your environment on as many as three levels: systemwide, on a group basis, and individually. See Chapter 16, Personalizing Your Environment, for instructions on creating a login file.

PRINTERS

Printers vary widely from site to site. If your terminal has a communication port, you can connect a printer locally and configure the printer using setup mode. On a standalone system, there may be only one or two printers. On a network or cluster, there may be thirty or forty printers connected to terminal servers and to various nodes. Users are generally allowed to send output to any printer on the system. Printers, print jobs, and print forms are covered in Chapter 13.

PERSONAL MAIL FILE

The first time you receive an electronic mail message, the system creates a private mail file which is usually located in your home directory. This mail file stores new and previously read messages and is a permanent part of your environment. Mail messages can be filed in folders, printed, extracted, forwarded, and manipulated in a variety of ways.

THE VMS ENVIRONMENT

As a VMS user, you are provided with a set of characteristics, privileges, and quotas that respectively define the group to which you belong, control the operations and commands you are permitted to use, and limit the amount of resources you can consume. You have a designated home disk and home directory where your personal files are stored. With suitable privileges, you may have access to files in other directories or on other disks. You may also be allowed to access files on magnetic tape.

Each time you log in, the system defines three "generic devices" for input, output, and error messages. These devices all default to the terminal, but can be selectively redirected by individual commands or applications. Each of these concepts is explained in detail in the discussion that follows.

User Authorization

The system manager creates and maintains a system authorization file that completely describes each user. Of the many fields defined for each user, those listed in Figure 5-2 are the most important. There may be additional controls requiring a secondary password, restrictions on the days and hours you can login, controls on whether or not you access VMS through a menu or at the system prompt, and controls that allow or restrict access to the network at your site.

```
Account       8 characters, the group you belong to
Username      12 characters, primary system access code
Password      31 characters, no spaces, personal access code
UIC           Combination of account and username
Device        Home disk
Directory     Home directory
Priority      How quickly you receive service from the CPU
Privileges    Control the operations you can perform
Quotas        Control the amount of resources you can consume
```

Figure 5-2. User Account Characteristics

USER IDENTIFICATION CODE (UIC)

Your UIC is a combination of your account and username. In general, your account reflects the department or group you belong to, and your username is some form of your personal name. Assume we have an account called ADMIN and a username MANAGER. The UIC for this individual is [ADMIN,MANAGER]. The group is ADMIN and the member is MANAGER. UICs are always enclosed in square brackets in this format.

Two employees, JSTATZ and GBOICE belong to the ADMIN group. The manager and employees are members of the ADMIN group, and the ADMIN group has three members. UICs for JSTATZ and GBOICE are in the same format as the manager as shown in Figure 5-3. Occasionally, the system manager may map a UIC to a single alphanumeric identifier that is the same as the username (*e.g.,* [SYSTEM]), but the double form which combines account and username is more common.

```
 Username          Account          Member          UIC

 -------------------------------------------------------------------
 MANAGER           ADMIN            MANAGER         [ADMIN,MANAGER]
 JSTATZ            ADMIN            JSTATZ          [ADMIN,JSTATZ]
 GBOICE            ADMIN            GBOICE          [ADMIN,GBOICE]
```

Figure 5-3. UIC Format

When you create a file, the system records your UIC in the file header. As the creator (owner), you can always access and control your files. If MANAGER creates a file, the file records the owner as [ADMIN,MANAGER]. If JSTATZ creates a file, the owner is [ADMIN,JSTATZ].

Members of the same group can normally read each other's files, but not change them. Users in other groups cannot access files belonging to the users in the ADMIN group unless the file owner gives special permission by changing the file protection to allow public access. For security reasons, most sites discourage this kind of file sharing.

The UIC is used in combination with file protection settings to implement basic VMS file security. You will learn how to examine the UIC of a file and how to change file protection to restrict or allow access to files in your directory.These subjects are discussed in greater detail in Chapter 11, File Protection and Security.

THE VMS PROCESS

At login, each user receives a separate, controlled environment called a "process," that is well insulated from the operating system and other users. The process defines, controls, and limits the environment for an interactive session based on authorization parameters. The system creates a process when you log in. Everything you do while logged in is done within the context of your process, and the system deletes your process when you log off.

Important process attributes include a set of devices, privileges, quotas, and a base priority. Devices identify your home disk and directory and establish your terminal as the primary location for input, output, and error messages. Privileges control the operations you can perform, quotas limit the amount of resources you can consume and your priority determines the order in which you receive the attention of the CPU.

Process Types

There are five kinds of processes: interactive, batch, network, subprocess, and detached. At login, the system creates an interactive process. Batch processes run in the background, usually at a lower priority than interactive processes. An interactive process communicates with a user via a terminal, while a batch process uses files for input and output.

When you do a remote login or use a network file specification to access data on a network node, the system uses a network process to manage your remote access. The subprocess is a special case covered in Chapter 10, File Manipulation, under the SPAWN command. Detached processes are used primarily by the operating system and are not covered in this book.

Process Devices

VMS uses a construct called a logical name to keep track of process devices: your home disk and directory, the source of input, and the destination for output and error messages. Every user process has the same set of devices and the same set of logical names. All these logical names start with "SYS$" which indicates they are system defined names. See Chapter 16, Personalizing Your Environment, for a full discussion of creating and using logical names.

Home Disk and Home Directory

When you are authorized, the system manager selects your home disk and directory and records these selections in the user authorization file. Each time you log in, you are placed in your home directory on your home disk. The reserved logical name SYS$LOGIN always points to your home disk and home directory.

Input, Output, and Error Devices

When you sit down at a terminal, there are two important paths for information flow between you and the system. First, there is a source of input to VMS, the place where you enter commands and utilities. Second, there is a place where the system sends output generated by commands, utilities, and applications. Although error messages are one kind of output, VMS makes a special case for the destination of error messages.

The source of input and the destination for output and error messages are called devices in VMS. Rather than tie a user to one or two specific devices, all commands use three standard "generic" devices for input, output, and error messages. These generic devices have distinctive system-defined names — SYS$INPUT, SYS$OUTPUT, and SYS$ERROR — and each process has the same set of three names (Fig. 5-4).

SYS$INPUT	Input device for commands and programs
SYS$OUTPUT	Output device for commands and programs
SYS$ERROR	Error message device for commands and programs

Figure 5-4. Generic Device Names

When you first log in, all three names point to your terminal, the normal device for input, output, and error messages during an interactive session. You may redefine any of these devices for a single command or series of commands. Because you normally use the terminal to enter commands, SYS$INPUT is seldom redefined.

However, SYS$OUTPUT is a different case. Because nearly all utilities and commands send output to SYS$OUTPUT, you can easily redefine SYS$OUTPUT to be a disk file, without having to modify the command in any other way. Rather than watching the output at your terminal, you can capture it in a disk file. This device independence allows great flexibility in how VMS commands are used.

For example, the DIRECTORY command normally lists files at your terminal, but you may want to capture the output in a disk file instead. You can do this using the /OUTPUT qualifier on the DIRECTORY command — this qualifier defines SYS$OUTPUT as a disk file for one execution of the DIRECTORY command.

Applications frequently change the definitions of these devices. Applications may redirect input from the terminal to a disk file and redirect VMS error messages to a file, rather than have the errors displayed on a user's terminal. They do this by defining SYS$INPUT and SYS$ERROR as disk files while the application is running.

Process Privileges

Some 30 VMS process privileges control what a process can do, which may include initializing or mounting disks or tapes, changing base priority, exceeding disk quota, accessing files with a different owner, or performing a disk backup or restore operation. The system manager, security manager, and system developers are generally the only users with elevated privileges. The majority of users require only two privileges to use VMS in a normal environment. These privileges allow a user to have two analogs of a "mailbox," a construct used by VMS to deliver mail to users (Fig. 5-5).

TMPMBX	Temporary mailbox needed to send/receive local MAIL
NETMBX	Network mailbox needed to send/receive remote MAIL

Figure 5-5. Normal User Privileges

At many installations, projects are managed by someone with greater expertise than other members of the group. Three privileges allow a project leader to manage files created by users in the same UIC group (Fig. 5-6).

```
GROUP          Can manage group processes
GRPNAM         Can create group logical names
GRPPRV         Can manage group file protection
```

Figure 5-6. Project Leader Privileges

Process Quotas

Process quotas control how the system allocates resources to each user, such as memory, CPU time, open files, and subprocesses. Quotas are maximum limits that apply to all resources. The use of process quotas varies from site to site. Normally, resource controls are placed on memory, priority, subprocesses and file usage. Disk space controls are regulated by a separate system utility. Figure 5-7 contains a list of some of the more common process quotas.

```
CPUTIME        Maximum CPU time a process can use
FILLM          Number of files that can be open
SHRFILLM       Number of shared files that can be open
PRCLM          Maximum number of subprocesses
PRIO           Default priority (4 for interactive processes)
WSDEFAULT      Starting memory allocation in pages
WSQUOTA        Maximum memory use on a busy system
WSEXTENT       Upper limit for memory use on a quiet system
```

Figure 5-7. Process Quotas

When your activity results in a request for more than the maximum amount authorized, you receive a "Quota Exceeded" error message. VMS users are frequently frustrated by this error message, as it seldom identifies which quota has been exceeded.

Process Memory Usage

In Figure 5-7, the "WS" in WSDEFAULT, WSQUOTA, and WSEXTENT stands for "working set," the VMS term that describes the amount of memory your process is allowed to use. Memory is managed in units of 512 bytes, each unit is called a page, and each quota reflects an upper limit on the number of pages. For example, a WSDEFAULT of 100 means your process can access one hundred pages of memory (equivalent to 51,200 bytes). The selection of 512-byte pages is no accident, but happens to be the same size as a unit of disk storage, which is called a disk block. Because a memory unit and a disk storage unit are the same size, moving data from disk to memory and back again requires very little overhead.

These three values are used in different ways, depending upon the memory demands of the command, utility, or application you initiate. The first quota, WSDEFAULT, controls the amount of memory made available when you log in and is generally smaller than the other two values. The second value, WSQUOTA, determines the maximum amount of memory your process can access on a busy system with very little uncommitted memory. This limit is set somewhere between 500 - 1500 on many systems. The third quota, WSEXTENT, defines the maximum number of memory pages you can access if the system is not very busy and has adequate memory available. WSEXTENT can range from 1024-5000 pages or more, depending upon the physical memory installed on the system, the space required by the operating system, and based on the system load during peak and off-peak processing cycles.

When you run a command or more sophisticated utility or program, your process is allowed to request additional memory as needed, up to the maximum values specified by WSQUOTA and WSEXTENT. In a similar fashion, when your process completes a command or application, unused memory is returned to the system, the actual memory in use is decremented, and your process can start adding pages once more. This cycle repeats continuously as long as you are active on the system, within the lower and upper limits defined by these memory quotas.

The system manager establishes these three quotas independently for each user and also selects systemwide upper limits that cannot be exceeded by any user. Although these limits can be increased, your initial memory quotas should be more than adequate for normal interactive usage.

Process Priority

Process priority controls the frequency and length of time each process accesses the CPU. In a multiprocessing system, each process uses a small fraction of the CPU's time to accomplish the compute part of command, utility, or program. Because the CPU is so fast, it appears to users that each one has the full attention of the system, when in reality, all processes are taking turns.

When processes request the attention of the CPU, they are placed on a list (queue) ordered by process priority. In VMS, process priority ranges from 0 to 31, where 0 is the lowest and 31 is the highest. Priorities 15 to 31 are reserved for realtime programs, powerfail notification, and device interrupts critical to the functioning of the system. Priorities 0 to 15 are assigned to timesharing activity. Interactive processes normally start with a base priority of 4. Batch processes run at priorities between 1 and 4, depending upon the site. A low priority restricts batch processes to executing only when the CPU has nothing else to do.

VMS has a dynamic priority adjustment algorithm that helps balance the CPU time apportioned to processes running at the same priority. This algorithm pays attention to the amount of compute time versus input and output activity from each process. Each time a request for data is issued, the requesting process is placed in a wait state until the requested information becomes available. If all processes stayed at the same base priority, those managing large amounts of data would be constantly waiting, and response time for those users would be very slow.

To counterbalance this potential problem, processes that have a small amount of compute work and a large amount of input and output gradually have their base priority elevated in small increments, to perhaps as high as 10 or 11. Processes that have a large amount of compute activity tend to stay at or close to the base priority, because they use more CPU time per access than the processes generating many I/O requests. Overall, this dynamic algorithm delivers about the same response time to all users when sufficient resources are available. Of course, if there are more users than the configuration can adequately support, all will experience slow response time, regardless of the priority adjustment algorithm.

RESOURCE ACCOUNTING

Each time you log off, the system makes an entry in the accounting file noting your UIC and terminal name, date and time of login, and a summary of resources consumed during the session. Many resources are tracked, the most important of which are elapsed time (length of time logged in), CPU time, maximum amount of memory used, number and size of I/O requests issued, the number of images (commands or programs) executed, and the number of pages printed.

At the end of the month, the system manager creates a resource accounting report that summarizes system use for all users by account and username. This report is typically used by the operations staff for several purposes. In companies that use a chargeback system to help support the data center, the monthly report summarizes the amount of resources each department uses and allows costs to be accurately prorated among departments using the data center.

Resource usage information is also important for tracking system usage trends to determine if the installation needs additional resources and the type of resources to add. The entries in the accounting file also provide a detailed record of who is using the system, at what time, and in what capacity. When security questions arise, the accounting file can be used to determine whether or not the system was compromised, along with the time, date and UIC used for unauthorized access.

SUMMARY

You have an account name for resource accumulation and billing purposes, as well as a username and password combination for logging in. Account and username together define your UIC. Your account usually corresponds to a group or department and username identifies you as a member of the group. When the system manager generates resource accounting summaries, reports are generally organized by department (group) and individuals within the group (members).

When you log in, you are placed in your home disk and directory. Part of the login sequence defines a standard set of devices for your home disk and directory (SYS$LOGIN), and for input, output, and error messages (SYS$INPUT, SYS$OUTPUT, and SYS$ERROR). When you first log in, these three devices point to your terminal. Certain commands or applications may temporarily reassign input, output, and error devices, or you can do so interactively by redefining these logical names.

The system records your UIC in the header of each file you create. As a file's owner, you usually have absolute control over it, although this may not be the case at sites with very high security controls. Members of the same group can easily share files, whereas members of other groups cannot. The UIC, in combination with a protection key, controls file access and forms the basis for VMS file security.

At login, the system creates a process for you that manages and controls your environment. Each process has a set of attributes including account, username, UIC, password, privileges, quotas, memory allocation, and base priority. Privileges control the operations you can perform and quotas limit the amount of resources you are allowed to consume. The process is also the base unit for scheduling the attention of the CPU, for resource allocation, and for resource accounting purposes.

At the end of a batch or interactive session, the system makes an entry in the system accounting file recording the amount and type of resources you consumed. The system manager summarizes this information, usually on a monthly basis, to track individual, group, and overall resource consumption.

## 6

Looking at the System

INTRODUCTION

New users develop a better understanding of both the personal and system environments by looking at the system with the SHOW command. SHOW understands more than 30 options and can display information about nearly every aspect of the computing environment. SHOW can display your process characteristics, the time and date, current directory location, a list of users logged in, jobs waiting in the print queue, and available print forms and printers to name a few. Other SHOW options examine the running system, display available memory and memory configuration information, and display information about the number, type, and characteristics of devices on the system.

Nearly every form of the SHOW command has a corresponding SET command that allows you to alter characteristics that directly impact your personal environment. Some of the more sophisticated SHOW commands, like examining terminal characteristics and print queue status, are covered in later chapters. SET commands are not collected in one chapter, but rather are described throughout this book wherever the appropriate subject occurs. See Appendix A for a summary of SHOW and SET commands.

USER ENVIRONMENT

As you read through the list in Figure 6-1 below, try each command. Not all details of each command are described here, but this list will familiarize you with the information available to every user. The various forms of SHOW have been grouped in two categories: those that display information about your personal environment and those that display information about the system environment. In the user environment category, we defer discussion of SHOW LOGICAL and

SHOW SYMBOL to Chapter 16, Personalizing Your Environment, where these subjects are discussed at length.

```
$ SHOW TIME          Current date and time
$ SHOW USERS         Users on the system or cluster
$ SHOW DEFAULT       Current disk and directory location
$ SHOW PROCESS       Process characteristics
$ SHOW TERMINAL      Terminal characteristics
$ SHOW LOGICAL       Predefined logical names
$ SHOW SYMBOL        Predefined commands
```

Figure 6-1. User Environment SHOW Commands

Checking the Time

SHOW TIME displays the current date and time in standard VMS format (DD-MMM-YYYY HH:MM:SS). DD is the day, MMM is the month in alpha format (*e.g.*, JAN is for January) and YYYY is the current year. HH is hours, MM is minutes, and SS is seconds (Fig. 6-2).

```
$ SHOW TIME          Command Format
$ SHOW TIME
  1-JAN-1990 08:39:20
```

Figure 6-2. SHOW TIME Command

Finding Other Users

You will use SHOW USERS frequently to look at other users on the system. If you do not provide a username as a parameter, this command displays a list of all interactive users and the type of processes that are active. You can supply a full username to see if a particular person is logged in. You can also supply a partial username and ask the system to display information on all usernames that start with the specified characters.

If you are on a cluster, this command reports all users logged into all nodes on the cluster. If you only want to see users logged into your node, use SHOW USERS/NODE. SHOW USERS/FULL generates a display that includes process name, process identification and terminal identification information. You can combine /NODE and /FULL to display detailed information on all users on a specific node on a cluster. Several forms of this command are included in Figure 6-3.

```
$ SHOW USERS [username]                        Command Format

$ SHOW USERS                                   ! VAXcluster
        VAX/VMS User Processes at 24-JAN-1990 09:19:22.05
     Total number of users = 6,  number of processes = 18


Username    Node      Interactive  Subprocess    Batch
ARDSCO      DVORAK         3
ARDSCO      EDISON         1
JIMALB      WAGNER         3
JIMGRE      HAYDEN         4
MARBRU      VERDI          6
TERWER      HANDEL         1

$ SHOW USERS /NODE                             ! This system only
       VAX/VMS User Processes at  8-JAN-1990 14:01:28.43
     Total number of users = 4,  number of processes = 6


Username       Interactive  Subprocess    Batch
GINABO             1             1
JIMGRE             2
VMSWIZ             1
SYSTEM             1

$ SHOW USERS J                                 ! Standalone system
         VAX/VMS User Processes at  8-JAN-1990 14:01:28.43
     Total number of users = 3,  number of processes = 8


Username       Interactive  Subprocess    Batch
JIMGRE             2
JEFTHU             2             1
JIMALB             3

$ SHOW USERS/FULL CAR                          ! Standalone system
         VAX/VMS User Processes at  9-JAN-1990 12:08:26.21
     Total number of users = 3, number of processes = 4


Username       Process Name        PID      Terminal
CARGOE         CARGOE              204024C6  VTA1287    LTA1321:
CARKEP         SIERRA    PLL175    204024D5  VTA1411    LTA1445:
CARKLE         CARKLE              20402916  VTA1442    LTA1476:
```

Figure 6-3. SHOW USERS Displays

Where Am I?

SHOW DEFAULT displays the current device and directory location (Fig. 6-4). When you use this command right after you log in, your home disk and directory are displayed. In this example, USERD: is the current disk and [MIS.VMSWIZ] is the current directory.

```
$ SHOW DEFAULT              Command Format
$ SHOW DEFAULT
  USERD:[MIS.VMSWIZ]
```

Figure 6-4. SHOW DEFAULT Command

When you change to a different directory, SHOW DEFAULT will return the new directory as your current location. Using directories and moving around in directories are covered in Chapter 9, Files and Directories.

Examining Process Characteristics

SHOW PROCESS displays characteristics, privileges, quotas, and memory usage information for your process (Fig. 6-5). SHOW PROCESS alone displays the date and time, your terminal name, username, UIC, base priority, and the disk and directory where you are currently working.

SHOW PROCESS/PRIVILEGE provides information about the privileges assigned to your process, SHOW PROCESS/QUOTA displays information about controls on the resources you can use, and SHOW PROCESS/MEMORY displays your memory usage statistics. SHOW PROCESS/ACCOUNTING displays a resource usage summary for the current session, and SHOW PROCESS/ALL displays two screens of information tracked for each process.

SHOW PROCESS has many other qualifiers that can be used to display various aspects of the user environment. You will normally use SHOW PROCESS to check for username, privileges and quotas, and possibly resource accounting information. Consult the HELP utility (explained in Chapter 8) for more information.

The process rights identifiers at the bottom of the display control whether or not you are allowed to use the system as an interactive, network, or batch user, and whether you have local or dialup access to the system. Other site-specific identifiers may also appear in this field. On a cluster or network, you will have an identifier that defines the node on which you are working. Node identifiers are used most frequently to restrict access to DEC layered products that are not licensed on all nodes in a cluster or network configuration.

```
$ SHOW  PROCESS [process-name]          Command Format

$ SHOW  PROCESS
24-JAN-1990 09:20:00.09   User: VMSWIZ    Process ID:   334000BB
                          Node: HAYDEN    Process name: "VMSWIZ"


Terminal:            RTA1:  (JECKYL::VMSWIZ)
User Identifier:     [MIS,VMSWIZ]
Base priority:       4
Default file spec:   MISDSK:[VMSWIZ]


Devices allocated:   HAYDEN$RTA1:

$ SHOW  PROCESS/PRIVILEGE
24-JAN-1990 09:20:09.19  User: VMSWIZ    Process ID:   334000BB
                         Node: HAYDEN    Process name: "VMSWIZ"
Process privileges:
  TMPMBX               may create temporary mailbox
  OPER                 operator privilege
  NETMBX               may create network device


 Process rights identifiers:
  INTERACTIVE
  REMOTE
 SYS$NODE_HAYDEN
```

Figure 6-5. SHOW PROCESS Command

Examining Terminal Characteristics

Terminals are fairly sophisticated pieces of equipment. The SHOW TERMINAL command displays some 40 soft characteristics that are enabled for the current interactive session. Some of the characteristics are set by the system manager and others are set by you. We learn how to examine and change several important terminal characteristics in Chapter 7, Digital Command Language.

SYSTEM ENVIRONMENT

More sophisticated users may wish to use other SHOW options to examine various aspects of the system environment: system processes, memory configuration and usage, devices, and nodes in the network or cluster configuration (Fig. 6-6).

```
$ SHOW QUEUE              Print and batch queues
$ SHOW SYSTEM             All processes on the system
$ SHOW MEMORY             VMS memory configuration information
$ SHOW DEVICES            All devices on the system or a detailed
                          description of a specific device
$ SHOW NETWORK            Nodes reachable from current system
$ SHOW CLUSTER            Nodes that are part of the cluster
```

Figure 6-6. System Environment SHOW Commands

Examining Queues

SHOW QUEUE lists each print and batch queue on your system. Print queues
store print requests until they can be directed to a printer and batch queues run
programs in background mode, usually at a lower priority than interactive users.
Chapter 13, Print Queues and Jobs, discusses print queues, print jobs, and print
forms in detail.

Examining System Characteristics

SHOW SYSTEM displays all processes active in the system, including interactive,
batch, network, and subprocesses. Batch, network, and subprocesses are identified by a single letter in the rightmost column of the SHOW SYSTEM display (B,
N, or S, respectively). SHOW MEMORY displays the total amount of physical
memory available in megabytes and pages, and shows how it is configured, including the amount permanently allocated to VMS. The amount VMS uses varies
from site to site, depending upon the system configuration.

Examining System Devices

If you need information about devices available on your system, use the SHOW
DEVICE command. SHOW DEVICE optionally accepts a physical or logical device
name as a parameter and displays information about the requested device or class
of devices. For example, SHOW DEVICE DU displays information about all
devices that begin with the letters DU. SHOW DEVICE DUA10 provides information on disk DUA10 only. You can specify any partial or full device name with this
command. Adding the /FULL qualifier results in more information than you ever
wanted to know about a device.

Figure 6-7 illustrates the use of both forms of the SHOW DEVICE command. The
first command displays information about the DU class of devices and returns a
single line describing each disk that falls into this category. There are two dif-

ferent forms of device names in this display: 1DUA12, 1DUA20, and so on, and USERA. The first form is called a "physical" device name and the second is a "logical name" created by the system manager. USERA is treated like an alias for the physical device 1DUA21. Users normally refer to disks using logical names because they are easier to remember and they also eliminate dependency on physical devices. Some sites may use only physical devices names, which is why they are mentioned here.

```
$ SHOW DEVICE DU
  Device                Device    Error   Volume     Free    Trans  Mnt
  Name                  Status    Count   Label      Blocks  Count  Cnt
  $1$DUA12:  (HSC015)   Mounted      0    WORKDISK1   295660    1     9
  $1$DUA20:  (HSC015)   Mounted      0    DATABASE1   416580   33     9
  $1$DUA21:  (HSC014)   Mounted     10    USERA       162036    2     9
  $1$DUA55:  (HSC014)   Online       0
  $1$DUA62:  (HSC015)   Mounted      7    SNAPSHOT    504969   13     9
  $1$DUS70:  (HSC015)   Mounted      0    LIBRARY     150632   18     9
  $1$DUS72:  (HSC015)   Mounted      0    VAXVMSRL5    22500  249     9

$ SHOW DEVICE/FULL USERA:
Disk $1$DUA21: (HSC014), device type RA82, is online, mounted, file-oriented
device, shareable, served to cluster via MSCP Server, error logging is enabled.

   Error count              3      Operations completed      11104914
   Owner process           ""      Owner UIC        [A000000,SYSTEM]
   Owner process ID  00000000      Dev Prot  S:RWED,O:RWED,G:RWED,W:RWED
   Reference count         70      Default buffer size            512
   Total blocks       1216665      Sectors per track               57
   Total cylinders       1423      Tracks per cylinder             15
   Host name         "HSC014"      Host type, avail         HS70, yes
   Allocation class         1
   Volume label       "USERA"      Relative volume number           0
   Cluster size             4      Transaction count               77
   Free blocks         152716      Maximum files allowed       121666
   Extend quantity          5      Mount count                      9
   Mount status        System      Cache name     "_$1$DUS72:XQPCACHE"
   Extent cache size       64      Maximum blocks in extent cache  15271
   File ID cache size      64      Blocks currently in extent cache  208
   Quota cache size       310      Maximum buffers in FCP cache    1128
   Min ret. period (days) 180      Max ret. period (days)         180

Volume status: subject to mount verification, write-through caching enabled.
Volume is also mounted on SOPHIE, ISHI, ARWEN, ATHENA, IRISH, TULL, GLUBBR,
        MIS3.
```

Figure 6-7. SHOW DEVICE Display

In Figure 6-7, "Mounted" status indicates the disk is available for use. One of the disks, 1DUA55, has a status of "Online," which indicates that it cannot be accessed at the present time. The Free Blocks column indicates the amount of free space on each drive. In the SHOW DEVICE/FULL example, the total number of blocks on the drive USERA is displayed, along with used blocks, the name of the host (which is an HSC70), error status, volume protection, and the cluster nodes on which the disk is mounted.

Although there are no hard and fast rules about physical device names, disks usually start with the designation DU, DR, DK, or DJ, and tape drives with MT, MS, MU, or MK. Direct-connect terminals are TT or TX devices, network terminals start with RT, and terminal server connections are normally designated as LTA devices. When virtual terminal support is enabled on your system, you are allowed to reconnect to your process when a session is disrupted. Virtual terminal sessions have a VTA device designation that translates to a physical device name of TT, TX, or LTA.

Examining the Network Environment

If your site has a network, VAXcluster, or Local Area VAXcluster, you can use two other SHOW commands to examine these extended configurations. Each network or cluster consists of multiple systems (nodes), each having a unique name. The SHOW NETWORK command displays the address, node name, and routing information for each system reachable from the current system (Fig. 6-8).

```
$ SHOW NETWORK

VAX/VMS Network status for local node 1.1010 MIS3 on 8-JUN-1989  14:42:54.33

        Node        Links  Cost  Hops   Next Hop to Node
    1.1010 MIS3       0     0     0     (Local)   -> 1.1010 MIS3
    1.1    DENHUB      0     0     0     (Local)   -> 1.1010 MIS3
    1.142  DNR001      0     3     1     UNA-0     -> 1.142  DNR001
    1.144  DNR002      0     3     1     UNA-0     -> 1.144  DNR002
    1.814  BACH        0     6     2     UNA-0     -> 1.1003 HARPO
    1.900  WAGNER      0     6     2     UNA-0     -> 1.1003 HARPO
    1.901  STRAUS      0     6     2     UNA-0     -> 1.1003 HARPO
    1.902  MOZART      0     6     2     UNA-0     -> 1.1003 HARPO
    1.903  HAYDEN      0     6     2     UNA-0     -> 1.1003 HARPO
    1.904  EDISON      0     6     2     UNA-0     -> 1.1003 HARPO
    1.905  CHOPIN      0     6     2     UNA-0     -> 1.1003 HARPO
                    Total of 11 nodes.
```

Figure 6-8. SHOW NETWORK Display

SHOW NETWORK displays names of other systems with DECnet links to the current CPU. If the system you are on can pass messages to other nodes (a routing node), this command displays the names of all nodes that can be reached from this system. On the other hand, if the system you are on can only receive messages (an end node), no network information will be displayed.

Examining the Cluster Environment

In its simplest form, SHOW CLUSTER displays the node names of the CPUs and HSCs in the cluster configuration (Fig. 6-9). SHOW CLUSTER displays the version of VMS for each CPU and the revision level of the software for each HSC. Many options are available that display disk activity, CPU activity, and other performance information about cluster nodes.

```
$ SHOW CLUSTER

        View of Cluster from system ID 2035   node: SYBIL


    +-------------------+---------+
    |      SYSTEMS      | MEMBERS |
    +--------+----------+---------+
    |  NODE  | SOFTWARE |  STATUS |
    +--------+----------+---------+
    | SYBIL  | VMS V5.0 | MEMBER  |
    | HSC014 | HSC V380 |         |
    | MIS3   | VMS V5.0 | MEMBER  |
    | HSC015 | HSC V380 |         |
    | ATHENA | VMS V5.0 | MEMBER  |
    | ISHI   | VMS V5.0 | MEMBER  |
    | JECKYL | VMS V5.1 | MEMBER  |
    | SOPHIE | VMS V5.2 | MEMBER  |
    | IRISH  | VMS V5.3 | MEMBER  |
    | TULL   | VMS V5.2 | MEMBER  |
    | HARPO  | VMS 5.1  | MEMBER  |
    | CHICO  | VMS 5.3  | MEMBER  |
    | ARWEN  | VMS V5.0 | MEMBER  |
    +--------+----------+---------+
```

Figure 6-9. SHOW CLUSTER Display

SHOW EXERCISES

1. Show your process. What is your UIC? Your account name? Your process name?

SHOW PROCESS displays your UIC, which is usually your account name and username in square brackets. Here, MIS is the account and VMSWIZ the user. Your
process name defaults to username unless otherwise specified.

```
$ SHOW PROCESS
8-JAN-1990 13:47:59.68   User: VMSWIZ          Process ID:   0000019F
                         Node: GROUCH          Process name: "VMSWIZ"

Terminal:              VTA24:  (SYBIL::VMSWIZ)
User Identifier:       [MIS,VMSWIZ]
Base priority:         4
Default file spec:     USERD:[MIS.VMSWIZ]
Devices allocated:     $1$VTA1970: (SYBIL)
```

2. Show your process privileges. What privileges do you have?

Normal users have TMPMBX and NETMBX. Local users have LOCAL and INTERACTIVE
identifiers. Network and cluster users also have a node identifier.

```
$ SHOW PROCESS/PRIVILEGE
8-JAN-1990 13:48:07.74   User: VMSWIZ          Process ID:   0000019F
                         Node: GROUCH          Process name: "VMSWIZ"

Process privileges:
 TMPMBX                 may create temporary mailbox
 NETMBX                 may create network device

Process rights identifiers:
 INTERACTIVE
 LOCAL
 SYS$NODE_GROUCH
```

3. Show your process accounting information. How long have you been logged in?

SHOW PROCESS/ACCOUNTING summarizes your resource use. Look at the "Connect
time" field in the display and compare it to the same field in number 10.

```
$ SHOW PROCESS/ACCOUNTING
8-JAN-1990 13:48:17.49   User: VMSWIZ          Process ID:   0000019F
                         Node: GROUCH          Process name: "VMSWIZ"

Accounting information:
Buffered I/O count:       936 Peak working set size:    1504
Direct I/O count:         220 Peak virtual size:        7233
Page faults:             8447 Mounted volumes:             0
Images activated:          24
Elapsed CPU time:      0 00:00:03.97
Connect time:          0 00:18:20.27
```

4. How many users are on the system?

SHOW USERS/FULL displays a summary line with the total number of users and
lists each user individually by username, process name, process id, and terminal name. If you omit /FULL, you see each username and the number and
type of processes being used.

```
$ SHOW USERS/FULL                           ! Standalone system
        VAX/VMS Interactive Users           8-JAN-1990 11:30:34.06
     Total number of interactive users = 13

   Username     Process Name      PID      Terminal
   BILBEI       BILBEI            2B20022E  LTA7:
   CHRORM       CHRORM            2B20061D  LTA117:
   DAVREI       DAVREI            2B2008FA  LTA194:
   DONBER       DONBER            2B200E14  LTA309:
   GINABO       Zapper            2B200E1E  RTA4:
   JEFTHU       JEFTHU            2B200D19  RTA1:
   JIMALB       KeepYoHandsOff    2B200E21  LTA311:
   JIMGRE       JIMGRE            2B200C3C  TNA12:
   MICBEI       M. BEIGHTOL       2B200CFE  LTA297:
   SCOCUR       SCOCUR            2B200D20  LTA306:
   TERWER       TERWER            2B200CFF  LTA298:
   TERWER       _LTA303:          2B200D0D  LTA303:

$ SHOW USERS
        VAX/VMS User Processes at  8-JAN-1990 14:01:28.43
     Total number of users = 2,  number of processes = 3

   Username    Interactive  Subprocess  Batch
   GINABO           1           1
   SYSTEM           1
```

5. How many disks are on the system? Disk devices names usually start with D.
   You may see DU, DK, DJ, DB, and DR drives, depending upon the disk models
   installed at your site.

SHOW DEVICE D returns information on all devices that start with D. The
physical device names appear in the first column. All these disks start
with "1" because they are cluster disks.

```
$ SHOW DEVICE D
  Device                  Device    Error  Volume       Free   Trans  Mnt
  Name                    Status    Count  Label        Blocks Count  Cnt
  $1$DUA0:    (HSC014)    Mounted     0    DATABASE     255944    1    22
  $1$DUA1:    (HSC014)    Mounted     0    S5KDSK        38420    4    22
  $1$DUA2:    (HSC014)    Mounted     0    HARPO_DUA2    51720    2    22
  $1$DUA4:    (HSC014)    Mounted     0    CNVDSK        85587   12    22
  $1$DUA5:    (HSC014)    Mounted     0    G3DSK        462576   14    22
  $1$DUA6:    (HSC014)    Mounted     0    CHICO_DUA6   148452    1    22
  $1$DUA7:    (HSC014)    Mounted     0    CHICO_DUA7   214824    2    22
  $1$DUA8:    (HSC014)    Mounted     0    HARPO_DUA8    64209    2    22
```

6. How many megabytes of memory does your system have?

SHOW MEMORY returns memory configuration information. Memory is shown in Mega-
Bytes (MB) and 512-byte pages on the first line. The last line displays the
amount of memory used by VMS.

$ SHOW MEMORY

```
                System Memory Resources on  8-JAN-1990 12:04:43.12
Physical Memory Usage (pages):     Total       Free     In Use    Modified
  Main Memory (128.00Mb)          262144     196713      65005         426

  Slot Usage (slots):              Total       Free   Resident     Swapped
    Process Entry Slots              310        253         57           0
    Balance Set Slots                240        185         55           0

Fixed-Size Pool Areas (packets):   Total       Free     In Use        Size
  Small Packet (SRP) List          10133        598       9535          96
  I/O Request Packet (IRP) List     4128        606       3522         176
  Large Packet (LRP) List            160         76         84        1648

Dynamic Memory Usage (bytes):      Total       Free     In Use     Largest
  Nonpaged Dynamic Memory        2981376    1401776    1579600     1255152
  Paged Dynamic Memory           1641984     893360     748624      881968

Paging File Usage (pages):                     Free  Reservable       Total
  DISK$JECKYL_SYS:[SYS0.SYSEXE]SWAPFILE.SYS   22296       22296       22296
  DISK$JECKYL_SYS:[SYS0.SYSEXE]PAGEFILE.SYS  259354      165353      300000
Of the physical pages in use, 28352 pages are permanently allocated to VMS
```

7. How many processes are currently running? Which process is yours?

SHOW SYSTEM displays several pieces of information about all processes. PID is
the process identification, a state of "HIB" means the process is hibernating,
"CUR" means the process is active, and "LEF" means the process is waiting for
input. The "Pri" column is process priority; as you scan this column, you can
see the dynamic priority adjustment algorithm at work. On the right side past
the last column, "S" signals a subprocess, "N" a network process and "B" a
batch process. Look for your process name in the second column.

$ SHOW SYSTEM

```
VAX/VMS V5.2  on node GROUCH   8-JAN-1990 13:48:47.79  Uptime  40 00:11:29
  Pid    Process Name    State  Pri    I/O       CPU      Page flts Ph.Mem
00000081 SWAPPER          HIB   16      0   0 00:00:06.92       0       0
00000085 ERRFMT           HIB    7  33449   0 00:11:46.83      93     140
00000086 OPCOM            HIB    9   1571   0 00:00:44.56    1004     157
00000087 AUDIT_SERVER     HIB   10     90   0 00:00:05.22    1345      93
00000088 JOB_CONTROL      HIB    8   1881   0 00:00:37.33     260     374
0000008F NETACP           HIB   10    557   0 00:20:23.33     387     425
00000090 EVL              HIB    6    157   0 00:09:43.62  867498      59 N
00000091 REMACP           HIB    9    295   0 00:00:02.00      89      58
0000019C SYSTEM           LEF    4    212   0 00:00:08.22     932     254
0000019F VMSWIZ           CUR    4    207   0 00:00:08.35    1051     223
```

8. Are you on a network? If so, how many nodes are linked to your system?

SHOW NETWORK displays the nodes linked to your system. You will either get a message indicating your node is a non-routing node and does not have any network information or a list of node addresses, names, and routing information.

```
$ SHOW NETWORK
VAX/VMS Network status for local node 1.1012 JECKYL on 8-JAN-1990 12:09:37.97
    Node        Links  Cost  Hops   Next Hop to Node
    1.1012 JECKYL    0     0    0    (Local)  -> 1.1012 JECKYL
    1.905  CHOPIN    1     4    1    BNA-0    -> 1.905  CHOPIN
    1.908  HAYDEN    0     4    1    BNA-0    -> 1.908  HAYDEN
    1.920  DVORAK    0     4    1    BNA-0    -> 1.920  DVORAK
    1.921  BRAHMS    0     4    1    BNA-0    -> 1.921  BRAHMS
    1.922  VERDI     0     4    1    BNA-0    -> 1.922  VERDI
    1.923  HANDEL    0     4    1    BNA-0    -> 1.923  HANDEL
                   Total of 7 nodes.
```

9. Are you on a cluster? How many cluster nodes are there? What are their names?

If you are not on a cluster, this command returns a single node name which is the name of the current node. On a cluster, identify the HSC nodes by the description in the software field. The explanations at right are not part of the display.

```
$ SHOW CLUSTER
View of Cluster from system ID 2036  node: JECKYL  8-JAN-1990   12:10:02
+-------------------+---------+
|      SYSTEMS      | MEMBERS |
+--------+----------+---------+
|  NODE  | SOFTWARE |  STATUS |
+--------+----------+---------+
| JECKYL | VMS V5.1 | MEMBER  |
| HSC014 | HSC V380 |         |      [HSC software revision level 380]
| HANDEL | VMS V5.2 | MEMBER  |
| ZEUSS  | VMS V5.2 | MEMBER  |
| ECKERT | VMS V5.2 | MEMBER  |
| MILLER | VMS V5.2 | MEMBER  |
| STRAUS | VMS V5.1 | MEMBER  |
| HAYDEN | VMS V5.2 | MEMBER  |
| WILLIE | VMS V5.1 | BRK_NON |      [Node is broken and not a member]
| TURING | VMS V5.2 | MEMBER  |
| CHOPIN | VMS V5.1 | MEMBER  |
| DOLLY  | VMS V5.1 | MEMBER  |
| EDISON | VMS V5.2 | NEW     |      [Node is asking to join the cluster]
| YOUNG  | VMS V5.1 | MEMBER  |
| BRAHMS | VMS V5.1 | MEMBER  |
| BABAGE | VMS V5.1 | MEMBER  |
| BELL   | VMS V5.2 | VMS BOOT|      [Node is booting and not yet available]
| WAGNER | VMS V5.2 | MEMBER  |
| NEUMAN | VMS V5.2 | MEMBER  |
+--------+----------+---------+
```

10. What time is it?

```
$ SHOW TIME
28-JAN-1990 12:05:05.42.
```

11. How long have you been logged in? What has changed from the first time you issued this command?

You should see an increase in the images activated which reflects the number of commands, utilities, and programs used and an increase in the connect time and elapsed time amounts.

```
$ SHOW PROCESS/ACCOUNTING

8-JAN-1990 13:48:17.49   User: VMSWIZ      Process ID:    0000019F
                         Node: GROUCH      Process name:  "VMSWIZ"

Accounting information:
  Buffered I/O count:      105  Peak working set size:    560
  Direct I/O count:         37  Peak virtual size:       3506
  Page faults:             811  Mounted volumes:            0
  Images activated:         46
  Elapsed CPU time:    0 00:00:06.33
  Connect time:        0 00:42:36.80
```

## 7

Digital Command Language (DCL)

INTRODUCTION

This chapter reviews the Digital Command Language (DCL), the rules for entering correct commands, and the ways in which parameters and qualifiers are used. Next is a quick lesson on command line editing, which involves using control characters to correct mistakes without retyping the entire command line. Becoming proficient with command line editing saves many keystrokes and improves your efficiency on the system. Last, we learn how to examine, interpret, and change terminal characteristics with the SHOW TERMINAL and SET TERMINAL commands.

COMMAND LANGUAGE RULES

VMS understands more than 200 different commands and a multitude of variations on each. Command language rules, collectively called the syntax of the language, ensure that commands have a standard format. When you understand the rules for constructing commands, they become predictable, which makes it easier for you to learn and expand your command skills. The general form of a DCL command, shown in Figure 7-1, includes a command, a qualifier, and a parameter. Items enclosed in square brackets are optional. Because everything but the command is enclosed in square brackets, the simplest VMS command may be only a single word.

```
$ COMMAND[/qualifier[/...]]    [PARAMETER[/qualifier][,...]]
```

Figure 7-1. DCL Command Format

More complicated commands require more information, and may be composed of several parts:

- The command indicates the operation to perform

- A command qualifier modifies or adds functionality to the way the command is performed

- A parameter which is the object on which the command is to operate

- A parameter qualifier modifies the way the command treats that parameter only

The ",..." notation represents a parameter list and appears frequently in command descriptions in the rest of this book. Wherever you see it, you can specify more than one parameter as long as each is separated from the previous one by a comma.

Separate commands and parameters by one or more spaces. Separate qualifiers from commands and parameters with a slash (/) and separate parameters from each other with a comma. You may enter commands in uppercase or lowercase, because the command interpreter translates all of them to uppercase.

Parameter Definition

A parameter is the name of an object that receives the action of a command. For example, to print a file, you enter both the PRINT command and the name of the file to be printed. In Figure 7-2, the file name DAILY.RPT is called a parameter. You can print many files with one command by typing several file names separated with commas on the command line.

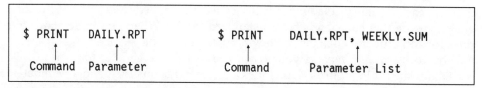

Figure 7-2. Command Parameters

Qualifier Definition

VMS provides a default operating method for all commands, although many other options may be available. Qualifiers override or add to the default operation. For example, the PRINT command normally prints a single copy of each file. To print three copies of both DAILY.RPT and WEEKLY.SUM, add a qualifier telling the command to generate multiple copies. The string **/COPIES=3** is called a command qualifier, because it follows the command and applies to every parameter (Fig. 7-3).

Figure 7-3. Command Qualifiers

To print DAILY.RPT on a laser printer, you add another qualifier to the command line (Fig. 7-4). This time, you use a parameter qualifier which instructs PRINT to manage one file differently than the other.

Figure 7-4. Command and Parameter Qualifiers

Command qualifiers affect each parameter in the list, are position independent, and can be combined in any order, as long as each is preceded by a slash. There may be several desirable qualifiers for a command. For example, to print three copies of each file, and to send both DAILY.RPT and WEEKLY.SUM to a laser printer place the /QUEUE=LASER qualifier immediately after the command (Fig. 7-5).

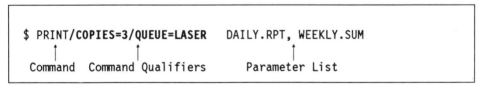

Figure 7-5. Multiple Command Qualifiers

Qualifier Values

Many qualifiers either require or allow you to specify a value rather than use a VMS default. In Figure 7-5 above, 3 is a value for the number of copies to be made. Depending on the qualifier, values are either integers or strings. A string can contain letters, numbers, special punctuation, and blanks. Enclose a string in double quotes (") to preserve the case of the text or embedded blanks.

Negative Qualifiers

You can negate nearly all qualifiers by preceding them with NO, which disables the effect of the qualifier. For example, you may not need a separator page with output printed on a laser printer. Although the PRINT command normally creates a separator page (the /FLAG qualifier is the command default), you disable it by using /NOFLAG on the PRINT command, as shown in Figure 7-6. Also, for your information, the HELP utility (covered in Chapter 8) does not index the negative form of qualifiers. If a negative form is accepted, it is included with the normal qualifier description.

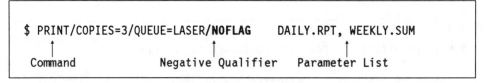

```
$ PRINT/COPIES=3/QUEUE=LASER/NOFLAG    DAILY.RPT, WEEKLY.SUM
        ↑                      ↑                     ↑
    Command          Negative Qualifier     Parameter List
```

Figure 7-6. Using a Negative Qualifier

COMMAND PROMPTING

If you forget the order in which a command expects parameters, or you forget to enter a parameter on the command line, VMS prompts for missing items by starting the next line with an underscore (Fig. 7-7). If you enter only PRINT, you are asked to supply a file name as shown below. If you enter the SHOW command without an option, VMS prompts you for the option.

```
$ PRINT              Command
_File:               VMS prompt

$ SHOW               Command
_What:               VMS prompt
```

Figure 7-7. Command Prompting

Novice users often forget to enter an entire command on one line, and then become confused as to why the command does not execute properly. Note that command line prompting always places an underscore (_) at the beginning of the prompt line to indicate the command is not yet complete. Paying attention to the prompt at the beginning of the line will save a lot of grief while you are learning.

CONTINUATION CHARACTER

Occasionally, you will enter a command that is too long to fit on a single line. You can continue a command from one line to the next by using the hyphen (-) continuation character. If the last character on the command line is a hyphen, VMS responds with the continuation prompt (_$) on the next line, at which point you finish entering the command (Fig. 7-8). Where command prompting automatically continues the command line for you, when you use a hyphen as the last character on the command line you are explicitly continuing the line yourself.

```
$ PRINT/COPIES=3  DAILY.RPT/QUEUE=LASER, -
_$ WEEKLY.SUM
```

Figure 7-8. Continuing a Command

COMMENT CHARACTER

The exclamation character "!" starts a comment. When this character is encountered, the command interpreter ignores the rest of the command line. Although the use of a comment in interactive mode has limited value, you may use comments in your login file or other command procedures (see Chapter 16, Personalizing Your Environment).

ABBREVIATIONS

You can abbreviate all VMS commands to four characters and many to two or three characters. You must enter enough of the command to uniquely identify it. For example, there are two commands that start with the characters REC — RECALL and RECOVER. For RECALL, you must enter RECA, and for RECOVER, RECO. You can also shorten qualifiers to four or fewer characters. As long as there are no conflicts in interpretation, you can use the shortest allowable string.

CONTROL CHARACTERS

You will use several control characters on a regular basis. In Figure 7-9, CTRL signifies the control key which is located on the lower left side of the keyboard. To enter CTRL/Z, press and hold CTRL (like you would SHIFT) and press the Z key. Although VMS treats CTRL/Y and CTRL/C the same way, these two control characters may be trapped and handled differently by command procedures and application packages.

```
Control Character      Action
-----------------------------------------------------------------
CTRL/Z                 Terminate input (HELP, CREATE, other input)
CTRL/Y                 Abort current procedure or program
CTRL/C                 Same as CTRL/Y
CTRL/O                 Stop/start terminal output
CTRL/T                 Show process status
CTRL/R                 Retype previous line
CTRL/W                 Refresh the screen (within an editor)
CTRL/S                 Disable terminal output (HOLD SCREEN/NOSCROLL)
CTRL/Q                 Enable terminal output
```

Figure 7-9. VMS Control Characters

CTRL/S and CTRL/Q are used to stop and start output to your terminal. This is equivalent to pressing the HOLD SCREEN key once to stop output and again to start output. You will only use these two control characters if you are working on a non-standard terminal. Most DEC terminals and compatibles have these two functions mapped to the HOLD SCREEN key which is the leftmost key in the top row of function keys. On a VT100 terminal, this key is labeled NOSCROLL.

Novice users frequently press the HOLD SCREEN key by accident. When no output is forthcoming from the VAX, it appears that something is drastically wrong. If you have used either HOLD SCREEN or CTRL/S, the LED light labeled Hold Screen on the upper right side of your keyboard will be illuminated. Press the key again and command echo and output will continue as expected.

CHANGING THE SYSTEM PROMPT

The standard VMS system prompt is the dollar sign ($). In a cluster or network configuration, the system manager may redefine the system prompt to be the node name, so users can distinguish one node from the other. You can also redefine the system prompt with the SET PROMPT command (Fig. 7-10).

```
$ SET PROMPT = string                 Command Format

$ SET PROMPT = nightowl:               Translates to uppercase
NIGHTOWL:
$ SET PROMPT= "Nightowl: "             Case and blanks preserved
Nightowl:
```

Figure 7-10. SET PROMPT Command

If the prompt you select has no blanks, specify the prompt string as shown in the first example. If you want to preserve the case of your prompt string or include blanks, you must enclose the prompt string in double quotes.

COMMAND LINE EDITING

Command line editing allows you to recall, modify, and reuse previously entered commands using a combination of arrow keys, control key functions, and the RECALL command. Line editing functions work at the system prompt and within utilities, although some utilities save only the last command. Once you become familiar with VMS commands, you will find that command line editing is an excellent timesaver and a great way to cut down on typing.

UP Arrow Key

The UP arrow key (or CTRL/B) recalls previously entered commands. Each time you press UP arrow, the next earlier command appears on the command line until you have recalled 20 commands or all the commands in the buffer.

Insert and Overstrike Mode

You use the LEFT and RIGHT arrow keys (or CTRL/D and CTRL/F) to position the cursor on the command line. When you make corrections, there are two ways line editing can work — insert mode or overstrike mode. In overstrike mode, the typed character replaces the character the cursor is resting on. In insert mode, the typed character is inserted directly to the left of the cursor.

Overstrike is the default on most terminals. Selecting one mode or the other is strictly a matter of individual preference. See Figure 7-13 for instructions on how to change your default editing mode. The default editing mode, whether insert or overstrike, is enabled with every new command line. On a command line, you can toggle between modes using CTRL/A, but when you start a new command, your terminal reverts back to the default editing mode.

Line Editing Control Characters

Figure 7-11 contains a list of all the control characters you can use with command line editing. To erase the whole command, use CTRL/U. To erase the word to the left of the cursor, use CTRL/J. An easy way to remember CTRL/H is that it returns the cursor to "home," the beginning of the line. Likewise, CTRL/E, for "end," places the cursor at the end of the line. When the command line is correct, the cursor does not have to be at the end of the line to enter the command. Simply press RETURN when the corrections are finished.

```
 ┌────────────────────────────────────────────────────────────────────┐
 │ Control Character           Function                                 │
 │ ------------------------------------------------------------------   │
 │ CTRL/A          ↑           Toggle between insert/overstrike mode    │
 │ CTRL/B or |                 Recall (up to last 20 commands)          │
 │ CTRL/D or ←─                Move cursor left                         │
 │ CTRL/E                      Move cursor to end of line (End)         │
 │ CTRL/F or ─→                Move cursor right                        │
 │ CTRL/H or BACKSPACE         Move cursor to beginning of line (Home)  │
 │ CTRL/J                      Delete word to left of cursor            │
 │ CTRL/U                      Delete from beginning of line to cursor  │
 └────────────────────────────────────────────────────────────────────┘
```

Figure 7-11. Line Editing Control Characters

Enabling Line Editing

Use SHOW TERMINAL to examine your terminal characteristics and look for the attribute "Line Editing" in the first column (Fig. 7-12). If it appears, line editing is enabled for your terminal. Immediately to the right of the Line Editing attribute, in the second column, either "Insert" or "Overstrike" appears. Line editing and Overstrike mode are usually enabled by default at system startup.

```
 ┌───────────────────────────────────────────────────────────────────────┐
 │ $ SHOW TERMINAL                                                        │
 │ Terminal: _RTA1:    Device_Type: VT200_Series      Owner: PSHARICK     │
 │ Remote Port Info: SYBIL::VMSWIZ                                        │
 │                                                                        │
 │   Input:   9600    LFfill:  0     Width:  80      Parity: None         │
 │   Output:  9600    CRfill:  0     Page:   24                           │
 │                                                                        │
 │ Terminal Characteristics:                                             │
 │   Interactive       Echo             Type_ahead      No Escape         │
 │   No Hostsync       TTsync           Lowercase       Tab               │
 │   Wrap              Scope            Remote          Eightbit          │
 │   Broadcast         No Readsync      Form            Fulldup           │
 │   Modem             No Local_echo    Autobaud        Hangup            │
 │   No Brdcstmbx      No DMA           Altypeahd       No Set_speed      │
 │   Line Editing      Insert editing   No Fallback     Dialup            │
 │   No Secure server  No Disconnect    No Pasthru      No Syspassword    │
 │   No SIXEL Graphics No Soft Characters No Printer Port Numeric Keypad  │
 │   ANSI_CRT          No Regis         No Block_mode   Advanced_video    │
 │   Edit_mode         DEC_CRT          DEC_CRT2                          │
 └───────────────────────────────────────────────────────────────────────┘
```

Figure 7-12. SHOW TERMINAL Command

To enable line editing or change from insert to overstrike mode, change your terminal characteristics with the SET TERMINAL command, as shown in Figure 7-13.

```
$ SET TERMINAL/LINE_EDIT/INSERT          For insert mode
                                         -- or --
$ SET TERMINAL/LINE_EDIT/OVERSTRIKE      For overstrike mode
```

Figure 7-13. Enabling Command Line Editing

COMMAND RECALL

Each user process has a command buffer that saves up to 20 commands. You can use UP arrow or CTRL/B to recall commands one at a time, but single-line recall can be inconvenient when the command you want is way back in the buffer. RECALL retrieves any of the last 20 commands in three ways: all commands, a single command by buffer line number, or a single command by string matching.

RECALL/ALL displays up to 20 commands with buffer line number. You can recall a command by line number, or, even better, you can recall a command using part of the string. For repetitive work, RECALL and line editing do almost everything. In Figure 7-14, you can see that the RECALL command is not stored in the command line buffer, for obvious reasons.

```
$ DIR  LIST.DAT
$ EDIT LIST.DAT                Original sequence of commands
$ TYPE LIST.DAT

$ RECALL/ALL                   Recall all commands
1 TYPE LIST.DAT
2 EDIT LIST.DAT
3 DIR  LIST.DAT

$ REC 2                        Recall second command
$ EDIT LIST.DAT

$ REC T                        Recall last command starting with T
$ TYPE LIST.DAT
```

Figure 7-14. RECALL Command

VMS MESSAGES

If you have been practicing commands, you no doubt have seen several VMS messages on your screen. Although the messages look confusing, all messages are presented in the standard format shown in Figure 7-15. Messages are issued for information and warning purposes, as well as for error conditions.

```
% Facility-L-Ident, Text

Facility     Command or utility issuing the message
L            Severity code
Ident        Message text abbreviation
Text         Descriptive text
```

Figure 7-15. VMS Message Format

The first clue that an error has occurred is the presence of a percent sign (%) on the line immediately following the command. All VMS messages begin with this character. Facility identifies the command or VMS module that detected the error. Next comes a one-letter code indicating the severity of the message (an "S" indicates the command performed successfully). The Ident portion of the message is the most cryptic, because it is an abbreviation of the message text. The last portion of a VMS message is the descriptive text. Figure 7-16 contains facility and ident examples and a complete list of severity codes.

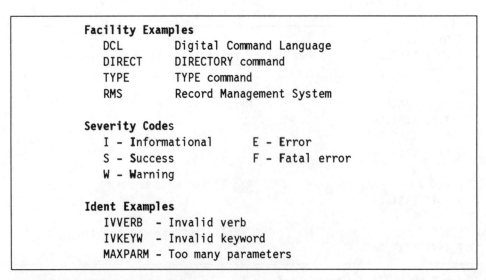

```
Facility Examples
    DCL          Digital Command Language
    DIRECT       DIRECTORY command
    TYPE         TYPE command
    RMS          Record Management System

Severity Codes
    I - Informational      E - Error
    S - Success            F - Fatal error
    W - Warning

Ident Examples
    IVVERB  - Invalid verb
    IVKEYW  - Invalid keyword
    MAXPARM - Too many parameters
```

Figure 7-16. VMS Message Fields

Often you will receive a message that has either an "I" for Information or "W" for Warning. VMS uses information and warning messages to indicate that a command or parameter was not entered properly. At other times, these messages are provided as a convenience for the user and can be safely ignored. Messages with either "E" or "F" indicate that a more severe error has occurred.

When you make a syntax error, VMS echoes the portion of the command that caused the error between backslashes (\) on the next line. If you look closely at what appears here, you can usually figure out the mistake you made. Figure 7-17 has two common error messages. The first is caused by a misspelling of the DIRECTORY command and the second is caused by an invalid option to the SHOW command. In both cases, the system presents part of the command in backslashes as an indicator of what went wrong (\DOR\ in the first example and \UP\ in the second).

```
$ DOR
%DCL-W-IVVERB, unrecognized command verb - check validity and spelling
\DOR\

$ SHOW UP
%DCL-W-IVKEYW, unrecognized keyword - check validity and spelling
\UP\
```

Figure 7-17. Sample Error Messages

With repeated exposure to messages, they become easier to decipher. Appendix B lists common error messages encountered by novice users. You can find a complete list of messages generated by VMS and possible corrective action in Volumes 6A and 6B of the General User documentation, labeled *System Messages and Recovery Procedures.*

TERMINAL CHARACTERISTICS

We had a brief look at terminal characteristics in the section on line editing. VMS stores over 40 soft terminal characteristics that control terminal operation. The system manager defines terminal characteristics at system startup., so you can expect your terminal to have the right speed setting and device type. Several features that you might want to change are shown in boldface in Figure 7-18.

You examine terminal characteristics with SHOW TERMINAL and modify them with SET TERMINAL and an appropriate selection of qualifiers. SET TERMINAL accepts an optional device name. If you are changing your own terminal characteristics, you can omit the the device name, because it defaults to your terminal.

Figure 7-19 lists some of the most commonly used qualifiers. You can also control some of these same characteristics in terminal setup mode.

```
$ SHOW TERMINAL
Terminal: _RTA1:    Device_Type: VT200_Series        Owner: PSHARICK
Remote Port Info: SYBIL::VMSWIZ

   Input:   9600    LFfill:  0    Width:  80    Parity: None
   Output:  9600    CRfill:  0    Page:   24

Terminal Characteristics:
   Interactive        Echo              Type_ahead        No Escape
   No Hostsync        TTsync            Lowercase         Tab
   Wrap               Scope             Remote            Eightbit
   Broadcast          No Readsync       Form              Fulldup
   Modem              No Local_echo     Autobaud          Hangup
   No Brdcstmbx       No DMA            Altypeahd         No Set_speed
   Line Editing       Insert editing    No Fallback       Dialup
   No Secure server   No Disconnect     No Pasthru        No Syspassword
   No SIXEL Graphics  No Soft Characters No Printer Port  Numeric Keypad
   ANSI_CRT           No Regis          No Block_mode     Advanced_video
   Edit_mode          DEC_CRT           DEC_CRT2
```

Figure 7-18. Examining Terminal Characteristics

```
$ SET TERMINAL [device-name]      Command Format

   /DEVICE=dev-type    Select a default set of characteristics based
                       on device type (most common is VT200 or VT300)
   /FORM               Terminal recognizes a form feed character
   /INSERT             Select insert mode for line editing
   /LINE_EDIT          Enable command line editing
   /NOLINE_EDIT        Disable command line editing
   /LOWERCASE          Characters are displayed in upper and lowercase
   /OVERSTRIKE         Select overstrike mode for line editing
   /TAB                Terminal recognizes a tab character
   /WIDTH=n            Set line width to n (either 80 or 132)
   /WRAP               Wrap lines longer than width
   /NOWRAP             Truncate lines longer than width
```

Figure 7-19. SET TERMINAL Qualifiers

Changing Terminal Characteristics

The first line in Figure 7-20 defines the terminal as a VT200-compatible device. From the lesson on command syntax at the beginning of this chapter, you know you can select several terminal characteristics with one command by combining qualifiers. The second line enables terminal recognition of tab and form feed characters and sets your terminal line width to 132 columns. The last line shows you how to reset terminal width to 80 columns and disable line wrap. To disable recognition of form feed or tab characters, use the negative form of these qualifiers (/NOFORM or /NOTAB) with the SET TERMINAL command.

```
$ SET TERM/DEVICE=VT200         Terminal is VT200 compatible
$ SET TERM/TAB/FORM/WIDTH=132   Terminal recognizes tab, form
                                feed, has 132-column display
$ SET TERM/WID=80/NOWRAP        80-column display, do not wrap lines
```

Figure 7-20. SET TERMINAL Command

DCL EXERCISES

1. Use setup mode to turn off keyclicks and the margin bell for your terminal. You may wish to reset these characteristics after you practice this exercise. How do you permanently save the new characteristics?

   - Press SET UP, use the cursor arrow to move to the "Keyboard" box and press ENTER
   - In the Keyboard menu position the cursor on the box that says "Keyclick." Press ENTER and verify the "No Keyclick" selection is displayed.
   - Move the cursor to the Margin Bell box and press ENTER until you see "No Margin Bell" setting.
   - Position the cursor on the "To Directory" box and press ENTER. You should now see the main Set-up Directory.
   - To permanently save your selections, place the cursor on "Save" and press ENTER.
   - Press the SET UP key to leave setup mode.

2. Use SHOW TERMINAL to display your terminal characteristics. What is your terminal name? What speed is your terminal running at?

   Terminal name and speed settings are in boldface in the SHOW TERMINAL display. The terminal name RTA2 indicates a remote login has been performed and the terminal speed is 9600 baud. The rest of the display has been omitted.

```
$ SHOW TERMINAL
Terminal:  _RTA2:       Device_Type: VT200_Series   Owner: VMSWIZ
Remote Port Info: SYBIL::VMSWIZ

Input:    9600      LFfill:  0      Width:  80      Parity: None
Output:   9600      CRfill:  0      Page:   24
```

3. Set your terminal width to 132 characters. You can do this in terminal setup mode or with the SET TERMINAL command.

```
In setup mode, select the "Display" menu and press ENTER. Move the cursor
to the box labeled "80 Columns" and press ENTER to select 132 columns.Then
press the SET UP key to exit setup mode. SET TERMINAL/WIDTH=132 does the
same thing.
```

4. Set the system prompt to Nightowl: and then to the string "Is it Friday?" In the first case, there is no space between the prompt and what you type. In the second, there is one space. Last, change the system prompt back to the default. If your default system prompt is highlighted (reverse video), you can only reset it by logging out and back in again.

```
$ SET PROMPT=Nightowl:
Nightowl: SET PROMPT = "Is it Friday? "
Is it Friday? SET PROMPT = "$ "
$
```

5. Is your terminal set up for command line editing?

```
The line editing and mode attributes are in boldface in the SHOW TERMINAL dis-
play. This terminal is in overstrike editing mode which is the system default.
```

```
$ SHOW TERMINAL
Terminal: _RTA2:       Device_Type: VT200_Series      Owner: VMSWIZ
Remote Port Info: SYBIL::VMSWIZ

Input:   2400    LFfill:  0    Width:  80       Parity: None
Output:  2400    CRfill:  0    Page:   24

Terminal Characteristics:
  Interactive      Echo              Type_ahead       No Escape
  No Hostsync      TTsync            Lowercase        Tab
  Wrap             Scope             No Remote        Eightbit
  Broadcast        No Readsync       No Form          Fulldup
  No Modem         No Local_echo     No Autobaud      Hangup
  No Brdcstmbx     No DMA            No Altypeahd     Set_speed
  Line Editing     Overstrike editing No Fallback     No Dialup
  No Secure server Disconnect        No Pasthru       No Syspassword
  No SIXEL Graphics No Soft Characters No Printer Port Numeric Keypad
  ANSI_CRT         No Regis          No Block_mode    Advanced_video
  Edit_mode        DEC_CRT           DEC_CRT2         No DEC_CRT3
```

6. Set your terminal width back to 80 characters. Recall the previous SET TERMINAL command and modify it using line editing control characters.

```
$ RECALL SET T                      [Pull back last SET command]
$ SET TERMINAL/WIDTH=80             [Change 132 to 80 and execute]
```

7. Type in the command SHOW USRRS followed by RETURN. You are supposed to enter the command incorrectly. What message do you get?

The "unrecognized keyword" message indicates the system does not understand the USRRS option. The facility issuing the message is DCL.

```
$ SHOW USRRS
%DCL-W-IVKEYW, unrecognized keyword - check validity and spelling
\USRRS\
```

8. Recall the previous command. Use CTRL functions to move the cursor to the beginning of the line and the end of the line.

Press the UP arrow or use CTRL/B to recall the previous command. Press CTRL/H to move to the beginning and CTRL/E to move to the end.

```
$ SHOW USERS
  ↑         ↑
CTRL/H    CTRL/E
```

9. Use CTRL functions to erase the word USRRS and the word SHOW.

Press CTRL/J to erase USRRS. Press CTRL/J again to erase SHOW. You can also erase the whole command line with CTRL/U.

```
$ SHOW USRRS↑                    $ SHOW USERS↑
          ↑                                ↑
        CTRL/J                          CTRL/U
$ SHOW↑                          $
     ↑
    CTRL/J
$
```

10. Recall the command again, change the word USRRS to USERS and execute the command.

Use UP arrow to recall the command. Use the LEFT arrow to position the cursor on the first R and type an E. If you are in overstrike mode, the E replaces the R and the word USERS should now be correct. Press RETURN to execute the command. Remember the cursor does not have to be at the end of the line to execute the command.

```
$ SHOW USRRS                     [Position the cursor on the R]
        ↑
$ SHOW USERS                     [Press E to correct the mistake]
                                 [RETURN to execute the command]
```

11. Set your terminal to the editing mode you like best for the rest of the exercises in this book.

```
$ SET TERMINAL/OVERSTRIKE     or     $ SET TERMINAL/INSERT
```

## 8

The HELP Utility

INTRODUCTION

The HELP utility provides excellent online documentation about commands, utilities, and many other subjects. The text of each command is taken directly from the master reference volume for commands in the VMS General User documentation, which means using HELP is the same as looking up information in the *DCL Dictionary*. In this chapter, you will learn how HELP information is organized and how to interpret and respond to HELP prompts. When you learn this utility well, you have most essential information available at your fingertips.

In HELP, each command and utility is indexed separately. The master HELP menu also lists many generic information subjects that group commands by function. When you understand the command language rules, it is easy to find your way through HELP documentation because the information is organized by commands, parameters and qualifiers.

HELP provides a short description of each command, accompanied by information on parameters and qualifiers where they are available. The text points out where qualifiers can be used on parameters, as well as on the command. HELP does not index the negative form of qualifiers — you find out if a qualifier can be negated by looking up the qualifier itself. There is usually one example of how to use each utility or command and there are multiple examples in many cases.

HELP INFORMATION ORGANIZATION

HELP information is organized in a multiple level tree structure as shown in Figure 8-1. The top level lists general categories and commands. Lower levels contain increasingly specific information. This organization mirrors the format of each VMS command, in that the command is described first, followed by information on parameters, qualifiers, and examples. Complex command structures like SHOW or topics like Specify may have as many as three or four lower levels of information.

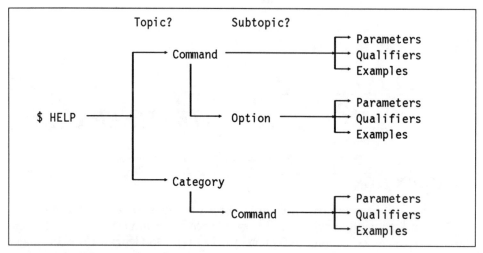

Figure 8-1. HELP Topic Organization

MAIN HELP SCREEN

You start the HELP utility with the HELP command. The master HELP screen, shown in Figure 8-2, includes an Instructions category and a Hints category in the first screen of the display. Next you are instructed to press RETURN. The second screen displays the master list of all commands and topics for which documentation is available. Last, you see a Topic? prompt at the bottom of the screen.

HELP PROMPTS

At the Topic? prompt, you can request information on any item listed in the menu. The Topic? prompt indicates you are at the top level in HELP. As you request HELP information on lower levels in the information tree, the prompt changes to Subtopic? preceded by the subject under which you are working. You can figure out how deep you are in the information tree by examining the number of subjects that appear in front of the Subtopic? prompt.

At the Topic? prompt, you can enter a single subject like SHOW or two or more related subjects like SHOW USERS. HELP displays a description of the command and the command qualifiers for which information is available. The next prompt you see is Subtopic?, which indicates you are at the command level in the information tree. For information about all qualifiers, enter "command_qualifiers," which you can abbreviate "com." For information about a specific qualifier, enter the qualifier preceded by a slash. To look at the examples, enter "examples." After the information is displayed, the Subtopic? prompt is repeated, which allows you to request more information about the same command.

```
$ HELP

The HELP command invokes the VAX/VMS HELP Facility to display information
about a VMS command or topic. In response to the "Topic?" prompt, you can:

 o Type the name of the command or topic for which you need help.

 o Type INSTRUCTIONS for more detailed instructions on how to use HELP.

 o Type HINTS if you are not sure of the name of the command or topic for
   which you need help

 o Type a question mark (?) to redisplay the most recently requested text.

 o Press the RETURN key one or more times to exit from HELP.

Additional information available:

:=              =               @               ACCOUNTING ALLOCATE  ANALYZE    APPEND
ASSIGN          ATTACH          AUTHORIZE       AUTOGEN    BACKUP    CALL       CANCEL
CLOSE           CONNECT         CONTINUE        CONVERT    COPY      CREATE     DEALLOCATE
DEASSIGN        DEBUG           DECK            DEFINE     DELETE    DEPOSIT    DIFFERENCE
DIRECTORY       DISCONNECT      DISKQUOTA       DISMOUNT   DUMP      EDIT       EOD
EOJ             Errors          EXAMINE         EXCHANGE   EXIT      FDL        GOSUB
GOTO            HELP            Hints           IF         INITIALIZE INQUIRE   INSTALL
Instructions                    JOB             LATCP      Lexicals  LIBRARY    LICENSE
Line_editing                    LINK            LOGIN      LOGOUT    MACRO      MAIL
MERGE           MESSAGE         MONITOR         MOUNT      NCP       NCS        ON
OPEN            PASSWORD        PATCH           PHONE      PRINT     PURGE      Queues
READ            RECALL          RECOVER         RENAME     REPLY     REQUEST    RETURN
RMS             RTL_Routines                    RUN        RUNOFF    ScriptPrinter
SEARCH          SET             SHOW            SORT       SPAWN     Specify    START
STOP            SUBMIT          Symbol_Assign              SYNCHRONIZE          SYSGEN
SYSMAN          System_Services                 TFF        TYPE      UIL        UNLOCK
V52_NewFeatures                 V53_NewFeatures            VIEW      WAIT       WRITE

Topic?
```

Figure 8-2. Main HELP Screen

It is not necessary to go through every menu level in HELP to look up lower level information. You can request information on a particular command and qualifier by entering both the command and qualifier with the HELP command or at the Topic? prompt. See the examples in Figures 8-3, 8-4, and 8-5. You can also enter a command or topic when HELP instructs you to "Press RETURN to continue." Then, instead of displaying the next screen for the previous subject, HELP presents information on the new topic you request.

To examine all information stored for the current topic or subtopic, enter an asterisk (*) at the prompt. To display the screen you have just viewed, enter a question mark (?). To back up one level, press RETURN. At the Subtopic? prompt RETURN brings you back to the Topic? prompt. At the Topic? prompt, RETURN exits HELP. Use CTRL/Z to exit HELP from any prompt.

COMMAND INFORMATION

For information on a specific command, enter the command name. Abbreviations are allowed — HELP displays the first command that matches the abbreviation. If more than one command matches the string you enter, information is presented for each command. To see all information stored for a command, enter the command followed by an asterisk (*). HELP responds with information about parameters, qualifiers, and examples. All three forms of command query are shown in Figure 8-3. Intervening lines of HELP text have been omitted.

You can use a shorthand technique to list all commands or qualifiers instead of wading throughseveral screens of introductory material. To display the main command menu, enter HELP XX or some other illegal command at the Topic? prompt. HELP responds with "No such command" and lists the valid subjects.

```
One Command              Ambiguous Command         Everything
------------------------------------------------------------------
$ HELP CREATE            $ HELP REC                $ HELP PRINT *
CREATE                   RECALL                    PRINT

. . . . . . . .          . . . . . . . .           Parameters
CREATE Subtopic?                                   . . . . . . . .
                         RECOVER                   Command_Qualifiers
                         . . . . . . . .           . . . . . . . .
                         Topic?                    Topic?
```

Figure 8-3. HELP Command Information

PARAMETER INFORMATION

For information on command parameters, you can either enter the command followed by "parameter" or request help on the command and then enter the word "parameter" at the Subtopic? prompt. Both forms of query are shown in Figure 8-4.

```
$ HELP PRINT                    $ HELP PRINT parameters
PRINT                           PRINT
..........                          Parameters
PRINT Subtopic? parameters      ..........
PRINT                           Topic?
  Parameters
  ..........
PRINT Subtopic?
Topic?
```

Figure 8-4. HELP Parameter Information

QUALIFIER INFORMATION

For information on a qualifier, you can ask for help on the command and then enter the qualifier (preceded by a slash) at the Subtopic? prompt, or you can enter the command followed by the qualifier at the Topic? prompt. Negative qualifiers are not indexed separately, but are included with the qualifier description whenever the negative form is recognized. For example, for information on the /NOWRAP qualifier, you must enter HELP SET TERM/WRAP and read the /WRAP description for instructions on how the negative form is used.

To see a description of all qualifiers for a command, enter "command_qualifiers." HELP responds with each qualifier and its description, which can result in a display several screens long. You can use a shorthand technique to see a list of legal qualifiers by entering /XX or some other illegal choice. HELP responds with "No such qualifier" and lists the legal choices for this command.

Most commands operate with one or more qualifiers enabled, even when they are not specified on the command line. This is called the command "default." HELP identifies default qualifiers by placing the word "default" after the qualifier or in the qualifier description.

Figure 8-5 illustrates four ways to ask for information on command qualifiers. You can first ask for information on the command and then request qualifier information at the Subtopic? prompt. You can also ask for information on a specifica qualifier or all qualifiers. And last, you can list all command qualifiers by entering an illegal qualifier with the command or at the Subtopic? prompt.

```
Command                          One Qualifier
-----------------------          -----------------------
$ HELP PRINT                     $ HELP PRINT/FORM
PRINT                            PRINT
                                   /FORM
..........
PRINT Subtopic? /FORM              ..........
PRINT                            Topic?
  /FORM

  ..........
PRINT Subtopic?
Topic?


All Qualifiers                   Qualifier choices
-----------------------          -----------------------
$ HELP PRINT command_qualifiers  $ HELP PRINT/XX
PRINT                            PRINT
 /AFTER                          No such qualifier
                                 Additional information
 ..........
 /BACKUP
                                 /AFTER     /BACKUP    ...
 ..........                      PRINT Subtopic?
Topic?
```

Figure 8-5. HELP Qualifier Information

EXAMPLE INFORMATION

HELP information usually includes an example category that illustrates the proper use of the command. If the command has many qualifiers, the examples normally demonstrate several of them. To see an example, enter the command name followed by the word "example" without the quotes.

GETTING HELP FOR THE SHOW COMMAND

The HELP SHOW display is illustrated in Figure 8-6. From the command description we see that, strictly speaking, the SHOW command does not conform to normal DCL syntax rules. Instead of parameters, we have "options" for the SHOW command. HELP SET displays a similar screen for the available SET options. This command and the SET command are the only two that use options. Many of the SHOW and SET options either accept or require a parameter (*e.g.*, SHOW USERS or SET TERMINAL). In this case, HELP contains a description of the parameter and how it is used.

```
$ HELP SHOW
SHOW

Displays information about the current status of the process, the
system, or devices in the system.

Format:

  SHOW option

Additional information available:

ACCOUNTING ACL       AUDIT    BROADCAST CLUSTER   CPU      DEFAULT
DEVICES    DISPLAY   ENTRY    ERROR     INTRUSION KEY      LICENSE
LOGICAL    MAGTAPE   MEMORY   NETWORK   PRINTER   PROCESS
PROTECTION QUEUE     QUOTA    RMS_DEFAULT         STATUS   SYMBOL
SYSTEM     TERMINAL  TIME     TRANSLATION         USERS
WORKING_SET

SHOW Subtopic?
```

Figure 8-6. HELP SHOW Display

The SHOW Subtopic? prompt at the bottom of the display indicates you are down
one level in HELP and can now ask for information on any of the options
displayed on the screen. To look up SHOW TIME, enter TIME at the SHOW Subtopic? prompt. Press RETURN for the Topic? prompt and RETURN a second time
to exit HELP.

OTHER HELP CATEGORIES

Hints

This subject provides information in 13 different categories, including batch and
print jobs, command procedures, contacting people, developing and executing
programs, files and directories, logical names, physical devices, the terminal environment, and the user environment (Fig. 8-7). Each category contains a list of
commands and a brief description of how it is used. For example, the user environment category describes the SHOW and SET commands you use to modify
and control your environment. The files and directories subject describes the commands you use to create, manipulate, and manage files.

```
$ HELP HINTS

HINTS

Type the name of one of the categories listed below to obtain a list
of related commands and topics. To obtain detailed information on a
topic, press the RETURN key until you reach the "Topic?" prompt and
then type the name of the topic.

Topics that appear in all upper case are DCL commands.

Additional information available:

Batch_and_print_jobs   Command_procedures   Contacting_people
Creating_processes      Developing_programs  Executing_programs
Files_and_directories   Logical_names        Operators_in_expressions
Physical_devices        System_management    Terminal_environment
User_environment

HINTS Subtopic?
```

Figure 8-7. HELP Hints Display

Specify

Hidden away in the Specify topic there is information of considerable value to
new VMS users. How to specify a date and time, construct legal expressions, how
to specify and interpret privileges, and the rules for file specification, file protection, UICs, integers and strings are all included (Fig. 8-8).

```
$ HELP SPECIFY

SPECIFY
 This help category contains information on the syntax of various
 entities used in DCL.

Additional information available:

Date_time   Expression   File_spec  Integer   Privilege  Protection
String       Symbol        UIC
SPECIFY Subtopic?
```

Figure 8-8. HELP Specify Display

Run-Time Library

For programmers, the RTL (Run-Time Library) topic describes callable system routines for math and string functions, generic date/time and other utility functions, parallel processing, and screen management. These descriptions are taken from the information contained in Volumes 5A and 5B, *Run-Time Library*, in the VMS Programming documentation set. Each routine is fully described, down to the number and type of parameters required for each call. You must preface each routine for which you are seeking help with the appropriate four-letter prefix (*e.g.*, LIB$, MTH$, PPL$, STR$, SMG$, OTS$).

Lexicals

The "Lexicals" topic describes the programming functions that can be used in DCL command procedures. These programming functions allow great sophistication in the way VMS commands are combined and used. Your LOGIN.COM file is probably the first command procedure you will create. As you become more sophisticated, you may want to use some of these functions to enhance your login file. In HELP, when you get to the Lexicals Subtopic? prompt, be sure to preface the function you are interested in with an F$.

Compilers

If your site has one or more DEC compilers, your HELP library will contain very complete documentation on the language syntax and semantics, as well as descriptions of valid expressions, transfer of control, and other language-specific features.

HELP EXERCISES

When you are practicing the exercises, pay attention to the prompt from the utility. The prompt tells you how many levels down the information tree you have traveled. Also, remember that you can abbreviate topics to the first unique string that identifies the command, parameter, qualifier, or example you wish to examine. Intervening lines of HELP text have been removed.

1. Review the rules for using the HELP utility by reading the information in the INSTRUCTIONS category. At the Topic? prompt, ask for help on HINTS.

```
$ HELP INSTRUCTIONS
INSTRUCTIONS
............
Topic? HINTS
HINTS
........
```

2. Ask for help on the SHOW command and redisplay the help screen you are looking at. Ask for information on SHOW USERS and look at the examples for this subject.

```
$ HELP SHOW                                [SHOW information]

SHOW

..........
SHOW Subtopic? ?                           [? displays the current screen]
SHOW

..........
SHOW Subtopic? USERS                       [SHOW USERS information]
SHOW
   USERS
..........
SHOW USERS Subtopic? examples              [Ask for examples]
SHOW
   USERS
     examples
     ..........
SHOW Subtopic?                             [Press RETURN]
Topic?
```

3. Next ask for help on Specify and then for Specify topic Date_time. How many levels down are you right now? Exit HELP with one control key.

```
Topic? SPECIFY
SPECIFY

..........
SPECIFY Subtopic? Date_time                [Date and time information]
SPECIFY
   Date_time
   ..........
   Absolute    Combination    Delta
SPECIFY Date_Time Subtopic? Absolute       [How to enter an absolute time]
SPECIFY
   Date_time
   Absolute                                [Three levels down in specify]
   ..........
SPECIFY Date_time Subtopic? CTRL/Z         [Exit HELP]
$
```

4. Start HELP again and ask for information on the SET command. Next ask for information on SET PASSWORD and then information on the /GENERATE qualifier. At the SET PASSWORD Subtopic? prompt, try the Up Arrow. What happens?

```
$ HELP SET                                 [SET information]
SET

..........
SET Subtopic? PASSWORD                      [SET PASSWORD information]
SET
```

```
      PASSWORD
      .........
 SET PASSWORD Subtopic? /GENERATE
 SET
   PASSWORD
     /GENERATE
     ........
 SET PASSWORD Subtopic? /GENERATE              [UP arrow recalls /generate]
```

5. Erase /GENERATE with one control character and enter a question mark. What happens? Now ask for all information that is available for this command.

Erase /GENERATE with CTRL/U which deletes all text on the command line. The question mark directs HELP to redisplay the current screen. You should see the main SET PASSWORD screen. The asterisk (*) displays all the information available for the current topic or subtopic, which in this case is SET PASSWORD, all qualifiers, and examples.

```
 SET PASSWORD Subtopic? /GENERATE
 SET PASSWORD Subtopic?                        [CTRL/U erases /GENERATE]
 SET PASSWORD Subtopic? ?                      [Redisplay SET PASSWORD screen]
 SET
   PASSWORD
   ..........
 SET PASSWORD Subtopic? *                      [* asks for everything]
 SET
   PASSWORD
     Command_Qualifiers                        [Enter CTRL/Y to abort HELP or
       /GENERATE                               any other command or utility]
       ..........
       /SECONDARY
       ..........
       /SYSTEM
       ..........
     Examples
     ..........
 SET PASSWORD Subtopic?                        [Press RETURN]
 SET Subtopic?
```

6. Exit the HELP utility. Next, ask for information on SET PASSWORD/GENERATE with one command. Which prompt do you see and why?

You see the Topic? prompt because HELP returns to the main prompt after the information you requested is displayed.

```
 $ HELP SET PASSWORD/GENERATE
 SET
   PASSWORD
     /GENERATE
     ..........
 Topic?
```

7. Ask for help on all the qualifiers available with the LOGOUT command. Which qualifier is used by default? How do you override the default operation?

```
Help qualifier information is accessed by the topic "command_qualifier".
The qualifier descriptions indicate which ones are used by default. In this
case, /BRIEF is the default. To override the default, use one or more
qualifiers on the command (e.g., LOGOUT/FULL or LOGOUT/HANGUP).
```

```
Topic? LOGOUT com
LOGOUT
   Command_Qualifiers
      /BRIEF                                  [LOGOUT default is /BRIEF]
      ..........
      /FULL
      ..........
      /HANGUP
      ..........
Topic?
```

8. How can you examine the examples stored for any command?

```
Enter the command followed by "examples" at the appropriate prompt.
```

```
Topic? LOGOUT ex      or      $ HELP LOGOUT ex
LOGOUT
   Examples
   ..........
Topic?
```

Files and Directories

INTRODUCTION

In this chapter, we review the full VMS file specification, including the remote file specification used to access files across a network. We discuss the DIRECTORY command which searches for and identifies files, and learn about using wildcards in a file specification. Then we delve into directory structures, your home directory, and creating new directories under your home directory. We also learn how to examine the current directory location with SHOW DEFAULT and how to use SET DEFAULT to move from one location to another using either an absolute or relative directory specification (path name). Last, we examine some of the more important date and time file attributes VMS stores in the header of each file and how to select files using these attributes.

VMS FILE SPECIFICATION

Because of the flexibility of VAX configurations, you may access files stored in many different locations — a local disk, a disk on a VAXcluster, a disk on a network node, or a tape drive in any of these configurations. There are six components in a full VMS file specification and the use of all six parts uniquely identifies a file in any configuration. Blanks are not allowed anywhere in a file specification and punctuation is required to separate each part of a file name (Fig. 9-1).

```
NODE::DEVICE:[DIRECTORY]NAME.TYPE;VERSION
```

Figure 9-1. VMS File Specification

Node

Node identifies a network or cluster node and can be a maximum of six characters long. The double colon (::) must be included to ensure that the network file specification translates correctly. See the Network File Specification section later in this chapter for a more complete description of network file access.

Device

Device name selects a disk, tape, or other mass storage peripheral, and must be followed by a colon (:). Device names can be up to 255 characters long, although in real life, they are much shorter.

Directory

Devices are typically organized into partitions called directories to keep user files separate from one another. The directory name, which selects one of these partitions, is a specific location on a disk or tape drive. A directory name is always enclosed in square brackets and can be up to 39 characters long, including A-Z, 0-9, the dollar sign ($), the underscore (_), and the hyphen (-).

Name and Type

Name selects one file in a directory. If there is more than one file with the same name, the file type, which is also called a file "extension", further identifies the file. The words file type and file extension are used interchangeably in the rest of this book. Name and type must be separated by a period (.) and can each be 39 characters long, including A-Z, 0-9, the dollar sign ($), underscore (_), and hyphen (-).

Version

Version numbers keep track of multiple copies of a file. Each time you modify a file, the system creates a new version. If there are several versions of the same file, it may be necessary to uniquely identify one of them by version number. Version is separated from type by a semicolon (;). Version numbers are integers in the range of 1-32767.

DEVICE NAMES

We introduced device names in Chapter 6, Looking at the System, in the SHOW DEVICE command. DUA0:, 1DUA21:, and USERA: are all legal forms of disk names. The first two are "physical" device names and the third is a "logical name" created by the system manager. VMS users normally refer to disks using logical names because they are easier to remember and they also eliminate dependency on physical devices.

When you are authorized as a VMS user, the system manager selects a home disk and home directory where your files will be stored. You normally create and manipulate files on this home disk in your home directory. You need only be concerned about device names in a file specification when you are allowed to access files on other disks or on magnetic tape. If you are always working on your home disk, you do not need to provide a device name as part of a file specification.

FILE VERSION USAGE

The first version of a file is version 1, the second version is 2, and so on. If you do not provide a version number as part of a file specification, the system automatically selects the highest numbered version, which is also the most recent. The only time you must supply a version number is with the DELETE command, which requires that you uniquely identify the file to be deleted.

You can use zero (0) as a version number to select the highest version of a file and a negative version number (*e.g.,* -1) to select earlier versions of a file. The negative number is subtracted from the highest version number to compute the target version number. For example, if you have five copies of a file called TEST.DAT, versions 1 through 5, the specification TEST.DAT;-1 refers to TEST.DAT;4, the next lower version number. This notation is especially useful in referring to the previous version of a file when you do not know the actual version number.

You can limit the number of versions of each file that are stored in your directory by setting a version limit on the file in the file header. Users find this automatic purging feature an effective aid in controlling the proliferation of files. Chapter 10 discusses this subject in detail under the heading Version Limit Controls.

FILE SPECIFICATION DEFAULTS

When you use a file specification, you can provide all six parts or, even better, you can let the system provide defaults for you. The system uses your current node, device, and directory as defaults whenever you omit any or all of them from a file specification. For example, the system assumes you are accessing files on the node you are logged in to, unless you specifically include a node name in a file specification. Likewise, your current disk and directory are provided for the device and directory portions whenever they are omitted.

When type is omitted from a file name, the extension supplied depends upon the command or utility you are using. Some commands provide a default file type and others do not. For example, the PRINT and TYPE commands use a default file type of .LIS, the RUN command uses .EXE, and the SORT and MERGE utilities use a file type of .DAT.

If your file type is the same as the default expected by the command, you can omit it from the file specification. There is no standard list of file type conventions; you learn them from experience. One easy way to discover command file type defaults is to enter the command and a file name without a type. If your file type is not the same as that expected by the command, the information message will contain the default type expected. Remember, however, that you do not need to know the rules if you always provide the type as part of a file specification.

The result of file specification defaults is that you need to provide only a file name and type in most instances. The system takes the parts you specify, applies defaults, and expands the file specification to include all portions except the node name. This expanded file specification always appears in command output and in information, error, and warning messages.

Figure 9-2 has five file specifications. The first example uses all six parts, so no defaults are applied. The second omits the node name, so the system assumes the file is on the current node. In the third example, the system provides the current device as a default. The current device and directory are defaulted on the fourth file name and, in the last example, the system uses the highest numbered version of the file, if more than one version exists.

```
Node  Device Dir   Name  Type Version
----------------------------------------
SYBIL::DUAO:[TEST]REPORT.LIS;23
        USERA:[TEST]REPORT.LIS;23
              [TEST]REPORT.LIS;23
                    REPORT.LIS;23
                    REPORT.LIS
```

Figure 9-2. Example File Specifications

NETWORK FILE SPECIFICATION

Occasionally, you may need to access a file on a network node. If you are unsure of the node name, use SHOW NETWORK to display the nodes reachable from your system. You select a network node by entering a node name, followed by a double colon, and then the file specification. The system manager may predefine your network access by providing an invisible username and password combination, or you may have to provide your network username and password explicitly.

Both forms of a network file specification are shown in Figure 9-3. With predefined network access, VMS logs you in to the remote system with the username and password defined by the system manager. If you are not automatically mapped to a username on the remote system, but are an authorized user, you can include your remote username and password with the file specification. When you include them, they appear right after the node name and must be enclosed in double quotes (").

```
NODE::name.type
NODE::[DIRECTORY]name.type
NODE::DEVICE:[DIRECTORY]name.type

NODE"username password"::name.type
NODE"username password"::[DIRECTORY]name.type
NODE"username password"::DEVICE:[DIRECTORY]name.type
```

Figure 9-3. Network File Specifications

VMS logs you in to the remote system with either the predefined or explicit username and password provided and puts you in the home directory for that username. If you are accessing a file in the home directory, you can omit device and directory from the file specification. Otherwise include the device and directory portions as needed. The remote file is then made available to you on the local node. When you are finished using the remote file, you are transparently logged out of the network node.

You can use a network file specification with most file manipulation commands (with CREATE, TYPE, COPY, RENAME, DELETE, EDIT, and so on), but network file access is much slower than accessing a file on the local node. When you need regular access to a remote file, it should be moved to the system you use most often.

LISTING FILES

DIRECTORY, usually abbreviated DIR, is one of the most heavily used VMS commands. You use it to list files in the current directory, another directory, or files in a directory on another device. In the command format in Figure 9-4, the file specification is enclosed in square brackets which means it is optional. DIR alone lists all files in the current directory in alphabetical order. Your current directory is always called your "default" directory and your current device is the "default" device.

If you include a parameter, it can contain any part or combination of parts of a file specification. DIRECTORY will use the specified parts to locate files that match. If no files match the specification or the directory is empty, the message "No Files Found" is issued. If the file you are looking up does not have a file type, you must include the period after the file name — otherwise DIRECTORY will not locate the file.

```
$ DIRECTORY [file-spec]     Command Format

$ DIR                       Files in the current directory
$ DIR TEMP.DAT              All versions of TEMP.DAT
$ DIR TEMP                  Files with a name of TEMP and any
                            type or version number
$ DIR .DAT                  Files with any name and .DAT type
```

Figure 9-4. DIRECTORY Commands

FILE NAME WILDCARDS

To aid in searching for files where you know only part of the name, use the asterisk (*) wildcard character which matches any string. The percent (%) wildcard matches any single character and is useful when file names are identical except for two or three characters. Use wildcards alone, together, or in combination with a partial file name to select and operate on a group of files (Fig. 9-5). Wildcards can be used in all parts of a file specification except the device name.

```
$ DIR *.*;*                 All versions of all files
$ DIR *.*                   Highest version of all files

$ DIR WPS*                  File names that start with WPS
$ DIR *JUN87.DAT            File names that end with JUN87

$ DIR [.*]                  Files one level down
$ DIR [.A*]                 Files in subdirectories starting with A

$ DIR SUM%.DAT              Files that start with SUM and any
                            character in the fourth position
$ DIR %%%.COM               Three-character names with type .COM
```

Figure 9-5. The * and % Wildcards

DIRECTORY STRUCTURES

A directory is a special type of file, similar to a catalog, that records the name, size, owner, and other information about each file created in that location. Directory files always have the file type .DIR and a version number of 1. Never create a non-directory file with a .DIR extension, and never change the file type or the version number of a directory file. If you have an ordinary text file with a .DIR extension or a directory file with any type but .DIR, you will run into problems.

A disk usually has directories organized in a tree structure. The example in Figure 9-6 shows a possible organization for users in an administrative department. The main department directory [ADMIN] is at the top of the tree. It functions as a group area where common and shared files are located. Each user in the department also has a personal or home directory where individual files are created and stored. This structure separates and protects the files of one user from those of other users in the group.

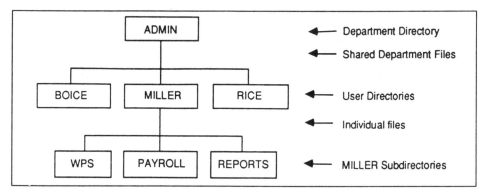

Figure 9-6. Directory Tree Structure

At user authorization time, the system manager creates the ADMIN group directory and a personal directory for each user in this group that is one level below the ADMIN directory. After logging in, each user is placed in his home directory in the second level of the tree. In this example, BOICE is placed in the BOICE directory, MILLER in MILLER, and so on. The directory file names are BOICE.DIR, MILLER.DIR, and RICE.DIR. When you refer to any of these directory locations, you must enclose the directory name in square brackets (*e.g.*, [.MILLER]). This notation is referred to as a "directory specification." Assume you are in the ADMIN directory which contains only three directory files when you issue the DIRECTORY commands in Figure 9-7. To look up files in a different directory, include the target directory name in square brackets.

```
$ DIR                 Displays BOICE.DIR, MILLER.DIR, and RICE.DIR
$ DIR .DIR            Displays BOICE.DIR, MILLER.DIR, and RICE.DIR
$ DIR BOICE           Displays BOICE.DIR

$ DIR [.RICE]         Displays files in the RICE directory
$ DIR [.MILLER.WPS]   Displays files in the WPS directory
```

Figure 9-7. The DIRECTORY Command in a Directory Tree

DISPLAYING YOUR DEFAULT DIRECTORY

SHOW DEFAULT displays your default device and directory location, which is the same as asking "Where Am I?" SET DEFAULT can change the default device, the default directory, or both. Remembering that the current directory is called the default directory, these commands start to make sense.

SHOW DEFAULT has no parameters or qualifiers. Using the tree structure in Figure 9-6, if you log in as ADMIN, SHOW DEFAULT displays USERA:[ADMIN]. If you log in as MILLER, SHOW DEFAULT returns USERA:[ADMIN.MILLER] and if you move to the WPS directory under MILLER, SHOW DEFAULT returns USERA:[ADMIN.MILLER.WPS] (Fig. 9-7). When you are lower than the top level in a directory tree, SHOW DEFAULT displays the device and all directory names concatenated with periods as they are encountered when moving down the tree.

```
$ SHOW DEFAULT                          Command Format

$ SHOW DEFAULT
  USERA:[ADMIN]                         Department shared directory
$ SHOW DEFAULT
  USERA:[ADMIN.MILLER]                  Miller's home directory
$ SHOW DEFAULT
  USERA:[ADMIN.MILLER.WPS]              Miller's WPS directory
```

Figure 9-8. SHOW DEFAULT Command

CHANGING YOUR DEFAULT DIRECTORY

You use SET DEFAULT to change your default device, default directory, or both. This moves you from one directory to another on the same disk, or to a new disk and directory. SET DEFAULT accepts a device name, a directory specification, or both (Fig. 9-9). If you use a device name with this command, it should be followed by a colon. However, if you are only allowed to access your home disk, you will never need to change devices.

If you are allowed to use other disks or tape drives, specify the device name with SET DEFAULT. If you specify a device name, but not a target directory, your current directory is combined with the device name to define the new location. If no such directory exists on the target device, the system issues the error message "Directory not found" when you attempt to reference a file in that location.

A directory specification may contain a single directory name or several directory names, concatenated with periods, to identify a lower level directory. The directory specifications used with SET DEFAULT in Figure 9-9 are identical to those returned by SHOW DEFAULT in Figure 9-8.

```
$ SET DEFAULT [device-name[:]][directory-spec]   Command Format

Changing Devices
$ SET DEFAULT USERA:                Move to a new disk
$ SET DEFAULT MUAO:                 Move to a tape drive


Changing Directories
$ SET DEFAULT [ADMIN]               Move to ADMIN directory
$ SET DEFAULT [ADMIN.MILLER]        Move to MILLER directory
```

Figure 9-9. SET DEFAULT Command

SET DEFAULT Goes Anywhere

SET DEFAULT accepts any device or directory name without validating that the device or directory exists. This means that you can SET DEFAULT to a non-existent location and never see an error message. The invalid location is discovered only when you actually try to access a file on a non-existent device or in a non-existent directory (Fig. 9-10). Do not be surprised if this happens to you once in a while, most commonly when you make a typing mistake in a directory name.

```
$ SET DEFAULT [TOMATO]
$ SHOW DEFAULT
%DCL-I-INVDEF, USERA:[TOMATO] does not exist
$ DIR
%DIRECT-E-OPENIN, error opening USERA:[TOMATO]*.*;* as input
-RMS-E-DNF, directory not found
-SYSTEM-W-NOSUCHFILE, no such file
```

Figure 9-10. SET DEFAULT Goes Anywhere

In Figure 9-10, both SHOW DEFAULT and DIRECTORY attempt to access the TOMATO directory. SHOW DEFAULT clearly states that the directory does not exist. The three messages returned by the DIRECTORY command are not quite as direct, but they convey the same information.

The first error message issued by DIRECTORY indicates an error occurred opening the TOMATO directory. You also see the file specification used by the command with VMS defaults applied. Next you see the RMS message (the Record Management System handles most file functions) "directory not found" which tells you that this directory does not exist. The last message, "no such file," is redundant but unavoidable.

CREATING DIRECTORIES

You make directories with the CREATE/DIRECTORY command. You must provide one directory specification, and you can create several directories if you include multiple directory specifications, separated by commas, on the command line (Fig. 9-11). Directories may be nested seven levels deep, plus the top directory for a maximum depth of eight levels. You are normally allowed to create directories, often called subdirectories, only below your home directory. You need elevated privileges to create a directory in a group area or at the top of a disk.

Suppose we want to add a MANAGER directory to the ADMIN tree in Figure 9-6 at the same level as the user directories. First, we move to ADMIN and use the directory specification [.MANAGER] to create the MANAGER directory. The period indicates that we are creating a directory below the current [ADMIN] location. The second CREATE/DIR command shows an equivalent way to accomplish the same thing by including ADMIN in the directory specification. We can also create a MEMOS subdirectory under the new MANAGER directory in two equivalent ways, as shown by the last two commands in Figure 9-11.

```
$ CREATE/DIRECTORY  directory-spec[,...]   Command Format

$ SET DEFAULT [ADMIN]                      Move to top directory
$ CREATE/DIR [.MANAGER]                    Create MANAGER under ADMIN
  -- or --
$ CREATE/DIR [ADMIN.MANAGER]              Equivalent command

$ SET DEFAULT [.MANAGER]                   New MANAGER directory
$ CREATE/DIR [.MEMOS]                      Create MEMOS under MANAGER
  -- or --
$ CREATE/DIR [ADMIN.MANAGER.MEMOS]        Equivalent command
```

Figure 9-11. CREATE/DIRECTORY Command

When you enter this command, if a directory of the same name already exists, the system issues an information message and does not create another one. You need elevated privileges to create a directory at the top of a device. If you accidentally end up at the top of a disk, CREATE/DIRECTORY will issue a protection violation error message. This error message is a clue that you are probably not in the correct location or that you made an error in the directory specification.

SEARCHING DIRECTORIES

Another wildcard called the ellipsis (...) can be used alone or with a directory specification to select all files in a directory tree. You should not confuse the ellipsis with the *.*;* wildcard. The ellipsis replaces a directory specification or is combined with another directory specification and the *.*;* substitutes for a file name, type, and version. As a directory specification, the ellipsis selects all lower directories and files in a tree, down to the very bottom level. It is not valid as a file specification for commands that operate on a single file or directory (*e.g.*, CREATE or SET DEFAULT).

Assume you are in the ADMIN directory when you issue the commands shown in Figure 9-12. The first example displays all files in the entire ADMIN tree. The second example lists all files in the BOICE directory and any lower levels, and the third example lists all files in the structure that starts with the REPORTS directory under MILLER.

```
$ DIR [...]                List all files in the ADMIN tree
$ DIR [.BOICE...]          List files in the BOICE tree
$ DIR [.MILLER.REPORTS...] List files in the REPORTS tree
```

Figure 9-12. Searching a Directory Tree

USING DIRECTORY SPECIFICATIONS

When dealing with directories, the directory specification may contain one or more directories depending upon the target location. It also changes based upon whether you are moving down, up, or laterally in a directory tree. In all cases, you must enclose the directory specification in square brackets.

In the ADMIN directory structure, we can see that there are six paths through the tree. Each path ends in a directory at the first, second, or third level. Each path is uniquely identified by spelling out the device on which the tree is located and the directories encountered along the way (Fig. 9-13). A lower level directory is always preceded by a period. Each time you see a period, you know you are going down one level in the tree.

Because the user directories are at the second level, each user directory specification has two names — ADMIN and the name of the home directory for that user. In the case of the subdirectories under MILLER which are three levels down, there are three directory names, concatenated with periods, in the directory specification.

```
Group Directory
USERA:[ADMIN]                          Top level directory


User Directories
USERA:[ADMIN.BOICE]                    BOICE directory
USERA:[ADMIN.MILLER]                   MILLER directory
USERA:[ADMIN.RICE]                     RICE directory


Miller Directories
USERA:[ADMIN.MILLER.WPS]               MILLER subdirectories
USERA:[ADMIN.MILLER.PAYROLL]
USERA:[ADMIN.MILLER.REPORTS]
```

Figure 9-13. Using Device and Directory Specifications

You can use any of these path names with the SET DEFAULT command. Remembering the rules for VMS defaults, you know that the device name USERA: is not necessary if it is the default device. Likewise, you do not have to provide the name of your default directory if you are interested in files in a directory immediately below your current location. With the required privileges or appropriate file protection, you can move to any directory in ADMIN using one of these path names with SET DEFAULT as shown in Figure 9-14.

```
$ SET DEFAULT USERA:[ADMIN]             Move to ADMIN

$ SET DEFAULT USERA:[ADMIN.MILLER]      Move to MILLER
$ SET DEFAULT USERA:[ADMIN.BOICE]       Move to BOICE

$ SET DEFAULT USERA:[ADMIN.MILLER.WPS]  Move to MILLER's WPS
```

Figure 9-14. SET DEFAULT Command

Moving Down in a Directory Tree

From the ADMIN directory, you can get to the BOICE directory or any other user directory in two equivalent ways. You can spell out the "absolute" specification of the target directory, or you can use a "relative" specification that says go down one level to BOICE. You use absolute and relative file specifications much the same way as you give a friend directions to your home.

You can either spell out every street and the direction to turn at each intersection, or you can tell your friend to go south two blocks, east six blocks, and south two blocks from his or her current location. The same concept applies to moving around in a directory tree. You can either spell out the full path name of your destination or provide a path relative to your current location. The commands in Figure 9-15 illustrate both forms of a directory specification.

```
$ SET DEFAULT USERA:[ADMIN.BOICE]       Absolute file specification
$ SHOW DEFAULT                          Display current location
  USERA:[ADMIN.BOICE]                   BOICE Directory

$ SET DEFAULT [ADMIN]                   Start from [ADMIN]
$ SET DEFAULT [.BOICE]                  Relative specification
$ SHOW DEFAULT                          Display current location
  USERA:[ADMIN.BOICE]                   BOICE directory
```

Figure 9-15. Using SET and SHOW DEFAULT

If this were the only way to move around in a directory tree, we would all work in a single level because of the typing involved. Fortunately, there are two shorthand notations that make this job easier.

Moving Up in a Directory Tree

In a directory specification, the hyphen (-) character takes the place of the next higher directory name. Because of the way a tree is constructed, a subdirectory has one unique parent directory. You can use the hyphen alone to move up one level or multiple hyphens to move up several levels (Fig. 9-16). The hyphen can also be combined with other directory names to identify a directory lateral to the current location.

```
$ SET DEF [-]       Move up one level
$ SET DEF [-.-]     Move up two levels
```

Figure 9-16. Moving Up in a Directory Tree

Moving Laterally in a Directory Tree

Two rules control moving laterally in a tree. If the target directory is at the top of a physical or logical device, specify the desired directory in square brackets (*e.g.*,

[ADMIN]). Because you normally are not allowed to access directories and files at the top of a disk, you will seldom use a directory specification of this form. If you are in a subdirectory under your home directory and want to move to a different subdirectory, you must first move up one level and then back down again. This requires that you combine the hyphen with the target directory name in the device specification for SET DEFAULT, as illustrated in Figure 9-17.

```
$ SHOW DEFAULT                     Current location
  USERA:[ADMIN.MILLER]             Home directory one level down

$ SET DEFAULT [.WPS]               Move from MILLER to WPS
$ SHOW DEFAULT                     Make sure
  USERA:[ADMIN.MILLER.WPS]         Two levels down

$ SET DEFAULT [-.PAYROLL]          Move from WPS to PAYROLL
$ SHOW DEFAULT                     Check location
  USERA:[ADMIN.MILLER.PAYROLL]     Two levels down

$ SET DEFAULT [-]                  Move up one level
$ SHOW DEFAULT                     To the MILLER directory
  USERA:[ADMIN.MILLER]             One level down
```

Figure 9-17. Moving Laterally in a Directory Tree

Moving to Your Home Directory

SYS$LOGIN is a logical name that points to your home directory. You can look at the definition with the command SHOW LOGICAL SYS$LOGIN. It displays the expanded file specification that includes your home device and home directory. Use this logical name with SET DEFAULT to return to your home directory from any location (Fig. 9-18).

```
$ SHOW LOGICAL SYS$LOGIN                     Examine the definition
  "SYS$LOGIN" =  "USERA:[ADMIN.MILLER]" (LNM$JOB_80C211D0)

$ SET DEFAULT SYS$LOGIN                      Move to your home directory
$ SHOW DEFAULT                               Check your location
  USERA:[ADMIN.MILLER]
```

Figure 9-18. Using SYS$LOGIN

DIRECTORY GUIDELINES

Every reference to a file causes the system to search a directory. When there are over 500 files in one directory, it is more efficient for you to create subdirectories and divide your files into two or more groups. It is more efficient to have files distributed among several directories than one directory with many files. This technique reduces file search time, especially when a storage structure is many levels deep.

VMS allows directory files to grow to a maximum of 1024 blocks. However, for performance reasons, directories should never exceed 127 blocks or contain more than about 500 files. When a directory file grows too large, it can become fragmented (non-contiguous) on the disk and fragmentation slows down directory search operations significantly. The file management system also stores directory files in memory to speed up file search operations. When a directory exceeds 127 blocks, it is not cached in memory, which also results in a performance slowdown. From the user perspective, it is hard to find one file name in 500, and easy to locate one in 50. Check the size of your directory files with the DIR/SIZE command.

FILE ATTRIBUTES

The system maintains four dates for each file in the file header: creation, modification, expiration, and backup dates. The creation date is the date and time you created the file, and modification date is the date and time you last changed the file. The backup date is the date the file was last backed up using the BACKUP utility — the recording of this date must be specifically requested by the system manager during a backup operation. Otherwise the field remains blank. The expiration date is a way of tracking files you do not use for extended periods of time. The system manager can implement expiration date processing on a disk by disk basis. Using the BACKUP utility, the system manager may copy files with expired dates to magnetic tape and then delete them from the disk to free up space.

Additional fields in the file header record the size of the file in blocks, the UIC of the file owner, file protection, file organization and record format, and security information. The DIRECTORY/FULL command displays these attributes, as well as several other types of information, as shown in Figure 9-19.

Files are stored in units of disk blocks and each disk block contains 512 characters. In this figure, the file size is represented as 2/2. The first number is the actual number of disk blocks that contain data and the second is the total number of disk blocks allocated to the file. For efficiency reasons, the system manager may direct the file management system to allocate disk space in multi-block increments, so more space is allocated to the file than is initially used. A file can grow up to the last allocated block before additional space is needed. If file space is allocated in increments of one block, these two numbers will be the same.

```
$ DIRECTORY/FULL LOGIN.COM

Directory USERB:[VMSWIZ]

LOGIN.COM;38                    File ID:  (375,4,0)
Size:           2/3            Owner:    [MIS,VMSWIZ]
Created:    8-JAN-1990 15:18:11.00
Revised:    8-JAN-1990 15:15:57.77 (2)
Expires:    <None specified>
Backup:     9-JAN-1990 02:42:27.14
File organization:  Sequential
File attributes:    Allocation: 3, Extend: 0, Global buffer count: 0
                    Version limit: 3
Record format:      Variable length, maximum 67 bytes
Record attributes:  Carriage return carriage control
RMS attributes:     None
Journaling enabled: None
File protection:    System:RWED, Owner:RWED, Group:RE, World:
Access Cntrl List:  None

Total of 1 file, 2/3 blocks.
```

Figure 9-19. DIRECTORY/FULL Display

EXAMINING FILE ATTRIBUTES

The DIRECTORY command has many qualifiers you can use to examine specific file attributes. Figure 9-20 includes some of the most frequently used qualifiers, but is not a complete list. Although /EXCLUDE has nothing to do with file attributes, it is handy when you want to omit one or more files from a DIRECTORY search. For example, when you are interested in all files except directory files, you might use DIR/EXCLUDE=.DIR.

```
/EXCLUDE=file-spec    Omit specified file(s) from search
/DATE                 Creation date
/SIZE                 Size in blocks (512 bytes)
/TOTAL                Total of files matching file-spec
/GRAND                One line summary of files matching file-spec
/OWNER                UIC of the file's owner
/PROTECTION           Protection key
/SECURITY             All security information
```

Figure 9-20. DIRECTORY Qualifiers

Occasionally you may want to send a directory listing to a file, rather than have it displayed on the terminal. There are several formatting controls available for the output file as shown in Figure 9-21. To capture DIRECTORY output in a file, use the /OUTPUT=file-spec qualifier and provide a file name in which the output will be stored. You can also control the number of file names on a line and include or omit the header and trailer lines that are normally included with the display.

```
/OUTPUT=file-spec      Save listing in file-spec
/HEADER                Include header line
/NOHEADER              Omit header line
/COLUMNS=n             Number of columns of file names
/TRAILER               Include trailer line
/NOTRAILER             Omit trailer line
```

Figure 9-21. DIRECTORY Formatting Qualifiers

Figure 9-22 contains two DIRECTORY examples using the /OUTPUT qualifier. The first command creates a file called ADMIN-FILES.LIS that contains a list of all files stored in the ADMIN tree. The second example creates a list of files in the current directory in a file called DOCS.LIS — the output file contains one file name per line and has no header or trailer line.

```
$ DIR/OUTPUT= ADMIN-FILES.LIS   [ADMIN...]
$ DIR/OUTPUT= DOCS.LIS/COLUMNS=1/NOHEADER/NOTRAILER [.MEMOS]
```

Figure 9-22. DIRECTORY Formatting Examples

SELECTING FILES BY DATE AND TIME

You can select files based creation, modification, expiration or backup date with date and time qualifiers on the DIRECTORY command. This is very convenient when you are trying to remember the name of a file you made yesterday. You use two qualifiers to control date and time matching — one indicates which of the four dates to select and the other is the date to compare against. Figure 9-23 lists the valid qualifiers. The DIRECTORY command requires that you include either /BEFORE or /SINCE whenever you use any of the four date and time qualifiers.

When you use date and time qualifiers, the DIRECTORY command assumes you want to access files using the file creation date (*i.e.*, /CREATED is the default), so you do not need to include it with the command. VMS uses the current date and time when you use /BEFORE or /SINCE without a date and time value.

```
/CREATED                          Match on creation date
/MODIFIED                         Match on modification date
/BACKUP                           Match on backup date
/EXPIRED                          Match on expiration date

/BEFORE = date_time               Select files before this date_time
/SINCE =  date_time               Select files after this date_time
```

Figure 9-23. DIRECTORY Date and Time Qualifiers

DATE AND TIME SPECIFICATION

The standard date and time specification is **DD-MMM-YYYY:HH:MM:SS**, which stands for Day-Month-Year:Hours:Mins:Secs. When specifying a date and time, the colon between the date field and the time field is mandatory. When the system reports the date and time, it uses a blank to separate the two fields.

You will encounter many situations where a date and time value is expected. You enter only the date fields that are different from today, because the system defaults omitted fields to the current date and time. For example, if you are interested in files created this year, you can omit the year from the date specification. VMS also recognizes three reserved words for a date and time value: YESTERDAY, TODAY, and TOMORROW. These keywords substitute for a date and time value in any command that accepts one.

Figure 9-24 illustrates the use of DIRECTORY date and time qualifiers and the three reserved words. The last two examples continue the command on the next line with the hyphen (-) character.

```
$ DIR/SINCE=YESTERDAY             Files created yesterday
$ DIR/SINCE                       Files created today
$ DIR/SINCE=TODAY                 Files created today

$ DIR/CREATED/BEFORE = 30-JUN     Files created before June 30
$ DIR/MODIFIED/SINCE = 1-JAN      Files changed since Jan 1
$ DIR/BACKUP/SINCE    = 15-AUG    Files backed up since Aug 15

$ DIR/SINCE  = 1-MAY -            Files created during May
      /BEFORE = 1-JUN
$ DIR/SINCE  = 1-OCT-1989 -       Files created Oct-Dec 1989
      /BEFORE = 1-JAN-1990
```

Figure 9-24. Selecting Files by Date and Time

FILE AND DIRECTORY EXERCISES

1. Use SHOW DEFAULT to display your current disk and directory location. How does this compare with your username?

   If you are at the top of a device, you will see a device name and single
   directory name enclosed in square brackets. The device name that appears is
   site specific and may be either a physical device name like DUA10 or
   1DUA44 or a logical name like USERD or PROD1. Your home directory is
   usually the same as your username. Here [VMSWIZ] is the home directory for
   user VMSWIZ.

   ```
   $ SHOW DEFAULT
     USERD:[VMSWIZ]
   ```

   If you are part of a group organized under a common group directory, you
   may see a device and two directory names. Here user VMSWIZ is part of a
   group that shares the ADMIN top level directory and [ADMIN.VMSWIZ] is the
   home directory for user VMSWIZ.

   ```
   $ SHOW DEFAULT
     USERD:[ADMIN.VMSWIZ]
   ```

2. If you see only a device and one directory from SHOW DEFAULT, skip to number 3. Otherwise, set your default up one level and enter the DIRECTORY command. What do you see?

   If this directory has group access enabled, you will see the directory
   files for other members of the group. Otherwise you will get a file protect
   violation when you try to list the files (see next exercise).

   ```
   $ SET DEFAULT [-]          [Move up one level]
   $ SHOW DEFAULT             [Look at where you are]
     USERD:[ADMIN]            [In the ADMIN directory]
   $ DIR                      [List files in this location]

   Directory USERD:[ADMIN]

   VMSWIZ.DIR;1     MILLER.DIR:1        RICE.DIR:1

   Total of 3 files.
   ```

3. Set your default up one level and examine the current location. Then use DIR to list the files in this location. Did you get a file protection violation?

   VMS indicates the top of a disk with the directory specification [000000].
   Without elevated privileges, you are prohibited from accessing files at
   this level.

   ```
   $ SET DEFAULT [-]          [Move up one level]
   $ SHOW DEFAULT             [Look at where you are]
   ```

```
    USERD:[000000]                              [The very top of the disk]
    $ DIR                                       [List files in this location]
%DIRECT-E-OPENIN, error opening USERD:[000000]*.*;* as input
-RMS-E-PRV, insufficient privilege or file protection violation
```

4. Return to your home directory and create the subdirectories in this tree structure diagram. Use command recall and command line editing to reissue the CREATE/DIR/LOG commands needed to reproduce this structure. Read the information message issued with each create operation.

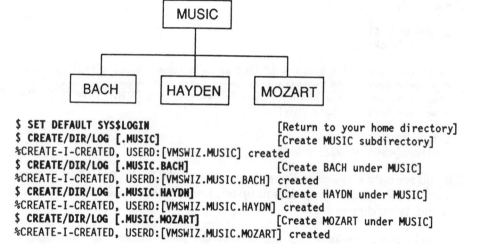

```
$ SET DEFAULT SYS$LOGIN                         [Return to your home directory]
$ CREATE/DIR/LOG [.MUSIC]                        [Create MUSIC subdirectory]
%CREATE-I-CREATED, USERD:[VMSWIZ.MUSIC] created
$ CREATE/DIR/LOG [.MUSIC.BACH]                   [Create BACH under MUSIC]
%CREATE-I-CREATED, USERD:[VMSWIZ.MUSIC.BACH] created
$ CREATE/DIR/LOG [.MUSIC.HAYDN]                  [Create HAYDN under MUSIC]
%CREATE-I-CREATED, USERD:[VMSWIZ.MUSIC.HAYDN] created
$ CREATE/DIR/LOG [.MUSIC.MOZART]                 [Create MOZART under MUSIC]
%CREATE-I-CREATED, USERD:[VMSWIZ.MUSIC.MOZART] created
```

5. Get a directory of this structure with one command.

```
$ SHOW DEFAULT                                  [Where are you?]
    USERD:[VMSWIZ]                              [Your home directory]
$ DIR [...]                                      [Ellipsis selects all files]

Directory USERD:[VMSWIZ]                         [Home directory files]

MUSIC.DIR;1

Total of 1 file.

Directory USERD:[VMSWIZ.MUSIC]                   [MUSIC directory files]

BACH.DIR            HAYDN.DIR            MOZART.DIR

Total of 3 files.
```

6. This exercise should familiarize you with using relative path names to move around in a directory tree. Set your default to the MUSIC directory and list the files. Then move to MOZART and check your location.

```
$ SHOW DEFAULT                          [Start from the home directory]
  USERD:[VMSWIZ]
$ SET DEFAULT [.MUSIC]                  [Move down one level to MUSIC]
$ SHOW DEFAULT                          [Are you there?]
  USERD:[VMSWIZ.MUSIC]                  [Yes]
$ DIR                                   [Any files here?]

Directory USERD:[VMSWIZ.MUSIC]         [Yes, three directory files]

BACH.DIR;1     HAYDN.DIR;1     MOZART.DIR;1

Total of 3 files.

$ SET DEFAULT [.MOZART]                 [Move down one level to MOZART]
$ SHOW DEFAULT                          [Are you there?]
  USERD:[VMSWIZ.MUSIC.MOZART]          [Yes]
```

7. Move up one level. Where are you? Move up one more level. Where are you now?

```
$ SET DEFAULT [-]                       [Move up one level]
$ SHOW DEFAULT                          [Where are you?]
  USERD:[VMSWIZ.MUSIC.MOZART]          [In MOZART]
$ SET DEFAULT [-]                       [Move up one more level]
$ SHOW DEFAULT                          [Where are you now?]
  USERD:[VMSWIZ.MUSIC]                  [In MUSIC]
$ SET DEFAULT [-]                       [Move up once again]
$ SHOW DEFAULT                          [Where are you?]
  USERD:[VMSWIZ]                        [Back in your home directory]
```

8. From your home directory, move to BACH and verify you are there. Then return to your home directory again. Use only one command for each of these operations.

```
$ SET DEFAULT [.MUSIC.BACH]             [Move to BACH]
$ SHOW DEFAULT                          [Where are you?]
  USERD:[VMSWIZ.MUSIC.BACH]            [In BACH]
$ SET DEFAULT [-.-]                     [Move up two levels]
$ SHOW DEFAULT                          [Where are you?]
  USERD:[VMSWIZ]                        [In your home directory]
```

File Attribute Exercises

These exercises assume you have completed the file and directory exercises earlier in this chapter. If you have not done the previous lesson you will not have directories and subdirectories to practice with.

1. Use DIR/FULL on the MUSIC directory. When was it created? Who is the owner? How big is it in disk blocks? Has it been backed up?

```
This directory was created on January 11, 1990 by username VMSWIZ. It is
```

currently using two disk blocks and has not been backed up. If you created MUSIC before today, you should see a date in the backup field.
```
$ DIR/FULL MUSIC.DIR
```

```
Directory USERB:[VMSWIZ]

MUSIC.DIR;1                      File ID:  (37245,6,0)
Size:           1/2        Owner:     [VMSWIZ]
Created:  11-JAN-1990 11:38:13.72
Revised:  11-JAN-1990 11:38:14.13 (1)
Expires:  10-JUL-1990 11:54:36.67
Backup:     <No backup recorded>
File organization:  Sequential
File attributes:    Allocation: 2, Extend: 0, Global buffer count: 0
                    No default version limit, Contiguous, Directory file
Record format:      Variable length, maximum 512 bytes
Record attributes:  No carriage control, Non-spanned
RMS attributes:     None
Journaling enabled: None
File protection:    System:RWE, Owner:RWE, Group:RE, World:E
Access Cntrl List:  None

Total of 1 file, 1/2 blocks.
```

2. Try a DIR/SIZE/OWNER [...]. What does this command do?

```
$ DIR/SIZE/OWN [...]
```

```
Directory USERB:[VMSWIZ]

MUSIC.DIR;1              1   [VMSWIZ]
LOGIN.COM;1             1   [VMSWIZ]

Total of 2 files, 2 blocks.

Directory USERB:[VMSWIZ.MUSIC]

BACH.DIR;1              1   [VMSWIZ]
HAYDN.DIR;1            1   [VMSWIZ]
MOZART.DIR;1          1   [VMSWIZ]

Total of 3 files, 3 blocks.

Grand total of 4 directories, 5 files, 5 blocks.
```

3. Try DIR/SIZE/GRAND [...]. How does this command compare with the previous one?

The /GRAND qualifier displays a one-line summary of the total number of directories and files.

```
$ DIR/SIZE/GRAND [...]
```

```
Grand total of 3 directories, 7 files, 7 blocks.
```

4. Store the list of all files in your entire directory tree in a disk file called MASTER.LIS.

```
$ DIR/OUTPUT=MASTER.LIS [...]
$ DIR MASTER.LIS
```

Directory USERB:[VMSWIZ]

MASTER.LIS;1

Total of 1 files.

5. Recall the last command and add the qualifiers to put one filename per line, with no header or trailer lines. Store the output in the same file as the previous command. What version does this output file have and why?

This command creates version 2 of MASTER.LIS because a file of the same name and type already exists in the directory.

```
$ DIR/OUTPUT=MASTER.LIS/NOHEADER/NOTRAILER/COL=1
$ DIR MASTER.LIS
```

Directory USERB:[VMSWIZ]

MASTER.LIS;2   MASTER.LIS;1

Total of 2 files.

6. How many files have you created today?

Both MASTER.LIS files and the MUSIC directory were created today.

```
$ DIR/SINCE
```

Directory USERB:[MIS.VMSWIZ]

MASTER.LIS;2   MASTER.LIS;1   MUSIC.DIR;1

Total of 3 files.

7. How many files in your directory were created before today if any?

Among others, you may have a mail file or a login file created earlier than today.

```
$ DIR/BEFORE
```

Directory USERB:[VMSWIZ]

EVE$INIT.EVE;1   LOGIN.COM;1   MAIL.MAI;1

Total of 3 files.

File Manipulation

INTRODUCTION

Now that you understand how to create directories and how to move around in a tree structure, you are ready to manipulate files and structures using CREATE, TYPE, COPY, RENAME, APPEND, DELETE, PURGE, RUN, SUBMIT, and SPAWN. File manipulation commands are easy to understand and use and many sophisticated operations are possible with each command using command qualifiers. Each command is accompanied by several examples, which you are encouraged to try as you read through the material. In the examples, you should substitute file names that are available on your system.

Most file manipulation commands have qualifiers that allow you to select files using the four dates recorded in the file header. For example, the TYPE command can display files created since a specific date and time and DELETE can remove files created before a certain date and time. You can freely use the date and time qualifiers reviewed at the end of Chapter 9, Files and Directories, with most of the commands covered in this section. Because they are so common, these qualifiers have been omitted from the individual command descriptions.

COMMAND AND PARAMETER DESCRIPTIONS

In the command descriptions in this chapter, most of the parameters are files. The use of a file as a parameter is designated by the word "file-specification" or "file-spec" in the command format at the top of each figure. Some commands accept only a directory name rather than a full file specification. In this case the parameter is noted as "directory-specification" or "directory-spec" in the command format. Remember you must always enclose a directory specification in square brackets ([]).

The notation [,...] appears frequently in the individual command descriptions. The square brackets indicate the item is optional, which means the command functions by itself, as well as with one or more parameters. The ",..." represents a parameter list, which means you can specify more than one parameter, as long as each is separated from the previous one by a comma.

In the TYPE command format in Figure 10-1, the file-spec parameter is not enclosed in square brackets, which indicates that one parameter is required. The [,...] notation indicates that you can optionally give TYPE a list of files. Most of the file manipulation commands operate equally well on one file or several files. You can operate on several files with one command when you use a wildcard as part or all of a file specification (*e.g.*, TYPE *.DAT or TYPE *.*).

```
$ TYPE   file-spec[,...]              Command Format

$ TYPE   REPORT.DAT                   TYPE one file
$ TYPE   MAR.DAT, APR.DAT, MAY.DAT    TYPE three files
```

Figure 10-1. The [,...] Notation

CREATING A NEW FILE

Use CREATE to make a file at the system prompt. After you enter the command, the cursor moves to the start of the next line and CREATE waits for you to enter text. When you are done entering text, use CTRL/Z to terminate input. This closes and saves the file and returns you to the system prompt, as shown in Figure 10-2.

```
$ CREATE file-spec[,...]              Command Format

$ CREATE TEST.DAT                     Make a file called TEST.DAT
A quick file                          Enter text for the file
CTRL/Z                                Terminate input and save file
$
```

Figure 10-2. CREATE Command

If a file of the same name already exists, CREATE will make a file with the same name and the next higher version number. CREATE does not use a file type default and date and time qualifiers do not apply to this operation.

DISPLAYING A TEXT FILE

Use TYPE to display a file at your terminal (Fig. 10-3). You can display the contents of several files by entering several file specifications on the command line. TYPE assumes a default file type of .LIS, if one is not provided. If you TYPE a long file, use CTRL/Y to terminate the display. You can type out a group of files by using a wildcard in the file specification (*e.g.,* TYPE TEST.* or TYPE *.*).

```
$ TYPE file-spec[,...]            Command Format

$ TYPE TEST.DAT                   Type one file
$ TYPE MAY.DAT, JUN.DAT           Type two files
$ TYPE/PAGE JUN*.DAT              Display one page at a time
$ TYPE DAILY                      Type DAILY files with type .LIS
```

Figure 10-3. TYPE Command

TYPE Qualifiers

TYPE has one useful qualifier, /PAGE, that displays text one screen at a time. You are prompted to press RETURN to see the next screen. TYPE does understand the date and time qualifiers, although they are seldom used with this command.

DUPLICATING A FILE

COPY duplicates a file in the same directory, a different directory, or on a different device and directory. You can change part or all of the file specification as part of the duplicating operation and can concatenate several input files into one output file. COPY requires two parameters, an input file and an output file — it duplicates the input file and stores the copy in the output file (Fig. 10-4). When you duplicate a file using the same name and type in the same directory, the system assigns the duplicate copy the next higher version number. If copied to a different directory, the version number of the duplicate is the same as the original.

Changing Version Numbers

Although you can change the version number in the output file, you must do this very carefully. Because all the file manipulation commands use the highest version of a file (which is normally the most recent), you can accidentally lose a file by selecting a version number lower than the highest version. Such a file can be deleted when automatic version limit controls are in force, or when you use the PURGE command to keep only the highest version of each file.

```
$ COPY input-file-spec[,...] output-file-spec Command Format

$ COPY TEST.DAT *                    Duplicate in same directory
$ COPY TEST.DAT TEST1.*              Change file name

$ COPY TEST.DAT *.TMP                Change file type
$ COPY TEST.DAT;97 *.*;1             Change version number

$ COPY TEST.DAT [-]                  Copy up one level, same name
$ COPY TEST.DAT [RICE]               Copy to another directory
$ COPY TEST.DAT USERB:[ADMIN]        Copy to new disk/directory

$ COPY *.*;* [.OLD]                  Copy all versions of all
                                     files to OLD directory
```

Figure 10-4. COPY Command

COPY Qualifiers

COPY understands date and time qualifiers and does not provide a default file type for the input file specification. The file type of the output file defaults to that of the input file. /LOG generates an information message for each file copied and is recommended for beginning users. When you use /CONFIRM, you must respond to a prompt to initiate each COPY operation — this qualifier is useful with a wildcard COPY operation (*e.g.*, COPY *.*).

Three qualifiers can improve file I/O performance in some cases, especially if a file is fragmented in serveral pieces. /ALLOCATION=n tells COPY to allocate a specific number of disk blocks to the duplicate copy, /CONTIGUOUS directs COPY to store the duplicate in physically contiguous disk blocks, and /EXTENSION=n extends the size of the duplicate by the number of blocks specified.

Duplicating a Directory Tree

You can duplicate a directory tree as easily as a single file if you enter a directory specification for the input and output files. If the directory you are copying does not contain subdirectories, the input file is the *.*;* wildcard specification and the output file is a directory specification. When the directory you are duplicating contains subdirectories, add an ellipsis (...) to the input and output directory specifications to select all lower level directories and files for the duplicating operation. If you omit the ellipsis from the output file specification, all files from the source directory tree are created at the same level in the target directory (*i.e.*, subdirectory structure is not maintained). The target directory that is to hold the duplicate tree must exist before you initiate the copy operation (creating directories is covered in Chapter 9).

Duplicating a directory tree requires only two commands, as shown in Figure 10-5. For these examples, assume you have a SOURCE subdirectory that contains two lower directories COM and LIB. You have created files in SOURCE and in the lower directories and are now ready to test your work. As part of the test operation, you want to duplicate the whole structure in another directory called TEST on the same level as the SOURCE directory.

From your home directory, you create the TEST directory and then copy the SOURCE structure to the TEST directory using the ellipsis with the input and output file specifications. The /LOG qualifier provides good feedback because it generates an information message for each file as it duplicated in the new location.

```
$ CREATE/DIR [.TEST]                      Make the target directory

$ COPY/LOG [.SOURCE...]*.*;* [.TEST...]    Duplicate the tree
%COPY-I-CREATED, USERB:[VMSWIZ.TEST.COM] created
%COPY-I-CREATED, USERB:[VMSWIZ.TEST.LIB] created
%COPY-S-COPIED, USERB:[VMSWIZ.SOURCE]DISCOVER.CC;23 copied to
USERD:[VMSWIZ.TEST]DISCOVER.CC;1  (36 blocks)
%COPY-S-COPIED, USERB:[VMSWIZ.SOURCE.COM]START.COM;12 copied to
USERD:[VMSWIZ.TEST.COM]START.COM;1 (6 blocks)
%COPY-S-COPIED, USERB:[VMSWIZ.SOURCE.COM]DEBUG.COM;9 copied to
USERD:[VMSWIZ.TEST.COM]DEBUG.COM;1 (2 blocks)
%COPY-S-COPIED, USERB:[VMSWIZ.SOURCE.LIB]LEARN.OLB;17 copied to
USERB:[VMSWIZ.TEST.LIB]LEARN.OLB;1 (108 blocks)
```

Figure 10-5. Duplicating a Directory Tree

CHANGING A FILE NAME

RENAME changes the directory, name, type, or version of a file. It requires an input file and an output file and changes the input file to the output file specification (Fig. 10-6). You can use RENAME to change the name of any file, including directory files. To change the name of a file, specify the current name as the input file and the new name as the output file. When you change the name, type, or version, the changed portion of the name is recorded in the directory in which the file is stored and the file remains in the same location.

RENAME is the most convenient way to move a file from one directory to another, instead of duplicating the file in a new directory and deleting the original. When you provide a new directory specification in the output file, the file is actually moved to the new directory. You change a directory name the same way you change an ordinary file — the current directory file name is the input file (*e.g.*, COMMANDS.DIR) and the new directory name is the output file (*e.g.*, COM.DIR). When you rename a directory file, you must include a file type of .DIR with both file specifications.

RENAME is very fast because it changes the file's directory entry and does not access the file itself. RENAME does not understand device names, so you cannot RENAME a file to a different disk. Use RENAME instead of COPY for all name modifications. You must have write access to the directory in which the file is stored to perform a RENAME operation. If you are changing the name of a directory file, you must have write access to the next higher directory.

```
$ RENAME input-file-spec[,...] output-file-spec    Command Format

$ RENAME TEMP.DAT TEST.*              Change file name
$ RENAME COMMANDS.DIR COM.DIR         Change directory name
$ RENAME COOKIE.EXE;243 *.*;1         Change version number

$ RENAME/LOG *.EXE [.EXECUTE]         Move files to lower directory
$ RENAME/CONFIRM OCT89.* [-]          Move files to higher directory
```

Figure 10-6. RENAME Command

RENAME Qualifiers

Use /LOG for an information message about each RENAME operation and verify name changes before they occur with /CONFIRM. This qualifier is also valuable when you initiate a RENAME operation using a wildcard file specification (*e.g.*, RENAME *.*).

COMBINING FILES

APPEND requires two parameters: an input file and an output file (Fig. 10-7). The contents of the input file are added to the end of the output file and the input file remains untouched. If you provide several input files, each input file is added to the end of the output file, in the order in which they appear on the command line. APPEND can process up to ten input files in a single command. Unless you ask for a new version, the output file version number remains the same.

APPEND is relatively slow command. When you need to combine many files or a few large files you should use the CONVERT utility, which is much faster (CONVERT/APPEND). Ask for HELP on CONVERT for more information.

```
$ APPEND input-file-spec[,...] output-file-spec  Command Format

$ APPEND FEB89.DAT   ANNUAL.RPT          Add FEB89.DAT to ANNUAL.RPT
$ APPEND MAR89.DAT,APR89.DAT ANNUAL.RPT  Add MAR89.DAT and APR89.DAT
                                         to ANNUAL.RPT
```

Figure 10-7. APPEND Command

APPEND Qualifiers

APPEND understands date and time qualifiers, /LOG, and /CONFIRM. Use /LOG to receive a message as each input file is added to the output file and /CONFIRM to verify each operation before it begins. If the output file does not exist, or you want to create a new version, place /NEW_VERSION after the output file.

DELETING FILES

DELETE eliminates files and directories. Deleting a directory is a multistep procedure covered in Chapter 11, File Protection and Security. Because a DELETE operation is dangerous, you must include a version number in your file specification to uniquely identify the file the system is to delete. If you want to delete the most recent version of a file a semicolon is sufficient, because the system provides the highest version number by default.

DELETE accepts one file specification or a parameter list (Fig. 10-8). You delete multiple files by entering all the file specs, separated by commas, on the command line. If an error occurs deleting one of the files, DELETE issues an information message and then processes any remaining files.

```
$ DELETE file-spec[,...]     Command Format

$ DELETE/CONFIRM TEMP.DAT;    Delete highest version  of TEMP.DAT
$ DELETE/CONFIRM TEMP.DAT;*   Delete all versions of TEMP.DAT

$ DELETE *.DAT;              Delete highest version, all .DAT files
$ DELETE *.DAT;*            Delete all versions of all .DAT files

$ DELETE/LOG  *.*;          Delete highest version of all files
$ DELETE/LOG  *.*;*         Delete all versions of all files
```

Figure 10-8. DELETE Command

DELETE Qualifiers

Use /CONFIRM to verify each delete operation and /LOG to see an information message for each file that is deleted. DELETE understands date and time qualifiers and /EXCLUDE=file-spec which omits the specified files from the delete operation.

DELETING OLD VERSIONS OF FILES

PURGE accepts zero, one or multiple file specifications. If you enter this command with no parameters, it deletes all but the highest version of each file in the current directory. If you provide one or more file specifications, PURGE deletes the lower numbered (older) versions of the specified files (Fig. 10-9). Use this command to clean up your directory on a regular basis.

```
$ PURGE [file-spec[,...]]        Command Format

$ PURGE/KEEP=2/LOG *.DAT         Keep two versions of .DAT files
$ PURGE/LOG *.DAT                Keep only the highest version
$ PURGE/LOG *.DAT,*.COM          Keep highest version of these files
$ PURGE/LOG                      Purge all files to one version
```

Figure 10-9. PURGE Command

PURGE Qualifiers

You can control the number of versions that remain with the /KEEP=n, which saves the highest n versions of each file — if you do not use /KEEP only a single copy remains. Use /CONFIRM to approve each delete operation and /LOG for a message when each file is deleted.

RUNNING PROGRAMS

RUN executes a program that is not part of VMS. Programs may be provided by an in-house department or purchased from a variety of vendors. Some vendors modify VMS to add their application to the master command table, in which case the RUN command is not necessary. If you have trouble starting an application, consult your system manager.

RUN accepts a single file specification which identifies the program you want to execute (Fig. 10-10). RUN expects a file type of .EXE (for EXEcutable), a standard that is followed at all VMS installations.

```
$ RUN file-spec                    Command Format

$ RUN CCALC                        Start the CCALC program
  /PROCESS_NAME=string             Process name to use
  /INPUT= file-spec                Input file (SYS$INPUT)
  /OUTPUT= file-spec               Output file (SYS$OUTPUT)
  /ERROR= file-spec                Message file (SYS$ERROR)
  /PRIORITY= n                     Priority at which to run job
```

Figure 10-10. RUN Command and Qualifiers

RUN Qualifiers

RUN has a large number of qualifiers that allow sophisticated control over the way a program is executed. Some of them are listed in Figure 10-10. You can use qualifiers to redirect input, output, and error messages, and to control resource quotas used by the running program. Some of the qualifiers require elevated privileges. You will probably not need any of these qualifiers for commonly used applications. If you do, see HELP RUN for a description of how they are used.

RUNNING A BATCH JOB

You may occasionally need to run a program in batch mode instead of interactively. Where the RUN command executes a program interactively, the SUBMIT command executes a program as a batch job. SUBMIT requires one parameter, which is the name of a command procedure procedure to be executed. A command procedure is a text file that has a file type of .COM and contains, at a minimum, a single line which is a RUN command and the name of the program you want to execute (Fig. 10-11). SUBMIT places your command procedure in the system batch queue in the next available position. When your job comes to the front of the queue, it starts.

```
$ SUBMIT  file-spec[,...]          Command Format

$ CREATE TEST.COM                  Create file TEST.COM
$ RUN REPORT                       First line is RUN command
$ EXIT                             EXIT signals end of procedure
CTRL/Z                             Close and save TEST.COM

$ SUBMIT/NOTIFY TEST               Submit batch job
  Job TEST (queue SYS$BATCH, entry 92) pending
```

Figure 10-11. SUBMIT Example

The system creates a batch log file in your home directory with the same name as the command procedure and a type of .LOG. Because a batch job logs in like an interactive process, the log file contains each line in the systemwide login file and each line from your personal login file. The log file also contains every line of your command procedure and may contain output generated by the program while it is running.

Running a batch job can be a sophisticated operation and the fine points of passing parameters, naming log files, submitting a job to run at a certain date and time, and so on are not included here. Check the HELP utility for a description of SUBMIT qualifiers and examples of how they are used.

USING A SUBPROCESS (SPAWN COMMAND)

SPAWN uses a VMS construct called a "subprocess" to give you another window into the operating system. SPAWN creates a child process from your parent process established at login time. The subprocess has identical process characteristics but is subordinate to your parent process. Subprocesses start with new memory quotas, but share most other quotas with the parent process.

Users are normally authorized to use a maximum of two subprocesses. (To check your subprocess quota, see PRCLM in the SHOW PROCESS/QUOTA display.) Many applications, including DEC's ALL-IN-1 office automation package, use subprocesses to maintain a tightly controlled user environment. Because each subprocess duplicates the resource use of the parent process, using two processes puts a double load on the system. SPAWN should be used selectively and with care.

SPAWN has one optional parameter, a VMS command (Fig. 10-12). Although SPAWN understands a large number of qualifiers, only three are included here. Without a parameter, this command creates a VMS process that attaches directly to your terminal and responds with the normal system prompt. When you log out of the subprocess, you return to your parent process.

```
$ SPAWN [command-string]      Command Format

   /NOWAIT                    Perform command independently
   /PROMPT= string            System prompt to use in the subprocess
   /NOTIFY                    Send message when subprocess completes
                              (use only with /NOWAIT)
```

Figure 10-12. SPAWN Command and Qualifiers

Figure 10-13 demonstrates the use of a simple SPAWN command. To start with, SHOW PROCESS displays a single process VMSWIZ running. After the SPAWN

command, SHOW PROCESS displays two processes, VMSWIZ and VMSWIZ_1.
The (*) indicates that the second process is active, so user VMSWIZ is interacting
with the subprocess rather than the parent process. After VMSWIZ logs out, the
system returns control back to the parent process.

```
$ SHOW PROCESS/SUBPROCESS
15-FEB-1990 17:32:29.58   User: VMSWIZ      Process ID: 42C00120
                          Node: DVORAK    Process Name: "VMSWIZ"
There is 1 process in this job:

 VMSWIZ (*)

$ SPAWN
%DCL-S-SPAWNED, process VMSWIZ_1 spawned
%DCL-S-ATTACHED, terminal now attached to process VMSWIZ_1

$ SHOW PROCESS/SUBPROCESS
15-FEB-1990 17:34:42.15   User: VMSWIZ      Process ID: 42C00121
                          Node: DVORAK    Process Name: "VMSWIZ_1"


There are 2 processes in this job:

 VMSWIZ
   VMSWIZ_1 (*)
$ LOGOUT
Process VMSWIZ_1 logged out at 15-FEB-1990 17:34:46.41
%DCL-S-RETURNED, control returned to process VMSWIZ
$
```

Figure 10-13. The SPAWN Command

Spawning a VMS Command

When you provide a command with SPAWN, the subprocess executes the command in one of two ways, depending upon whether or not you use the /NOWAIT
qualifier. If you enter the first command in Figure 10-14, the DIRECTORY command is executed while you wait. This mode does not have an obvious application for the general user.

The second SPAWN command in Figure 10-14 creates a subprocess and passes the
DIRECTORY command to it as input. The /NOWAIT qualifier tells the system to
return control to the parent process immediately after the subprocess starts. The
subprocess exists until the DIRECTORY command completes and then it disap-

/NOTIFY and indicates the subprocess is gone. This mode allows you to continue your interactive session while the subprocess is off working on its own. The /OUTPUT qualifier on the DIRECTORY command saves the listing in a file — without it, the output goes into the bitbucket.

```
$ SPAWN DIR/OUT=CLASS.LIS [.CLASS...]
%DCL-S-SPAWNED, process VMSWIZ_1 spawned
%DCL-S-ATTACHED, terminal now attached to process VMSWIZ_1
%DCL-S-RETURNED, control returned to process VMSWIZ

$ SPAWN/NOWAIT/NOTIFY DIR/OUT=CLASS [.CLASS...]
%DCL-S-SPAWNED, process VMSWIZ_1 spawned
$
Subprocess VMSWIZ_1 has completed
```

Figure 10-14. SPAWN Examples

SPAWN *and the* MAIL *Utility*

When you use SPAWN from within the MAIL utility, a subprocess attaches to your terminal and presents the system prompt. At this point you are free to enter VMS commands, a technique that is useful for any number of reasons. For example, from MAIL, you can SPAWN a process, start the editor, and create or modify a mail distribution list without losing the context of your mail session. When you are finished with the editor, you log out and return to the MAIL> prompt. MAIL is described in Chapter 14.

CHANGING FILE ATTRIBUTES

SET FILE can modify nearly 30 different file attributes including file ownership, version limits, and the backup attribute on normal files and directory files. You can only modify these attributes if you own the file or have control access granted by an Access Control List (covered in Chapter 11, File Protection and Security).

Changing File Ownership

To modify the owner field, you must own the file or have write access to the file and to the directory in which the file is stored. Changing the owner of a directory requires write access to the next higher directory as well. Both operations are illustrated in Figure 10-15. See Chapter 11 for more information about file protection and security controls.

```
$ SET FILE/OWNER=UIC    file-spec[,...]        Command Format

$ SET FILE/OWN=[ADMIN,STATZ] ADMIN.DIR         New owner for ADMIN.DIR
$ SET FILE/OWN=[ADMIN,STATZ] USERS.LIS         New owner for USERS.LIS
```

Figure 10-15. Changing File Ownership

Version Limit Controls

To control disk space consumed by users and applications, many system managers restrict the number of versions of each file that can be stored on the disk at one time. Even if your site does not use version controls on a systemwide basis, you might want to set your own version limits to help control the proliferation of files. This is quite useful in the software development environment where files tend to multiply in large quantities on a regular basis. Once set, the system takes care of deleting older files that exceed the version limit you have selected.

Version limit controls can be applied to a directory or to individual files. A directory version limit controls the number of versions maintained for each file created in that directory and a file version limit controls the number of copies of that file only. If version controls have been set, the DIRECTORY/FULL command displays this information.

Files can have an arbitrary limit on versions or a version limit of zero which allows a maximum of 32,767 copies. When version control is implemented, a limit of three to five versions is common. For example, if a file has a version limit of three and there are already three versions (;1, ;2, and ;3), when you create the fourth version the system automatically deletes version number 1. If a directory has a version limit of three, the system permits each file stored in that directory to have at most three versions. In a directory with a version limit of 1, only a single copy of each file is maintained.

Establishing Version Limits

All files can have the same version limit, whether controlled by a directory or individually. Files can also have different version limits, depending upon what makes the most sense. There are two commands used to modify the version limit attribute, SET FILE/VERSION and SET DIRECTORY/VERSION. Since the two commands perform the same function, only SET FILE/VERSION is discussed here.

Figure 10-16 illustrates using SET FILE/VERSION to set a version limit on a particular file, on all files in a directory, and on a directory file. If you do not specify a value with this command, the value defaults to zero, which is equivalent to setting the version limit to the maximum of 32,767.

```
$ SET FILE/VERSION_LIMIT =n  file-spec    Command Format

$ SET FILE/VERS=1  ANNUAL.REPORT          Version limit of 1
$ SET FILE/VERS=3  [...]*.*;*             Set all files to a
                                          version limit of 3
$ SET FILE/VERS=1  WORK.DIR               Restrict all files in this
                                          directory to one version
```

Figure 10-16. Controlling Version Limits

Changing the Backup Attribute

The system manager makes "backup" copies of all files on a daily and weekly basis at most installations. Occasionally you will create files that are very large and temporary, or easily reproducible (*e.g.*, plot files). You can use the /NOBACKUP qualifier to mark such files as not requiring a backup. If you decide later on that you want a backup copy, you reset this attribute with SET FILE/BACKUP as shown in Figure 10-17.

Changing this attribute should be done intelligently. If you mark a file as not needing backup and then accidentally delete it, you will not be able to restore the file. Eliminating files from a backup operation reduces backup time at sites where system backup is a shared responsibility. At large sites with an operations staff, the system manager usually overrides the nobackup attribute, so the files are backed up anyway.

```
$ SET FILE/BACKUP    file-spec           Command Format
$ SET FILE/BACKUP    SEP89.DAT           Enable backup for SEP89.DAT

$ SET FILE/NOBACKUP  file-spec           Command Format
$ SET FILE/NOBACKUP  AUG89.JNL           Disable backup for AUG89.JNL
```

Figure 10-17. Controlling the Backup Attribute

FILE MANIPULATION EXERCISES

1. Use CREATE to make a file in your home directory called COMPOSERS.ONE that contains three lines, one line with the name of each composer in the directory tree you created in Chapter 9 exercises. TYPE the file to make sure the names are correct.

```
$ CREATE COMPOSERS.ONE                  [Create the file]
bach                                    [Enter one composer per line]
haydn
mozart
CTRL/Z                                  [Terminate input]
$ TYPE COMPOSERS.ONE                    [Display the file]
bach
haydn
mozart
$
```

2. COPY COMPOSERS.ONE to a file called COMPOSERS.TWO in your home directory. Use the /LOG qualifier to see the full file specification of the input and output files.

```
$ COPY/LOG COMPOSERS.ONE *.TWO
%COPY-S-COPIED, USERB:[VMSWIZ]COMPOSERS.ONE;1 copied to USERB:[VMSWIZ]
COMPOSERS.TWO;1 (1 block)
```

3. Use DIRECTORY to search for all files that start with COMPOSERS, any extension. How many files are there?

```
There should be two COMPOSERS files, one made by CREATE and the other by
the COPY operation.
```

```
$ DIR COMPOSERS

Directory USERB:[VMSWIZ]

COMPOSERS.ONE;1     COMPOSERS.TWO;1

Total of 2 files.
```

4. Set your default to the MUSIC directory. Copy both COMPOSERS files from your home directory to the MUSIC directory. Use the /LOG qualifier to verify the names of the input and output files. What relative file spec do you use for the COPY input file?

```
$ SET DEFAULT [.MUSIC]                  [Move to MUSIC]
$ SHOW DEFAULT                          [Where are you?]
  USERB:[VMSWIZ.MUSIC]                  [In MUSIC]
$ COPY/LOG [-]COMPOSERS.* *             [Duplicate COMPOSERS files]
%COPY-S-COPIED, USERB:[VMSWIZ]COMPOSERS.ONE;1 copied to USERB:[VMSWIZ.MUSIC]
COMPOSERS.ONE;2 (1 block)
%COPY-S-COPIED, USERB:[VMSWIZ]COMPOSERS.TWO;1 copied to USERB:[VMSWIZ.MUSIC]
COMPOSERS.TWO;2 (1 block)
%COPY-S-NEWFILES, 2 files created
```

5. In the MUSIC directory, use RENAME/LOG to change COMPOSERS.ONE to COMPOSERS.THREE. Which COMPOSERS files are still here?

   ```
   COMPOSERS.TWO and COMPOSERS.THREE are in this directory.

   $ RENAME/LOG COMPOSERS.ONE COMPOSERS.THREE
   %RENAME-I-RENAMED, USERB:[VMSWIZ.MUSIC]COMPOSERS.ONE;2 renamed to
   USERB:[VMSWIZ.MUSIC]COMPOSERS.THREE;1
   $ DIR COMPOSERS

   Directory USERB:[VMSWIZ.MUSIC]

   COMPOSERS.THREE;1          COMPOSERS.TWO;1

   Total of 2 files.
   ```

6. In the MUSIC directory use RENAME/LOG to move COMPOSERS.THREE to the BACH directory.

   ```
   $ RENAME/LOG COMPOSERS.THREE [.BACH]
   %RENAME-I-RENAMED, USERB:[VMSWIZ.MUSIC]COMPOSERS.THREE;1 renamed to
   USERB:[VMSWIZ.MUSIC.BACH]COMPOSERS.THREE;1
   ```

7. Use RENAME/LOG qualifier to move COMPOSERS.TWO to HAYDN.

   ```
   $ RENAME/LOG COMPOSERS.TWO [.HAYDN]
   %RENAME-I-RENAMED, USERB:[VMSWIZ.MUSIC]COMPOSERS.TWO;2 renamed to
   USERB:[VMSWIZ.MUSIC.HAYDN]COMPOSERS.TWO;1
   ```

8. Look at the MUSIC directory. Are there any files left? Which ones and why?

   ```
   There are no COMPOSERS files left in the MUSIC directory because the RENAME
   commands actually move the files to the HAYDN and BACH directories.

   $ DIR

   Directory USERB:[VMSWIZ.MUSIC]

   BACH.DIR;1          HAYDN.DIR;1          MOZART.DIR;1

   Total of 3 files.
   ```

9. Move to the BACH directory and make sure COMPOSERS.THREE is there. Duplicate this file in the BACH directory. Use the DIRECTORY command to verify there are two copies.

   ```
   $ SET DEFAULT [.BACH]
   $ DIR COMPOSERS

   Directory USERB:[VMSWIZ.MUSIC.BACH]
   ```

```
COMPOSERS.THREE;1

Total of 1 file.
$ COPY COMPOSERS.THREE *                    [* uses same name and type]
$ DIR COMPOSERS

Directory USERB:[VMSWIZ.MUSIC.BACH]

COMPOSERS.THREE;2    COMPOSERS.THREE;1

Total of 2 files.
```

10. Recall the previous command and repeat it. How many versions of the file COMPOSERS.THREE are now in BACH?

```
$ COPY COMPOSERS.THREE *
$ DIR

Directory USERB:[VMSWIZ.MUSIC.BACH]

COMPOSERS.THREE;3    COMPOSERS.THREE;2    COMPOSERS.THREE;1

Total of 3 files.
```

11. COPY all versions of the file COMPOSERS.THREE from BACH to MOZART. Use the /LOG qualifier to see the files being duplicated. What relative file specification do you use for the output file? Are the files in each directory the same (number of files, names, and version numbers)?

```
$ COPY/LOG COMPOSERS.THREE;* [-.MOZART]
%COPY-S-COPIED, USERB:[MIS.MUSIC.BACH]COMPOSERS.THREE;3 copied to USERB:
[MIS.MUSIC.MOZART]COMPOSERS.THREE;3    (1 block)
%COPY-S-COPIED, USERB:[MIS.MUSIC.BACH]COMPOSERS.THREE;2 copied to USERB:
[MIS.MUSIC.MOZART]COMPOSERS.THREE;2    (1 block)
%COPY-S-COPIED, USERB:[MIS.MUSIC.BACH]COMPOSERS.THREE;1 copied to USERB:
[MIS.MUSIC.MOZART]COMPOSERS.THREE;1    (1 block)
%COPY-S-NEWFILES, 3 files created
```

12. Use PURGE/LOG to eliminate the lower versions of COMPOSERS.THREE in the BACH directory. How many files are deleted? Which file is left and why?

```
PURGE deletes the two lower versions and saves only the most recent version
of a file. The only file left should be COMPOSERS.THREE;3.
```

```
$ PURGE/LOG COMPOSERS.THREE
%PURGE-I-FILPURG, USERB:[MIS.MUSIC.BACH]COMPOSERS.THREE;2 deleted (2 blocks)
%PURGE-I-FILPURG, USERB:[MIS.MUSIC.BACH]COMPOSERS.THREE;1 deleted (2 blocks)
%PURGE-I-TOTAL, 2 files deleted (4 blocks)
```

13. Set your default back to your home directory. Use PURGE/LOG to reduce all files in the MUSIC structure to one version. Which files, if any, are removed by the PURGE command?

PURGE deletes the lower version of MASTER.LIS and the two lower versions of COMPOSERS.THREE in the MOZART directory.

```
$ SHOW DEFAULT
   USERB:[MIS.MUSIC.BACH]
$ SET DEFAULT [-.-]
$ SHOW DEFAULT
   USERB:[MIS]
$ PURGE/LOG [...]
%PURGE-I-FILPURG, USERB:[MIS]MASTER.LIS;1 deleted (2 blocks)
%PURGE-I-FILPURG, USERB:[MIS.MUSIC.MOZART]COMPOSERS.THREE;2 deleted (2 blocks)
%PURGE-I-FILPURG, USERB:[MIS.MUSIC.MOZART]COMPOSERS.THREE;1 deleted (2 blocks)
%PURGE-I-TOTAL, 3 files deleted (6 blocks)
```

File Protection and Security

INTRODUCTION

This chapter reviews UIC-based file security and file protection codes, and explains how you examine and change file protection with the SHOW PROTECTION and SET PROTECTION commands. These concepts ensure that you understand how to protect files, how to permit or deny access to different categories of users, and how to delete directories and directory structures properly.

VOLUME PROTECTION

VMS provides three levels of disk file protection: disk protection, directory protection, and individual file protection. A disk can be mounted as a public volume, a group volume, or a private volume. Most disks are initialized and mounted as public volumes available to all users at a site. Where sensitive information is an issue, a system manager may enforce security controls by having an individual or group own either a fixed or removable disk. When removable disks are used, the disk is loaded during work hours and stored in a safe after hours. Magnetic tapes have only one level of protection, called volume protection, to control access. For proper security, magnetic tapes should be initialized with a protection code to deter unauthorized access.

DIRECTORY PROTECTION

Directory protection implements the second level of file security. A directory can be public, group owned, or owned by an individual. The protection on a directory controls who has access to files stored there. If a directory prohibits public access, only the owner (and possibly members of the owner's group) can access the files.

FILE PROTECTION

Each file has a file protection code that controls access to that file only. Even though directory protection permits access to files by one or more categories of users, the individual file protection may deny access to that same category of user. The individual file protection ultimately determines who can and cannot access your files. All files can have the same protection, or protection can vary based on the contents of each file. Optional additional protection is available using a fourth level of security called an Access Control List (ACL), described later in this chapter.

VMS is installed with a standard protection code that applies to each file that it creates. This code is the same for all files on the system, whether directories or ordinary files. When the system manager creates your home directory, the default protection code is applied. When you create new files, the same default protection code is used. However, if you change the protection on a file, the next version of the file inherits its protection from the previous version.

UNDERSTANDING FILE PROTECTION

File protection is based on file ownership and four types of access. When you are authorized, the system manager gives you an account and a username which together form your UIC (see Chapter 5). A UIC is represented as a pair of numbers or strings enclosed in square brackets. The first element is the group and the second element is a member of the group. Although most system managers choose to express UICs as a pair of alphanumeric identifiers, some may use only a single identifier that corresponds to a username.

Some example UICs are shown in Figure 11-1. The numeric form is a holdover from earlier versions of VMS (prior to version 4). Most sites have discarded the numeric form in favor of the more readable alphanumeric representation.

```
[200,001]              Numeric representation
[ADMIN,MANAGER]        Paired alphanumeric representation
[JSTATZ]               Single alphanumeric representation
```

Figure 11-1. UIC Representation

UICs fall into four categories: system, owner, group, and world (Fig. 11-2). The system manager reserves the lowest numbered groups for system users with elevated privileges (*e.g.*, system manager or field service). Groups numbers above the largest system value are assigned to users. Department employees generally belong to the same group and different departments belong to different groups. A user who is not a system user or a member of your group falls into the world category.

```
      UIC Groups    Description
      SYSTEM        Any system UIC
      OWNER         Creator of the file
      GROUP         Members of the file owner's group
      WORLD         All other users


      Types of File Access
      READ    WRITE    EXECUTE    DELETE
```

Figure 11-2. UIC Groups and File Access

File Protection Code

VMS recognizes four types of file access: read, write, execute, and delete. VMS constructs the file protection code by specifying the type of access permitted to each category of user. The VMS file protection code combines UIC categories with file access types in the order shown in Figure 11-3: system, owner, group, and world. Each UIC category is allowed or disallowed read, write, execute, and delete access in the protection code. If any field is blank, the system denies access for that category of users.

```
      (S:RWED,  O:RWED,  G:RWED,  W:RWED)

      S - System Access    R - Read Access
      O - Owner Access     W - Write Access
      G - Group Access     E - Execute Access
      W - World Access     D - Delete Access
```

Figure 11-3. File Protection Code Format

In a standard VMS system, the default protection code is **(S:RWED, O:RWED, G:RE, W)** which allows read, write, execute, and delete access by system users and the owner of the file and read and execute access for members of the owner's group. All other UICs (*i.e.,* the world category of users) are prohibited from accessing a file with this protection code.

Read access allows you to COPY, PRINT, and TYPE a file. Execute access lets you run a program or execute a command procedure. Write access allows you to modify a file (with EDIT or under program control), and delete access allows you to DELETE, EDIT, PURGE, and RENAME a file. Figure 11-4 contains examples of protection codes that you might use with the SET PROTECTION command. The last two are not generally useful, but are valid.

```
    Private access          (S:RWED,O:RWED,G,W)
    Group read access       (S:RWED,O:RWED,G:RE,W)
    Group write access      (S:RWED,O:RWED,G:RWE,W)
    Group delete access     (S:RWED,O:RWED,G:RWED,W)
    Public read access      (S:RWED,O:RWED,G:RWED,W:RE)
    Public write access     (S:RWED,O:RWED,G:RWED,W:RWE)
    Uncontrolled access     (S:RWED,O:RWED,G:RWED,W:RWED)
```

Figure 11-4. VMS File Protection Codes

USING THE FILE PROTECTION CODE

The system determines who is allowed to access a file by comparing the UIC of the file's owner with the UIC of the process requesting access. If the two UICs match, owner access is granted. If the requesting UIC is in the same group as the file owner, the system grants the access specified in the group field. When the requesting UIC is not the owner or a member of the owner's group, it is either a system UIC or a UIC in the world category. The standard protection code normally prohibits world access to files. System users can access most, if not all, files and have elevated privileges that allow them to bypass file protection when necessary.

Access Control List security controls modify the way VMS grants access to files. Because ACLs are tested first, if the requesting process passes the ACL test, the normal UIC based security checks are not performed. ACLs are discussed in more detail later in this chapter.

Default Protection

You can examine the default protection code that applies to all new files with SHOW PROTECTION. You change the default protection mask for your files with SET PROTECTION/DEFAULT (Fig. 11-5).

```
$ SHOW PROTECTION                        Command Format
$ SET PROTECTION=(code)/DEFAULT          Command Format
```

Figure 11-5. SET and SHOW PROTECTION Commands

When you use SET PROTECTION to change the default protection applied to all new files, you only specify the part of the protection code that is to be changed. All other fields will remain the same. You do this by including the initial for that UIC category and the type of access permitted. To deny access, include the initial by itself. For example, to permit all four types of access to group members, use the protection code "G:RWED." To deny group access, use "G" by itself. Examining and changing default file protection are illustrated in Figure 11-6.

```
$ SHOW PROTECTION
  SYSTEM=RWED, OWNER=RWED, GROUP=RE, WORLD=NO ACCESS

$ SET PROTECTION=G:RWED/DEFAULT
$ SHOW PROTECTION
  SYSTEM=RWED, OWNER=RWED, GROUP=RWED, WORLD=NO ACCESS

$ SET PROTECTION=G/DEFAULT
$ SHOW PROTECTION
  SYSTEM=RWED, OWNER=RWED, GROUP=NO ACCESS, WORLD=NO ACCESS
```

Figure 11-6. SET and SHOW PROTECTION Examples

The first time you create a file, it inherits the default protection code. When you change the default protection mask, the new protection applies only to files created after it has been changed. Files existing before you issue the command are not affected by the new settings. If you are creating a new version of an existing file, the new version inherits its protection from the previous version.

Changing File Protection

SET PROTECTION changes both default protection and the protection code for a specific file or directory (Fig. 11-7). You can also use the SET FILE command covered at the end of the previous chapter with the /PROTECTION=(code) qualifier to modify the file protection code.

```
$ SET PROTECTION=(code) file-spec[,...]   Command Format

$ SET PROT=O:RWED SOURCE.DIR              Change directory protection
$ SET PROT=(G:RWE,W:R) ANNUAL.REPORT      Change file protection
```

Figure 11-7. SET PROTECTION Command

When you modify the file protection code for an existing file, there is one small trick. Specify only the part of the protection code that you want to change. Omitted parts of the protection code remain the same. To disable access for any UIC category, use only the letter for that category. In Figure 11-8, the first SET

PROTECTION command grants full access to members of the file owner's UIC group. The second SET PROTECTION command disables group access to the same file.

```
$ DIR/PROTECTION    REPORT.DAT                 Examine file protection
REPORT.DAT          (RWED, RWED, RE , )

$ SET PROT=G:RWED   REPORT.DAT                 Unrestricted group access
$ DIR/PROTECTION    REPORT.DAT
REPORT.DAT          (RWED, RWED, RWED, )

$ SET PROT=G        REPORT.DAT                 No group access allowed
$ DIR/PROTECTION    REPORT.DAT
REPORT.DAT          (RWED, RWED, , )
```

Figure 11-8. Changing File Protection

There is never any reason to disable system access to files. It is important that operators and the system manager have access to files for daily and weekly backup purposes. If you bar the system from reading files, the system manager can use a special privilege to access them anyway.

For security purposes, remember that directory protection poses the first barrier for a user seeking access to your files. If a directory does not allow world access, nobody can look at the files stored there. If it does allow world access, you can still protect files by removing world access from the individual file protection codes. Never use a protection code that grants world write or delete access.

ACCESS CONTROL LISTS

The /ACL qualifier displays the Access Control List associated with a file. An ACL is a special security list created by the system manager that is attached to a file that needs additional protection or to a file that must be shared by users in different UIC groups. The list contains one or more identifiers, each associated with a specific kind of access for one or more UICs. An identifier can be used either to permit or deny access to a file.

The identifier that appears in the ACL is granted to the users who need to access the file. This procedure is analogous to creating special keys for a file — if there is a key on the file and the system manager has given you the same key, you can access the file as specified in the ACL, even though you do not own the file and are not a member of the file owner's group. This technique allows users in different groups to share a file without permitting world access to the file. ACLs permit one user to read the file, another to write and delete the file, and yet another to control the file as if he or she were the owner. When an ACL is on a directory, it is usually propagated to all files stored in the directory. An ACL on a file may also be propagated to higher numbered versions of the file.

When a file has an ACL, VMS determines whether or not to grant access by performing ACL tests before the normal UIC checks. If the requesting process passes the ACL test, file access is granted. If the ACL does not grant the requesting process access or specifically denies access by that UIC, the normal UIC based security checks are made. Access is then permitted or denied based on the result of the UIC comparison and the file protection code. ACLs are administered and controlled by users with elevated privileges and are of minimal concern to the new user.

EXAMINING FILE OWNERSHIP AND PROTECTION

The DIRECTORY command has four qualifiers that display file ownership and security information: /OWNER, /PROTECTION, /ACL, and /SECURITY. The /SECURITY qualifier is equivalent to a combination of the first three qualifiers. In Figure 11-9, we examine the owner and protection on three kinds of files — a data file, a directory file, and a personal mail file.

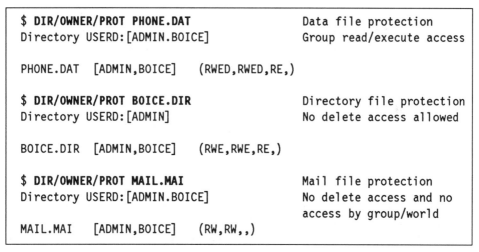

```
$ DIR/OWNER/PROT PHONE.DAT            Data file protection
Directory USERD:[ADMIN.BOICE]         Group read/execute access

PHONE.DAT  [ADMIN,BOICE]    (RWED,RWED,RE,)

$ DIR/OWNER/PROT BOICE.DIR            Directory file protection
Directory USERD:[ADMIN]               No delete access allowed

BOICE.DIR  [ADMIN,BOICE]    (RWE,RWE,RE,)

$ DIR/OWNER/PROT MAIL.MAI             Mail file protection
Directory USERD:[ADMIN.BOICE]         No delete access and no
                                      access by group/world
MAIL.MAI   [ADMIN,BOICE]    (RW,RW,,)
```

Figure 11-9. File Ownership and Protection

The directory file does not allow owner delete access, which is different than an ordinary file. To delete a directory, you must change the protection code to allow owner delete access. Mail files also have a special file protection. To keep them private, each mail file permits only system and owner read and write access. This protection prohibits other users from accessessing your mail and prevents you from accidentally deleting your mail file.

DELETING A DIRECTORY

Now that you understand how file protection works, you are ready to review the procedure for deleting a directory. You can use the DELETE command to delete a directory if and only if

- the directory protection code allows owner delete access, and

- the directory contains no files.

When you try to delete a directory, a file protection violation occurs because directory files are created without system and owner delete access. Owner delete access is purposely not allowed to make you very conscious of a directory delete operation. You must modify the protection code to permit owner delete access and delete all files in the directory before you can delete the directory file itself.

Figure 11-10 illustrates the procedure you use to delete a directory below your home directory. Assume you are in your home directory when these commands are issued. The first command to delete SOURCE.DIR fails with a file protection violation because the directory does not allow owner delete access. After you change the protection code, you issue the DELETE command again.

The second time, you get an error message that indicates that the directory is not empty and cannot be deleted. To avoid another file protection violation, you modify protection to allow owner delete access on all files and then use a wildcard delete command. If all files permit owner delete access, this step is not necessary. Once the directory is empty, you delete the directory file itself.

```
$ DELETE SOURCE.DIR;
%DELETE-W-FILNOTDEL, error deleting PUB1:[PSHARICK]SOURCE.DIR;1
%RMS-E-PRV, insufficient privilege or file protection violation

$ SET PROTECTION=O:RWED SOURCE.DIR
$ DELETE SOURCE.DIR;
%DELETE-W-FILENOTDEL, error deleting PUB1:[SHARICK]SOURCE.DIR:1
%RMS-E_MKD, ACP could not mark file for deletion
%SYSTEM-F-DIRNOTEMPTY, directory is not empty

$ SET PROT = O:RWED [.SOURCE]*.*;*
$ DELETE [.SOURCE]*.*;*
$ DELETE SOURCE.DIR;
```

Figure 11-10. Deleting a Directory

DELETING A DIRECTORY TREE

The procedure for removing a directory tree that contains subdirectories is almost identical to the one used for deleting a single directory. To delete an entire structure, change the protection code on all lower level directories and files to allow owner delete access. Then you issue the wildcard DELETE command once for every level in the tree.

Assume that the SOURCE directory from the previous figure now contains two subdirectories, LIB and COM, and two other files. In Figure 11-11, the first command adds an ellipsis to the directory specification to change file protection for all files in the tree, including the LIB and COM directory files. Then you use two wildcard DELETE commands — the first one removes all files in the LIB and COM subdirectories and the files in SOURCE. The second DELETE command removes the two subdirectories. Last, you move up one level, change the protection on the SOURCE directory file and delete it as well.

```
$ DIR [.SOURCE]
USERD:[VMSWIZ.SOURCE]

COM.DIR;1          LIB.DIR;1              TERM.C;18        MENU.C;24

Total of 4 files.

$ SET PROTECTION=O:RWED [.SOURCE...]*.*;*    Owner Delete access

$ DELETE [.SOURCE...]*.*;*                    LIB, COM, and *.C files
$ DELETE [.SOURCE...]*.*;*                    LIB and COM directories

$ SET PROT=O:RWED SOURCE.DIR                  Change SOURCE protection
$ DELETE SOURCE.DIR;                          Delete SOURCE directory
```

Figure 11-11. Deleting a Directory Tree

When there are additional levels in a tree, you issue the wildcard DELETE command until all the lower level directories have no files and are themselves deleted. If the error "Directory is not empty" occurs, repeat the DELETE command. Once you remove files from a lower level directory, the directory itself can be deleted.

This in turn causes a higher directory to be empty, which allows you to delete the next higher one, and so on. The last step in this procedure is eliminating the top level directory whose entire structure has been deleted. To change the file protection of this directory, you move up one level in the tree to access the directory file itself. After you change protection on the top level directory, it can also be deleted.

This procedure works for directories below a directory that you own or control. You probably do not have the privileges required to delete a directory at the top of a logical or physical device. If such a directory must be deleted, contact the system manager.

WHEN TO CHANGE FILE PROTECTION

With the exception of deleting directories, it is seldom necessary to change file protection. There are, however, a few good reasons to do so.

- A group development project may require that common files have RWED access by all group members, so everyone can modify and delete them.

- If you are updating your resume or working on a job evaluation, you may want to prohibit access by all but system users.

- You may want to allow a user not in your group to copy a file or run a program or command procedure in your directory. To share a file, the directory and file protections must permit world read access.

- If the default protection code is too permissive or too restrictive, you can change it with SET PROTECTION=(code)/DEFAULT.

The best way to avoid file protection problems when sharing a file with a user in another group is to mail the file to that person. MAIL can transmit a copy of any text file, which then becomes the property of the receiver.

FILE PROTECTION EXERCISES

1. What is your default protection code? Write it down so you can reset it later.

```
$ SHOW PROTECTION
SYSTEM=RWED, OWNER=RWED, GROUP=RE, WORLD=NO ACCESS
```

2. Compare the protection code on the MUSIC directory with another file in your directory. Are they different? If so, why?

```
$ DIR/PROTECT MUSIC.DIR
Directory USERB:[VMSWIZ]

MUSIC.DIR;1          (RWE,RWE,RE,E)

Total of 1 file.
```

3. Set your default protection to permit group execute and delete access.

```
$ SET PROTECT = G:RWED/DEFAULT
$ SHOW PROTECTION
SYSTEM=RWED, OWNER=RWED, GROUP=RWED, WORLD=NO ACCESS
```

4. Create a one-line file called PROTECT.LIS. Compare its protection code with the composers file you created earlier. Are they the same or different? Why?

> The new file PROTECT.LIS has G:RWED access and COMPOSERS.ONE has G:RE access. When you change the default protection code, all new files use the new code and old files keep the original protection.

```
$ CREATE PROTECT.LIS
This is a test file to illustrate how the default protection works.
CTRL/Z
$ DIR/PROT PROTECT.LIS, COMPOSERS.ONE

Directory USERB:[VMSWIZ]

COMPOSERS.ONE;1       (RWED,RWED,RE,)
PROTECT.LIS;1         (RWED,RWED,RWED,)

Total of 2 files.
```

5. Reset your default protection to the original setting.

```
$ SET PROT=G:RE/DEFAULT
$ SHOW PROTECTION
SYSTEM=RWED, OWNER=RWED, GROUP=RE, WORLD=NO ACCESS
```

6. Try to delete MUSIC.DIR created in the Chapter 9 exercises. What happens?

> MUSIC contains three directory files and cannot be deleted until the lower directory files are gone.

```
$ DELETE/LOG MUSIC.DIR;
%DELETE-W-FILNOTDEL, error deleting USERB:[VMSWIZ]MUSIC.DIR;1
-RMS-E-MKD, ACP could not mark file for deletion
-SYSTEM-F-DIRNOTEMPTY, directory file is not empty
```

7. Delete the BACH, HAYDN, and MOZART subdirectories. What procedure do you follow?

> You use the ellipsis with SET PROTECTION to change the protection code on each file, including directory files. Then you use the same directory specification with DELETE to remove files in each subdirectory. Once the files are gone, use DELETE a second time to remove the directory files.

```
$ SET PROT=O:RWED [.MUSIC...]*.*;*          [Owner delete access]
$ DELETE/LOG [.MUSIC...]*.*;*               [Select whole tree]
%DELETE-W-FILNOTDEL, error deleting USERB:[VMSWIZ.MUSIC]BACH.DIR;1
-RMS-E-MKD, ACP could not mark file for deletion
-SYSTEM-F-DIRNOTEMPTY, directory file is not empty
%DELETE-I-FILDEL, USERB:[VMSWIZ.MUSIC]COMPOSERS.ONE;1 deleted (2 blocks)
%DELETE-W-FILNOTDEL, error deleting USERB:[VMSWIZ.MUSIC]HAYDN.DIR;1
-RMS-E-MKD, ACP could not mark file for deletion
-SYSTEM-F-DIRNOTEMPTY, directory file is not empty
```

```
%DELETE-W-FILNOTDEL, error deleting USERB:[VMSWIZ.MUSIC]MOZART.DIR;1
-RMS-E-MKD, ACP could not mark file for deletion
-SYSTEM-F-DIRNOTEMPTY, directory file is not empty
%DELETE-I-FILDEL, USERB:[VMSWIZ.MUSIC.BACH]COMPOSERS.THREE;3 deleted (2 blocks)
%DELETE-I-FILDEL, USERB:[VMSWIZ.MUSIC.HAYDN]COMPOSERS.TWO;1 deleted (2 blocks)
%DELETE-I-FILDEL, USERB:[VMSWIZ.MUSIC.MOZART]COMPOSERS.THREE;3 deleted (2 blocks)
%DELETE-I-TOTAL, 6 files deleted (12 blocks)
$ DELETE/LOG [.MUSIC...]*.*;*
%DELETE-I-FILDEL, USERB:[VMSWIZ.MUSIC]BACH.DIR;1 deleted (2 blocks)
%DELETE-I-FILDEL, USERB:[VMSWIZ.MUSIC]HAYDN.DIR;1 deleted (2 blocks)
%DELETE-I-FILDEL, USERB:[VMSWIZ.MUSIC]MOZART.DIR;1 deleted (2 blocks)
%DELETE-TOTAL, 3 files deleted (6 blocks)
```

8. Now that the MUSIC directory is empty, can you delete it?

> This time you get a file protection violation because MUSIC does not allow owner delete access.

```
$ DELETE/LOG MUSIC.DIR;
%DELETE-W-FILNOTDEL, error deleting USERB:[VMSWIZ]MUSIC.DIR;1
%RMS-E-PRV, insufficient privilege or file protection violation
```

9. Change the file protection code on MUSIC.DIR to allow owner delete access.

```
$ SET PROT=O:RWED MUSIC.DIR
$ DIR/PROT MUSIC.DIR
Directory USERB:[VMSWIZ]

MUSIC.DIR;1             (RWE,RWED,RE,E)

Total of 1 file.
```

10. Now delete the MUSIC directory. What happens this time? Use the DIRECTORY command to verify that the entire structure is gone.

```
$ DEL/LOG MUSIC.DIR;
%DELETE-I-FILDEL, USERB:[VMSWIZ]MUSIC.DIR;1 deleted (2 blocks)
$ DIR MUSIC
%DIRECT-W-NOFILES, no files found
```

The EVE Text Editor

INTRODUCTION

This chapter covers the EVE editor, which is the most popular text editor provided with VMS. EVE provides over 150 editing functions — some of them are mapped to the grey editing keys and function keys and others are entered as commands. EVE supports multiple file editing, multiple windows, and has an extensive online HELP utility. EVE also provides a direct interface to VMS, which allows you to read your mail and execute other commands without terminating your edit session.

EVE OVERVIEW

EVE, which stands for Extensible VAX Editor, is implemented using the Text Processing Utility (TPU). TPU is both a language and a utility. Developers use the TPU language to implement general or specialized editors by combining editing primitives into more sophisticated operations. Editing functions are defined, named, optionally mapped to keys on a keyboard, and processed into an initialization file. TPU then operates with whatever commands are included in the initialization file. The standard TPU interface defines the editing language called EVE. When you start the TPU editor, it uses the EVE initialization file at most VMS installations.

The word extensible comes from the fact that EVE is easily modified to suit individual editing needs. You can create specialized editing functions with the DEFINE KEY and LEARN commands. DEFINE KEY binds a command to a key or CTRL/key combination on the keyboard. In LEARN mode, the editor remembers each keystroke in a sequence and maps the sequence to the key of your choice. Once you define custom editing functions, they can be permanently saved and automatically loaded when you start the editor.

EVE starts with 16 functions mapped to the grey editing keys and function keys. You can optionally use the SET KEYPAD EDT command to map additional functions to the keys on the numeric keypad. EDT functions round out the basic set of EVE commands already defined for the editing keypad and function keys, with some duplication of function.

EVE has several features that support multiple file editing. Files can be concurrently mapped to the screen in separate windows. The size of each window can be independently controlled, as can the margins and scrolling region. When multiple buffers are active, operating on or saving the contents of one buffer does not impact any other buffer.

The EVE DCL command creates a subprocess that attaches to your edit session in a separate edit buffer called DCL. The DCL command you enter and any output that normally comes to your screen are stored in the DCL buffer. This feature allows you to capture and edit the output from any command, program or application. Programmers find the DCL command a wonderful productivity feature because programs can be edited, compiled, linked, and run without leaving the editor environment. Simply switching buffers allows the programmer to check the status of a compile or test run and make corrections as necessary.

TEXT BUFFERS

EVE manages text by storing it in a work area called a buffer. When the editor is started with a file name, the contents of the file are loaded into a text buffer of the same name. The editor displays the current buffer name on the status line at the bottom of the screen at all times.

If you load a second file with the GET FILE command, a second text buffer is created for the new file. SHOW BUFFERS lists all user buffers that you have created during an editing session. The BUFFER command accepts a buffer name and maps that buffer to the active window, which effectively puts you into another text file.

SYSTEM BUFFERS

There are also several system buffers maintained during an editing session. You can display a list of these buffers with the SHOW SYSTEM BUFFERS command. Just as you can switch among user text buffers, you can also access system buffers using the BUFFER command. Many system buffers are read only, which means you are not allowed to make changes in these buffers. However, you can save the contents of any system buffer using the WRITE command. Also, do not delete system buffers, as they are required for proper editor operation.

Looking at system buffers can be informative. The INSERT HERE buffer contains text you have removed from a document that will be inserted with the INSERT key. The COMMANDS buffer records the commands you have executed during your editing session. The HELP buffer keeps the last screen of text displayed by EVE's HELP utility and the MESSAGES buffer keeps a list of all messages issued by EVE during your editing session. $DEFAULTS$ contains the list of default characteristics (*e.g.*, margins) active for all buffers.

THE HELP KEY AND THE HELP UTILITY

Extensive online documentation is available via the HELP key or the HELP command. The HELP key displays a diagram of EVE editing keys and allows you to ask for information on any key in the diagram by pressing the appropriate key. The HELP command responds with a list of topics or information about the topic you request. To use the HELP command, press the DO key and type HELP at the Command: prompt.

EVE HELP works like VMS HELP and uses the same Topic? and Subtopic? prompts. Terminate each HELP request with RETURN. Use NEXT SCREEN and PREV SCREEN to scroll back and forth in the HELP text. To exit HELP (either the key or the command), press RETURN.

When you enter the first HELP command, EVE creates a new buffer called HELP that stores the output of your last information request. The buffer name also appears on the status line. The HELP buffer is a system buffer that remains until you terminate your edit session. If you want to read the same information again, you can move to the HELP buffer with a BUFFER HELP command. In this buffer, you can use any of the EVE editing functions to scroll through the text, cut and paste sections into your main text file and so on. You can also save HELP information in a file with the WRITE command. EVE buffer, file, and window commands are listed later in this chapter in Figure 12-11.

Figure 12-1 is the display presented in response to the HELP command. It can take months to learn even half of what is available from the EVE editor. Start with editing and numeric keypad functions and dig through HELP when you want to learn more. When you examine information about a specific command, you will find excellent examples and a list of additional related subjects. EVE help documentation is well organized, very complete and very easy to use.

STARTING AND LEAVING THE EDITOR

Although the editor is called EVE, there is no EVE command — refer to Chapter 16, Personalizing Your Environment, for instructions on creating your own EVE command. Instead you start the editor with EDIT/TPU file-spec. If you provide a file name and the file exists, it is loaded into a buffer of the same name.

List Of Topics (Commands)

For help on EVE topics, type the name of a topic and press RETURN.

    o For a keypad diagram, press HELP.
    o For help on VAXTPU builtins, type TPU and press RETURN.
    o To exit from help and resume editing, press RETURN.

EDITING TEXT

Change Mode	Erase Word	Restore Character
Copy	Insert Here	Restore Line
Cut	Insert Mode	Restore Selection
Delete	Overstrike Mode	Restore Sentence
Erase Character	Paste	Restore Word
Erase Line	Quote	Select
Erase Previous Word	Remove	Select All
Erase Start Of Line	Restore	Store Text

SEARCHES

Find	Set Find Case Noexact	Set Wildcard VMS
Find Next	Set Find Nowhitespace	Show Wildcards
Find Selected	Set Find Whitespace	Spell
Replace	Set Wildcard Ultrix	Wildcard Find
Set Find Case Exact		

CURSOR MOVEMENT AND SCROLLING

Bottom	Mark	Move Right	Set Cursor Free
Change Direction	Move By Line	Move Up	Set Scroll Margins
End Of Line	Move By Page	Next Screen	Start Of Line
Forward	Move By Word	Previous Screen	Top
Go To	Move Down	Reverse	What Line
Line	Move Left	Set Cursor Bound	

GENERAL-PURPOSE COMMANDS

Attach	Do	Help	Recall	Reset	Show	Tab
DCL	Exit	Quit	Repeat	Return	Spawn	

FILES AND BUFFERS

Buffer	Open Selected	Set Journaling
Delete Buffer	Previous Buffer	Set Journaling All
Get File	Recover Buffer	Set Nojournaling
Include File	Recover Buffer All	Set Nojournaling All
New	Save File	Show Buffers
Next Buffer	Save File As	Show System Buffers
Open	Set Buffer	Write File

Figure 12-1. EVE HELP Display

WINDOWS AND DISPLAY

Delete Window	One Window	Set Width	Shrink Window
Enlarge Window	Previous Window	Shift Left	Split Window
Next Window	Refresh	Shift Right	Two Windows

FORMATTING AND CASE CHANGES

Capitalize Word	Insert Page Break	Set Paragraph Indent
Center Line	Lowercase Word	Set Right Margin
Fill	Paginate	Set Tabs
Fill Paragraph	Set Left Margin	Set Wrap
Fill Range	Set Nowrap	Uppercase Word

KEY DEFINITIONS

Define Key	Set Gold Key	Set Keypad VT100
Learn	Set Keypad EDT	Set Keypad WPS
Remember	Set Keypad NoEDT	Set Nogold Key
Set Func Key DECwindows	Set Keypad NoWPS	Show Key
Set Func Key NoDECwindows	Set Keypad Numeric	Undefine Key

CUSTOMIZING

@	Set Noclipboard
Define Menu Entry	Set Nodefault Command File
Extend All	Set Nodefault Section File
Extend EVE	Set Noexit Attribute Check
Extend This	Set Nopending Delete
Save Attributes	Set Nosection File Prompting
Save Extended EVE	Set Pending Delete
Save System Attributes	Set Section File Prompting
Set Clipboard	Show Defaults Buffer
Set Default Command File	Show Summary
Set Default Section File	TPU
Set Exit Attribute Check	Undefine Menu Entry

INFORMATIONAL TOPICS

Abbreviating	EDT Differences	New Features
About	Gold Keys	New User
Attributes	Initialization Files	Position Cursor
Canceling Commands	Journal Files	Prompts And Responses
Choices Buffer	Keypad (diagram)	Quick Copy
Command Files	Keys (list)	Ruler Keys
Control Keys	List Of Topics	Scroll Bars
DECwindows Differences	Mail Editing	Section Files
Defaults	Menus	Status Line
Dialog Boxes	Message Buffer	Typing Keys
Editing Command Lines	Mouse	Windows
EDT Conversion	Names For Keys	WPS Differences

Example 12-1. EVE HELP Display *(continued)*

If the file does not exist, the editor creates a buffer with the name you enter on the command line. If you enter text and exit EVE, the editor stores your text in the file name provided. Alternatively, you can start the editor without a file name, enter text, and specify a file name when you exit.

The status line on the bottom of the screen verifies the name of the file loaded, tells you whether you are using insert or overstrike mode, and the direction in which you are moving in the file. The [End of file] marker appears at the bottom of the file, after the last line of text. If you are creating a new file, the screen is empty and this marker appears on the first line.

EXIT Command

There are two ways to leave the editor, EXIT or QUIT. EXIT saves a new version of the file if any changes were made. Exit the editor with either CTRL/Z or by pressing function key F10, which is defined as the EXIT command. These two functions are identical. An information message from EVE informs you if a new version of the file is created. If no changes were made, EVE does not save a new version and the original file remains untouched.

QUIT Command

The second way to leave the editor is using QUIT, which never saves a new version of the file. Use QUIT if you did not change the file or when you do not want to save changes you made. Press the DO key, and enter QUIT in response to the Command: prompt at the bottom of the screen. Terminate the command with the RETURN key. EVE will ask you for confirmation that you do not want to save changes before exiting.

THE DO KEY

There are more than 150 commands in EVE and 16 standard editing keys that are automatically defined. To enter a command that is not already bound to a key, use the DO key on the top row of the editing keypad. Pressing this key causes a Command: prompt to appear at the bottom of the screen, below the status line. (Some commands may prompt for more information.) Enter the command and complete it with RETURN. You can abbreviate all EVE commands to the shortest string that uniquely identifies each command. Where there are several commands that match the abbreviation you enter, EVE displays the choices and asks for clarification.

EDITING FUNCTIONS

EVE understands five sets of editing keys: the control keys used with line editing, the arrow keys, the grey editing keypad keys, the function keys across the top of the keyboard, and optionally, functions that are mapped to the numeric keypad by the SET KEYPAD EDT command. The standard keyboard editing keys, sometimes called the mini-keypad, are illustrated in Figure 12-3 on the next page.

Line Editing Control Characters

All line editing control characters and several additional control combinations can be used in EVE (Fig. 12-2). Insert and overstrike modes and control key combinations are covered in more detail in Chapter 7, Digital Command Language, under Command Line Editing.

Keystrokes	Edit Function
CTRL/A	Toggle between insert/overstrike mode
CTRL/B or ↑	Recall (up to last 20 commands)
CTRL/E	Move cursor to end of line (end)
CTRL/H or **BACKSPACE**	Move cursor to beginning of line (home)
CTRL/I	Insert tab character
CTRL/J	Delete word to left of cursor
CTRL/K	Start a learn sequence
CTRL/L	Insert a page break
CTRL/M	Insert a carriage return
CTRL/R	Terminate a learn sequence
CTRL/U	Delete from beginning of line to cursor
CTRL/W	Repaint the screen
CTRL/V	Insert a quote
CTRL/Z	Exit the editor

Figure 12-2. Line Editing Control Characters

GOLD Key Functions

In the diagrams in Figure 12-3 (Eve Editing Keys) and Figure 12-4 (Numeric Keypad), many keys have two labels. The top function is activated by pressing the key. The bottom function, called a GOLD function, is in boldface. A GOLD function is activated by pressing the GOLD key, followed by the editing key (keys should not be pressed simultaneously).

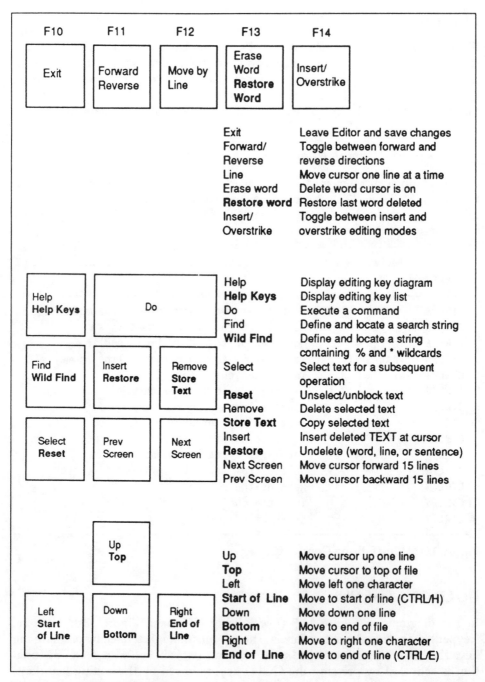

Figure 12-3. EVE Editing Keys

To use the GOLD functions, you must first define a GOLD key. Press DO and enter the command **SET GOLD KEY PF1**. This defines PF1 on the numeric keypad as the GOLD key. PF1 is the normal choice. However, you are free to choose another keypad or function key for this purpose.

Do not let the HELP key confuse you. The diagrams displayed are different, depending upon whether or not you have defined a GOLD key. If you press the HELP key before you define a GOLD key, the key diagrams only contain a single function. If you define a GOLD key and then press the HELP key, the key diagrams display both standard and GOLD functions.

Grey Editing Keys and Function Keys

Examine your keyboard and the labels on the grey editing keys — the labels describe functions standard with the EVE editor. Additional functions are defined on function keys F10 through F14 on VT200 and VT300 keyboards and an interface also exists for the older style VT100. If you have defined a GOLD key, you can use the GOLD functions shown in boldface in Figures 12-3 and 12-4. Otherwise these functions are not available.

There are no GOLD functions for the DO (F16), PREV SCREEN (E5) and NEXT SCREEN (E6) keys. If you have two or three editing commands you use all the time, you can define them as GOLD functions on any of these keys (GOLD/F16, GOLD/E5, and GOLD/E6). This places the functions you use all the time in a very convenient location. Key definitions are covered later in this chapter.

USING THE NUMERIC KEYPAD

The EDT text editor has been around for at least a decade and there are many VMS users that prefer EDT to the newer editors. In deference to this large number of EDT fans, EVE comes with a standard EDT editing interface that uses the numeric keypad on the right side of the keyboard. Many novice users find the numeric keypad functions quite useful in getting started.

To set up the numeric keypad with EDT functions, press the DO key and enter the command **SET KEYPAD EDT**. This command assigns a normal and a GOLD function to each key. It is not necessary to define the GOLD key as PF1 when using the EDT keypad, because SET KEYPAD EDT defines it for you. The GOLD function is the lower label shown in boldface on each key in Figure 12-4.

On the numeric keypad, you can reach most functions without ever repositioning your right hand. Cursor positioning works by line (0 key), word (1 key), character (3 key), and end of line (2 key). Delete/restore functions also work on a line (PF4), word (minus), character (comma), and end of line (GOLD 2) basis. After an hour or two of practice, you can easily learn the essential keys. Figure 12-5 contains a

short description of each numeric keypad function. Some of these functions duplicate functions on the grey editing keys, so choose the key that is easiest for you
to remember.

PF1 Gold Key	PF2 Help **Key Defs**	PF3 FndNxt **Find**	PF4 Del L **Res L**
7 MovByPag **Do**	8 Sect **Fill**	9 Append **EDT Repl**	- Del W **Res W**
4 Forward **Bottom**	5 Reverse **Top**	6 Remove **Ins Here**	, Del C **Res C**
1 Word **ChngCase**	2 EOL **Del Eol**	3 Char **SpecIns**	ENTER
0 Line **Open Line**		. Select **Reset**	Return **Subs**

Figure 12-4. Numeric Keypad Diagram

Because the numeric keys combine several EVE functions in one or two
keystrokes, these definitions are usually easier to remember than the equivalent
EVE commands. For example, EVE does not have a preprogrammed function to
move forward or backward by word. There is an EVE command called Move-by-
Word that you can enter with the DO key, but it is very inconvenient to move
around in your text buffer this way. On the numeric keypad, this function is
mapped to the "1" key (labeled Word), which eliminates the need for typing in
the command.

EVE does not have a single function to delete the line the cursor is on. You must
select and highlight the line and press REMOVE, which requires at least three
keystrokes if you don't make any mistakes. This sequence of commands is
mapped to the PF4 key on the numeric keypad and is called DEL L (delete line).
The same is true for a delete from the cursor to the end of the line — without the
numeric keypad, you must use several keystrokes. On the numeric keypad, press
GOLD 2 for this function. End-of-line is abbreviated EOL in the keypad diagram
and wherever this function is referenced.

```
Key Label      Function      Description
--------------------------------------------------------------------
PF1            Gold          Select the gold function
PF2            Help          Display key diagram
               KeyDefs       Display list of key definitions
PF3            FndNxt        Find next string
               Find          Define and locate first search string
PF4            Del L         Delete line
               Res L         Restore line

7              MovByPag      Move cursor to next page break
               Do            Enter a typed command
8              Sect          Next screen/previous screen analog
               Fill          Format line, paragraph, or block of text
9              Append        Remove and add to removed or stored text
               EDT Repl      Replace string with removed or stored text
Minus          Del W         Delete word
               Res W         Restore word

4              Forward       Set a forward direction
               Bottom        Position cursor at end of buffer
5              Reverse       Set a reverse direction
               Top           Position cursor at top of buffer
6              Remove        Remove highlighted text
               Ins Here      Insert previously removed or stored text
Comma          Del C         Delete character
               Res C         Restore character

1              MovByWord     Move cursor to next word
               ChngCas       Reverse case
2              EOL           Move cursor by end-of-line position
               Del EOL       Delete text from cursor to end-of-line
3              MovByChar     Move cursor one character
               SpecIns       Insert control character

0              MovByLine     Move cursor to beginning of next line
               Open Line     Insert blank line
Period         Select        Start a select operation
               Reset         Cancel a select operation
Enter          Return        Equivalent to RETURN key
               EDT Subs      Same as EDT Replace
```

Figure 12-5. Numeric Keypad Functions

MOVING FORWARD AND BACKWARD

Many editing functions work in either a forward or backward direction in your text file (*e.g.*, searching or replacing a string). The arrow keys control cursor movement and set either a forward or backward direction for edit operations. You can also use function key F11 which toggles between forward and reverse and, if you have activated the numeric keypad, FORWARD (4 key) and REVERSE (5 key) also toggle directions. The current direction is always displayed on the status line.

EVE starts with the direction set to forward. Pressing F11 once selects the reverse direction and pressing it a second time toggles to the forward direction. When a direction is defined, it remains in effect until a new direction is selected.

To move a line at a time, use F12, which, in the forward direction, moves the cursor using the end of line position and in the backward direction by the beginning of the line. On the numeric keypad key, END-OF-LINE (2 key) moves in the current direction to the next end-of-line position, and LINE (0 key) moves in the current direction to the next beginning-of-line position.

To move the cursor to the bottom of file, use GOLD DOWN arrow; to move it to the top of the file, use GOLD UP arrow. On the numeric keypad, BOTTOM (GOLD,4) positions the cursor at the bottom of the file and TOP (GOLD,5) moves the cursor to the top of the file.

Figure 12-8 summarizes cursor movement operations using numeric keypad keys. A direction key is included for each operation, which makes it a two-key action. If the proper direction is already set, you can omit FORWARD (4 key) or REVERSE (5 key) and just press LINE (0), WORD (1) , END-OF-LINE (2), or CHARACTER (3) on the keypad. The equivalent Move-by-Word and Move-by-Character EVE functions must be entered with the DO key. EVE HELP has information on EVE and EDT equivalent functions.

Action	Keys	Action	Keys
Forward Line	4,0	Backward Line	5,0
Forward Word	4,1	Backward Word	5,1
Forward EOL	4,2	Backward EOL	5,2
Forward Char	4,3	Backward Char	5,3
Bottom of File	GOLD,4	Top of File	GOLD,5
End-of-line(EOL)	2		

Figure 12-6. Numeric Keypad Cursor Movement

DELETE/RESTORE FUNCTIONS

Use the DELETE key to delete the character to the left of the cursor. To delete a word, position the cursor at the beginning of the word and press function key F13 (defined as ERASE WORD). To delete a line or block of text, position the cursor at the beginning of the text, press SELECT and use cursor arrows to highlight the text to be deleted. Then press REMOVE to delete the text. Use INSERT to restore the last REMOVE operation (word, line, or block of text) and RESTORE to undo the last ERASE WORD or ERASE LINE operation.

The numeric keypad has several delete functions that eliminate the need for highlighting the text that is to be removed. Delete line, word, and character functions are positioned vertically on the keypad: DEL L (PF4), DEL W (minus), and DEL C (comma). Where the DELETE key deletes the character to the left of the cursor, DEL C on the keypad deletes the character the cursor is resting on. To delete text from the cursor position to the end of a line, press GOLD EOL (GOLD,2).

To restore the previously deleted line, word, or character, press GOLD followed by the delete function you used initially. For example, to delete the current line, position the cursor at the beginning of the line and press PF4. To restore this line, press GOLD PF4. To restore a word, press GOLD, DEL W (GOLD,minus) and to restore a character press GOLD DEL C (GOLD,3). These keystrokes are summarized in Figure 12-7.

Action	Keys	Action	Keys
Delete Line	PF4	Restore Line	GOLD, PF4
Delete to EOL	GOLD,2	Restore Line	GOLD, PF4
Delete Word	Minus	Restore Word	GOLD, Minus
Delete Char	Comma	Restore Char	GOLD, Comma

Figure 12-7. Numeric Keypad Delete/Restore Functions

STRING SEARCHING

You can search for one or all occurrences of a string in your text file. Searching begins at the current line, in the current direction, and stops at the next occurrence of the string. Press FIND and enter the search string at the Forward Find: prompt at the bottom of the screen. EVE highlights the string wherever it is found. This same action is initiated by pressing FIND on the numeric keypad (GOLD, PF3).

If the string is located in the reverse direction, EVE displays a message to that effect and asks if you "Want to Go There?" Respond to the prompt with either yes or no. If the string is not found, the message "Could not find:" followed by the search string is displayed.

To locate the next occurrence of the same string, press the FIND key twice. The first time you are asked for a search string and the second key press tells FIND to use the previously defined string. You can also use FNDNXT (PF3) on the numeric keypad.

STRING REPLACING

Use REPLACE to substitute one string for another. You can direct REPLACE to substitute one, many, or all occurrences of the source string. To enter this command, press DO and enter REPLACE at the Command: prompt. You can enter the whole command on one line or enter REPLACE and wait for EVE to prompt for the old string and the new string.

Although the numeric keypad also provides a REPLACE function (GOLD, 9 or GOLD, ENTER), it requires first predefining the replace string and storing it in the INSERT HERE buffer. Then you use a two-key sequence to replace each occurrence. The EVE REPLACE function is much easier to use.

The first command in Figure 12-8 replaces the word sun with the word moon and the second command replaces the "The Bards Tale" with "Kings Quest." When you do a phrase replacement, enclose each phrase in double quotes ("). The replace operation replaces one, many, or all occurrences of the old string based on your response to the REPLACE prompts listed in this figure.

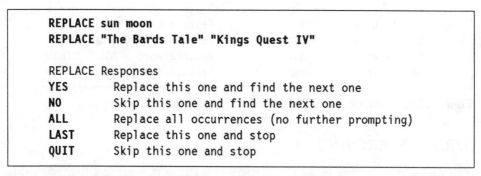

```
REPLACE sun moon
REPLACE "The Bards Tale" "Kings Quest IV"


REPLACE Responses
YES       Replace this one and find the next one
NO        Skip this one and find the next one
ALL       Replace all occurrences (no further prompting)
LAST      Replace this one and stop
QUIT      Skip this one and stop
```

Figure 12-8. REPLACE Command Options

REPLACE is case sensitive. When both strings are lowercase, EVE matches the case appropriately for each replacement. For example, if EVE finds a capitalized version of the old string, it is replaced by a capitalized version of the new string. If the old string contains any uppercase letters, the search and replacement are exact.

REMOVE AND INSERT OPERATIONS

You use SELECT, REMOVE, and INSERT for cut and paste operations. Position the cursor at the start of the text to be moved. Press the SELECT key and position the cursor at the end of the text to be moved. The selected text is highlighted on the screen. If you highlight the wrong text, press SELECT a second time to terminate the select operation. Use REMOVE to delete the highlighted text. The removed text is temporarily stored in the system INSERT HERE buffer. To insert that text at a new location, position the cursor at the new location and press INSERT.

The numeric keypad has these same functions — SELECT is the period key, REMOVE is the 6 key, and INSERT is GOLD 6. To start a select operation from the numeric keypad, press the period key. Move the cursor until the text to be removed is highlighted. Press REMOVE (6 key) to remove the text, position the cursor at the new location, and press INSERT (GOLD 6) to insert the text.

GOLD REMOVE copies highlighted text into the INSERT HERE buffer without deleting the highlighted text from the document. This is useful if you are duplicating the same text in several locations in your text file. There is no analog of this function on the numeric keypad.

You can insert removed text in several different locations with multiple INSERT operations. The text remains in the INSERT HERE buffer until it is overwritten by a new REMOVE operation. This means you can perform other editing functions between insert operations without losing the removed text. If you want to modify the removed text before inserting it into the document, switch to the INSERT HERE buffer (BUFFER INSERT HERE) and make the necessary edit changes. Then return to the main editing buffer, position the cursor, and press INSERT.

You can remove several pieces of text and append them together in the INSERT HERE buffer. The first block of text is removed using the REMOVE key. Select the next block of text and use APPEND (9 key) on the numeric keypad to add this text to the end of the first block. The whole block can then be inserted with a normal insert operation.

EDITING MULTIPLE FILES

EVE has several functions that facilitate editing several files concurrently. Briefly, there is a command to load another text file, a command to switch from one buffer to another, a command to write out the contents of the current buffer, and a command that allows you to map two or more buffers to the screen at the same time. You can edit as many files at one time as you can reasonably manage and you can create new empty buffers with the BUFFER command.

Loading Two Text Files

To load two files into two windows on the screen, press DO and enter each command in the procedure below. Complete each command with RETURN. If you are editing multiple files, you cannot leave the editor without being asked if you want to save the contents of all modified buffers. Respond yes to the prompt for each buffer you want to save.

- Start the editor with the first file name

- Enter the SPLIT command, which divides the screen into two windows. The file you started with is displayed in both windows.

- Use GET FILE to load and map the second file to the active window.

- Use a WINDOW command to switch from one to the other.

Many of the commands used to manipulate files, buffers, and windows are listed in Figure 12-9. GET FILE loads a text file into another buffer, INCLUDE FILE loads a text file into the current buffer at the current cursor position and WRITE FILE save the contents of the current buffer.

SHOW BUFFER lists all the user buffers you have created and the BUFFER command allows you to switch from one buffer to another. If you do not provide a buffer name, the BUFFER command prompts you for one. You can abbreviate the desired buffer name to the minimum unique string. You can also use the BUFFER command to create a new working buffer — if the buffer you specify does not exist, EVE creates it and makes it the active buffer.

```
Get File file-spec        Load file into another buffer
Include File file-spec    Load file into current buffer
WRite File                Write buffer to disk

SHow Buffers              List all user buffers
BUffer  buffer-name       Make this buffer the active buffer

ONe Window                Display one window on the screen
SPLit Window              Divide screen into two windows
Delete Window             Delete active window

OTher Window              Move cursor to the other window
Previous Window           Move cursor to previous window
Next Window               Move cursor to next window

Capitalized letters show the minimum command string you can use.
```

Figure 12-9. File and Window Commands

When there are two windows on the screen, switch between them with the OTHER WINDOW command. When there are more than two windows, switch among them using NEXT WINDOW and PREVIOUS WINDOW or the BUFFER command. When you have two or more windows on the screen, you delete the active window with the DELETE WINDOW command. This command removes the window from your screen but does not delete the buffer, which means your text is still there. If you regularly edit multiple files, you may find it convenient to map frequently used window and buffer commands to the keyboard using the DEFINE KEY command.

CUSTOMIZING EVE

EVE has 16 out of 150 commands mapped to the keyboard. All other EVE commands are entered using the DO key and typing the command at the prompt. In EVE, there are two ways to map editing commands to the typing keys, control key combinations, function keys and keypad keys.

- Use DEFINE KEY to bind functions to other keys

- Use LEARN to remember and bind a sequence of keystrokes to a key

You can define new functions each time you start the editor or you can make them a permanent part of your version of EVE when you save the commands in a "section file" using the SAVE EXTENDED EVE command. Each time the editor is started, EVE processes the saved definitions before the editing session begins.

Defining Custom Editing Keys

Use DEFINE KEY to attach a command to a key or CTRL/key combination on the keyboard. Use SHOW KEY to examine a definition and UNDEFINE KEY to remove a definition. If EVE has a definition for the key you UNDEFINE, the key reverts to that definition. You must include a key name with all three commands (Fig. 12-10).

```
DEFINE KEY key-name   command        Create definition
SHOW KEY key-name                    Display one definition
UNDEFINE KEY key-name                Remove one definition
HELP KEYS                            Display all definitions
```

Figure 12-10. Key Definition Commands

You can create definitions for the GOLD key, editing keypad keys, numeric keypad keys, and function keys. Figure 12-11 contains some example key definitions—the command can be entered in lower, upper, or mixed case with identical results.

```
DEFINE KEY=F17          DCL
DEFINE KEY=f18          QUIT

DEFINE KEY=CTRL/G       GET FILE
DEFINE KEY=CTRL/W       WRITE FILE

DEFINE KEY=KP7          LOWERCASE
DEFINE KEY=GOLD/KP7     UPPERCASE
DEFINE KEY=KP8          CENTER LINE
```

Figure 12-11. DEFINE KEY Examples

Most EVE key names are identical to the label on the keys. The EVE Help topic "Names for Keys" displays the names of the exceptions and is reproduced in Figure 12-12 for convenience. You can find out which keys are not definable from the Help topic "TPU nondefinable keys."

For example, F1 through F5 are reserved, and you cannot redefine RETURN, SHIFT, or CTRL. You also cannot redefine the typing keys, but can define CTRL/typing key combinations. When creating a key definition, you can press DO and type the whole command on one line or you can enter DEFINE KEY and respond to the EVE prompts for the key name and the definition.

Key name	Label	Key name	Location
F15	Help	**MINUS**	numeric keypad
F16	Do	**COMMA**	numeric keypad
E1	Find	**PERIOD**	numeric keypad
E2	Insert Here	KP0-KP9	numeric keypad
E3	Remove		
E4	Select	**UP**	up arrow
E5	Prev Screen	**LEFT**	left arrow
E6	Next Screen	**DOWN**	down arrow
BS_KEY	Backspace	**RIGHT**	right arrow
DEL_KEY	⟨x⟩ or Delete	**M1DOWN**	left mouse button-press
LF_KEY	Linefeed	**M1UP**	left mouse button-release
RET_KEY	Return		
TAB_KEY	Tab		

Figure 12-12. Definable Keys and Key Names

The LEARN Command

LEARN (or CTRL/K) is a great time saver for repetitive operations. LEARN instructs the editor to remember every keystroke until you terminate the sequence with CTRL/R. EVE then asks you to press the key you want to define. Repetitive operations that normally take many keystrokes, like creating columns by inserting tabs, capitalizing all paragraph titles, or inserting page breaks every 60 lines, can be mapped to a key as a single editing function.

LEARN remembers keystrokes and not commands, so it is best to have all the commands you are going to use in the LEARN sequence already defined as keys on the keyboard. Results are not guaranteed when you enter DO commands while a LEARN recording sequence is in progress, because the carriage return occasionally gets in the way.

Suppose you want to define a function that advances to the next line and centers the text on that line. You first define CENTER LINE as a key (*i.e.*, DEFINE/KEY KP8 CENTER LINE) on the numeric keypad. Then start the LEARN sequence with CTRL/K. Press CTRL/H to return the cursor to the beginning of the line, DOWN arrow to advance to the next line, and KP8 to center the line. Terminate the recording sequence with CTRL/R and select a key to hold the definition (you might want to reuse KP8). You now have a function that centers the next line in your text file.

If you make a mistake entering a LEARN sequence, press CTRL/R to terminate the recording and press RETURN at the "Press the key you want to use to do what was just learned" prompt. EVE responds with the message "Key sequence not remembered" because you are not allowed to redefine the RETURN key.

Saving Custom Key Definitions

After you define the same keys a few times you will want to save your definitions permanently. There are two ways to accomplish this. The first way is to create a text file called EVE$INIT.EVE in your home directory and place EVE commands in the file, one per line. The simplest initialization file might have a single line that contains the command SET KEYPAD EDT. More complex files might contain several key definitions, margin and tab settings, and so on. Each time EVE starts, the definitions in the initialization file are processed.

The command SAVE EXTENDED EVE stores all your current definitions in a processed form in a "section file" which is loaded at EVE startup. The next time you start the editor, the "compiled" commands in the section file are loaded. If you have many editing commands to perform, the second method is more efficient. Ask for HELP on Section Files and Initialization Files for information on where and how to save permanent custom definitions, which definitions take precedence, and the order in which EVE processes the definition files.

ADDITIONAL EDITING FUNCTIONS

DCL Command

To execute a DCL command, press the DO key and enter DCL followed by the command you want to run (*e.g.*, DO DCL DIRECTORY). EVE creates a subprocess to execute the command and creates a DCL text buffer in which the command and any screen output from the command are stored. If you switch to this buffer (BUFFER DCL), you can edit, select, remove and insert this text into another buffer like any other text file.

For example, while editing a file, you can execute a DCL command to run a report from a spreadsheet. The command and the report are stored in the DCL buffer. You can use SELECT, REMOVE, and INSERT HERE to move the report from the DCL buffer into the main editing buffer where it becomes a permanent part of your text file. If the command output contains formatting or control characters, you may have to delete them or substitute for them before saving the text file permanently.

There is one restriction that applies when you run a command, utility or application from an EVE DCL subprocess. When the command or program requires interactive input, you must enter each input with a separate DO DCL command. For example, you can start the MAIL utility with a DCL MAIL command. To read a new message, you enter the command DCL READ/NEW — READ/NEW is passed to the subprocess and is read as input by the MAIL utility. MAIL executes the READ/NEW command and displays your next message on the screen. Because it is screen output, the message is also stored in the DCL buffer. When the READ/NEW command finishes, control returns to the editor. You terminate MAIL by passing it the EXIT command (DCL EXIT).

So, the normal interactive dialog you expect when you run utilities and applications at the system prompt is segmented into individual commands, each of which starts with DCL. Although this dialog seems cumbersome, access to VMS and other applications from within the editor more than offsets the disadvantages of this form of interaction.

Text Formatting

EVE has commands to control margins, screen width, and center the text on the line where the cursor is located (Fig. 12-13). Screen width, controlled by the SET WIDTH command, determines whether you have large or small text on your display (80 or 132 columns). Do not confuse screen width with the amount of text that can appear on each line. In EVE each line of text can be 960 characters long, which far exceeds the terminal display capacity. Screen width controls how much of each line is visible, rather than the amount of text on each line.

Buffer margins are controlled by SET LEFT MARGIN and SET RIGHT MARGIN. They also determine the amount of text that fits on a line, as well as the starting and ending column position for each line. When you choose a left margin and a line of text wraps, it starts at the left margin, rather than at the first column position. When you choose a right margin, text wraps at the right margin setting. The right margin is also the boundary for text formatting when you use the FILL command.

```
SET WIDTH 80            Set screen width to 80 characters
SET WIDTH 132           Set screen width to 132 characters

SET LEFT MARGIN n       Left margin at column position n
SET RIGHT MARGIN n      Right margin at column position n

CENTER LINE             Center text on current line
FILL                    Align highlighted text
```

Figure 12-13. Formatting Commands

Automatic Fill

FILL insures that characters do not go beyond a certain right margin and evens out short and long lines by reformatting text to place the maximum number of words on each line. First make sure your right margin is correct. To fill a paragraph, position the cursor anywhere in the paragraph and press FILL (GOLD, 8) on the numeric keypad or press DO and enter the FILL command manually. To fill a larger block of text, first highlight the text and then use the FILL command. When you fill several paragraphs, EVE preserves the blank lines between them.

Horizontal Scrolling

Use shift commands to horizontally scroll your screen right or left an arbitrary number of characters (Fig. 12-14). This function is useful when you only have 80 columns on your display but are editing longer lines. EVE supports a maximum line length of 960 characters.

```
SHIFT RIGHT n           Shift display right n columns
SHIFT LEFT  n           Shift display left n columns
```

Figure 12-14. Horizontal Scroll Commands

Changing Case

Use SELECT to highlight the text to be changed. EVE has three functions to choose from as shown in Figure 12-15. You might want to define a key to use the function you use most often.

LOWERCASE WORD	Change text to all lowercase
UPPERCASE WORD	Change text to all uppercase
CAPITALIZE WORD	Capitalize first character in each word

Figure 12-15. Changing Case Commands

REPEAT Command

REPEAT expects a number and performs the very next command you enter that number of times. You can also use the GOLD key to enter a repeat count. Press GOLD, enter the repeat value, and then press the key you want repeated. For example, if you want to delete the next ten words in your buffer, press GOLD, type 10 using the numeric typing keys, and then press DEL W (minus). This causes the DELETE WORD command to be performed ten times.

You might also want to repeat a custom key definition several times. For example, you might define a key to do a CENTER LINE, and advance to the beginning of the next line. Then you can perform an arbitrary number of CENTER LINE commands by entering a repeat count before you press the custom key.

Inserting Control Characters

Occasionally, you may need to enter control characters into your text file. You enter a page break (form feed character) with CTRL/L and carriage return with CTRL/M. The GOLD key can be used to enter control characters that are not already defined. You press the GOLD key, type in the decimal equivalent of the control character you want to insert, and then press GOLD SPECINS (GOLD, 3).

SPECINS, which stands for special insert, inserts the corresponding control character into your editing buffer. When there are control characters in your text file, line feeds, page breaks, returns, and vertical tabs are displayed using special graphics characters. Most terminal manuals and some of the VMS manuals contain a list of decimal equivalents for control characters — control codes are usually below a decimal 30 value.

RECOVERING A FILE

When an editing session is interrupted by a system or equipment failure, you can easily recover your text file. EVE keeps a journal file of all your editing keystrokes in a file with the same name as the file you started with and a file type of .TJL. If the editor is terminated abnormally, this file will appear in your directory.

To insure a successful recovery, always make a copy of the journal file before you recover your file. EVE deletes the journal file after a recover operation, even if the recovery fails. If you do not make a copy of the journal file, you are asking for trouble. Start the recovery operation using the same edit command, but add the /RECOVER qualifier. The complete recovery procedure is illustrated in Figure 12-16.

```
1. Original File            TEST.DAT

2. Original Command         $ EDIT/TPU TEST.DAT
3. Journal File name        TEST.TJL

4. Duplicate Journal File   $ COPY TEST.TJL *

5. Recovery Command         $ EDIT/TPU/RECOVER TEST.DAT
6. Delete Extra TJL file    $ DELETE TEST.TJL;*
```

Figure 12-16. EVE File Recovery Procedure

When you start the recovery operation, EVE applies every single keystroke to the original file. Take your hands away from the keyboard and do not type anything until all changes from the journal file have been applied and the screen is quiet. The recovery looks like a disaster while it is taking place because all your keystrokes are applied in a very short period of time.

A brief editing session recovers in just a couple of minutes. A two hour editing session can take ten minutes to restore. When the recovery is complete, EVE deletes the highest version of the journal file. If the recovery is successful, save the recovered file and delete the other copy of the journal file. If the recovery is not successful, which you determine only by examining the file, duplicate the journal file again and repeat the procedure.

In VMS version 5.3 and above, edit file recovery is initiated by the EVE RECOVER command — the /RECOVER qualifier is no longer used. In EVE, ask for help on RECOVER to review the procedure for recovering text files and buffer modifications.

SUMMARY

We have reviewed many of the most frequently used editing commands, but there are probably 60 or 70 more that we have not yet covered. All the commands are very well documented in EVE's HELP utility. To see if a command exists for something not covered in this chapter, use HELP to direct you to the appropriate subject. As you become more skilled, you will find yourself creating many key definitions and possibly even defining new functions using a combination of EVE commands. Refer to HELP information on Section Files and Initialization Files for a description of how EVE can be tailored to your individual needs by defining standard and custom editing functions.

EDITING EXERCISES

Editing relies heavily on interactive feedback and is difficult to illustrate in a serial description without every keystroke, screen, and message. The main editing commands are included with each exercise, along with an explanation of the expected results.

1. Start the editor with a file called TEST.DAT. What message does the editor give you? Type in a few lines and exit the editor. Is this file now in your directory? What version number does it have?

When you start the editor, EVE tries to locate TEST.DAT in the current directory. You see an information message "Editing new file. Could not find: TEST.DAT." When you exit, EVE informs you of the number of lines written to the file and the full file specification. Locate TEST.DAT with the DIR command — because it is a new file, it has a version number of 1.

```
$ EDIT/TPU TEST.DAT
My first EVE text file
CTRL/Z
$ DIR TEST.DAT

Directory USERD:[VMSWIZ]

TEST.DAT;1

Total of 1 file.
```

2. Start the editor again with TEST.DAT. What message do you see this time? Delete all the text in the file.

This time EVE locates TEST.DAT, responds with the full file specification, and loads it into a buffer of the same name. To delete all the text in the file, position the cursor at the top of the file. Press SELECT and move the cursor to the bottom of the file with GOLD, DOWN arrow. This highlights all text in the file. Press REMOVE to delete the text. The file should now be empty.

```
$ EDIT/TPU TEST.DAT
```

3. This time QUIT the editor. What message do you see? Is TEST.DAT still in your directory? Type out the file to see what is there — is it empty? Why or why not?

Press the DO key, enter QUIT at the Command: prompt, and complete QUIT with RETURN. EVE asks you to verify that you do not want to save your changes. Respond yes to this prompt. Even though you deleted all the text, QUIT instructs the editor to discard the file, rather than saving the changes. The original file (version 1) is still in your directory.

```
$ DIR TEST.DAT
Directory USERA:[ADMIN.VMSWIZ]

TEST.DAT;1

Total of 1 file.
$ TYPE TEST.DAT
My first EVE file.
```

4. The document on the next page appeared several years ago with no author, no publication, and no one to credit. It has introduced much needed levity in my VMS classes over the years and is a fun way to start learning the editor. Type it in and save it as GLOSSARY.TXT.

```
$ EDIT/TPU GLOSSARY.TXT
. . . . . . .
CTRL/Z
```

5. Edit GLOSSARY.TXT and try the editing operations in the list below. Use the grey editing keys, EVE commands, or numeric keypad functions. Two possible sets of keystrokes are presented for each edit operation — the first column uses EVE keys and commands entered with the DO key. The second column uses numeric keypad functions exclusively.

A direction key is included with most of the key sequences — if the correct direction is already set, you can omit this key from the sequence. Use F11 to toggle between forward and reverse or the 4 key for forward and the 5 key for reverse on the numeric keypad.

If you do not want to use the numeric keypad, you must define a GOLD key with SET GOLD KEY PF1 to use the editing sequences shown. To use the numeric keypad enter the command SET KEYPAD EDT, which defines a GOLD key and all the numeric keypad keys. Check the status line to verify your current direction.

Action	EVE keys	Numeric Keypad
Move to the end of the file	GOLD, ↓	PF1, 4
Move to the start of the file	GOLD, ↑	PF1, 5
Move forward one line at a time	F11, F12	4, 0
Move backward one line at a time	F11, F12	5, 0
Move forward one word at a time	DO move by word	4, 1
Move backward one word at a time	DO move by word	5, 1
Move forward one character at a time	→	4, 3
Move backward one character at a time	←	5, 3
Delete any line	DO erase line	PF4
Restore the line you just deleted	DO restore line	PF1, PF4
Delete any word	F13	Hyphen
Restore the word immediately	GOLD, F13	PF1, hyphen
Delete any character	DELETE key	Comma
Restore the same character	DO restore char	PF1, Comma
Highlight the PROGRAMMER section	SELECT	Period,0
Remove the PROGRAMMER section	REMOVE	6
Insert it in the same position	INSERT	PF1, 6
Go to the top of the file	GOLD,↑	PF1, 5
Insert the PROGRAMMER section	INSERT	PF1, 6
Delete this section at the top of the file		
Highlight block of text	Select,↓	Period, 0
Delete highlighted text	REMOVE	6
Search for all occurrences of "talks"	FIND	PF1, PF3
Define and locate string "talks"	talks RETURN	talks,ENTER
Locate next occurrence	FIND, FIND	PF3
Replace "talks" with "babbles"	DO replace	
Define replace string	talks, babbles	
Start replace operation	Replace all occurrences	
Replace "babbles" with "talks"	DO replace	
Define replace string	talks, babbles	
Start replace operation	Replace all occurrences	
Change SYSTEMS ANALYST titles to lowercase		
Move to top of file	GOLD,↑	PF1, 5
Highlight title	SELECT, GOLD →	Period, 2
Change Case	DO lowercase	PF1, 1
Use CTRL Y to abort the editor	CTRL/Y	CTRL/Y
Make a copy of the journal file	COPY GLOSSARY.TJL *	
Start TPU up with /RECOVER and watch	EDIT/TPU/RECOVER GLOSSARY.TXT	
EXIT the editor	CTRL/Z	

A Glossary of Data Processing Terms - Anonymous

DATA PROCESSING MANAGER
Leaps tall buildings in a single bound
Is more powerful than a locomotive
Is faster than a speeding bullet
Walks on water
Gives policy to God

DATA PROCESSING SUPERVISOR
Leaps short buildings in a single bound
Is more powerful than a switch engine
Is just as fast as a speeding bullet
Walks on water if the sea is calm
Talks with God

SENIOR SYSTEMS ANALYST
Leaps short buildings with a running start and favorable winds
Is almost as powerful as a switch engine
Is faster than a speeding BB
Walks on water in an indoor swimming pool
Talks with God if a special request is approved

SYSTEMS ANALYST
Barely clears a quonset hut
Loses tug of war with locomotives
Can fire a speeding bullet
Swims well
Is occasionally addressed by God

LEAD PROGRAMMER
Makes high marks on the wall when trying to leap buildings
Is run over by locomotives
Can sometimes handle a gun without inflicting self-injury
Dog paddles
Talks to animals

SENIOR PROGRAMMER
Runs into buildings
Recognizes locomotives two out of three times
Is not issued ammunition
Can stay afloat with a life jacket
Talks to walls

MAINTENANCE PROGRAMMER
Falls over doorstep when trying to enter building
Says "Look at the Choo Choo"
Wets himself with a water pistol
Plays in mud puddles
Mumbles to himself

PROGRAMMER
Lifts buildings and walks under them
Kicks locomotives off the track
Catches speeding bullets in his teeth and eats them
Freezes water with a single glance
He is God

Print Queues and Jobs

INTRODUCTION

VMS allows you to control many aspects of a print job, including the device it is printed on, the time it is started, the number of copies, the form to use, and which pages to print. Because there are many printers and many options, printing a file can be a sophisticated operation. This chapter introduces several concepts and some terminology relating to queues, devices, and print forms. In VMS, printing and queues are inseparable topics.

We begin with a quick review of print queues, identifying the various printers on your system (SHOW QUEUE/DEVICE), looking at jobs waiting in a print queue (SHOW QUEUE/ALL), and understanding queue status. Next, we discuss the PRINT command and some of its 40 qualifiers. Then we learn how to display the predefined forms at your site (SHOW QUEUE/FORM) and how to use forms with the PRINT command (PRINT/FORM). Last, we review the commands for locating a print job (SHOW ENTRY) and deleting a print job (DELETE/ENTRY) from a print queue.

PRINT QUEUE OVERVIEW

VMS manages print jobs using a "queue," which is nothing more than a list of print jobs in the order in which they are received. Every VMS system has both logical and physical print queues. A logical queue, also called a "generic" queue, is a temporary holding queue for print requests. Each logical queue is associated with one or more physical queues that actually transfer files to output devices.

The standard PRINT command places a print job in the systemwide logical queue. When the print job comes to the front of the list, the system transfers it to a physical queue which outputs the print job on a specific print device. Each physical print queue is also called a "device queue" because it is associated with a specific device (*e.g.*, a departmental laser printer).

The number of queues varies widely from site to site. An installation may have 20 to 30 print queues supporting high-speed production printers and a variety of letter-quality devices. Sites with terminal servers usually have printers located on servers to make printers more available to the user community. Print queues are generally available to all users, unless specifically prohibited by the system manager.

Each print queue has a name and one or more characteristics that control queue operation. Characteristics define how jobs are ordered in the queue (*e.g.*, by time of arrival, number of pages, priority) and the default form used with every print job (number of lines per page and the standard font where applicable). You can override these default characteristics by using qualifiers on the PRINT command.

The system normally queues print jobs based on process priority and time of request and processes them in the order received. However, the system manager may control printers differently to provide better service. For example, the system manager may restrict large print jobs to high-speed printers and small jobs to letter-quality or laser printers, or may allow small jobs to print ahead of large ones on certain devices.

EXAMINING PRINT QUEUES

SHOW QUEUE is one of the most complicated VMS commands. This command examines print and batch queues and queue characteristics, lists print and batch jobs, and displays print forms. (Batch jobs are created with the SUBMIT command which is covered briefly in Chapter 10, File Manipulation.) Use SHOW QUEUE alone to list all print (and batch) queues, SHOW QUEUE/DEVICE for print queues only, and SHOW QUEUE with a queue name for information on a specific queue (Fig. 13-1).

SHOW QUEUE has several useful qualif ers. /FULL displays characteristics associated with a queue, /ALL lists all jobs waiting to be processed, and /FORM lists all predefined print forms at your installation. Each form of this command is discussed separately in the text that follows.

```
$ SHOW QUEUE [queue-name]      Command Format

   /DEVICE                     Display all print queues
   /FULL                       Display queue characteristics
   /ALL                        Display all jobs in the queue
   /FORM                       Display all predefined forms
```

Figure 13-1. SHOW QUEUE Command

If you are a new user, it is nice to know how many printers are on your system. Since each printer is associated with either a logical or physical print queue, when you examine the print queues you also know which printers are available. There are three types of print queues: generic queues, terminal queues, and server queues. A print request to a generic queue may end up on one of several devices, whereas a print request to a terminal or server queue is output to that specific device only.

You use SHOW QUEUE/DEVICE to list all available print queues. Figure 13-2 is a display generated at a mid-size VAXcluster. On anything other than a small standalone system, you can expect to find many such queues in the display.

```
$ SHOW QUEUE/DEVICE
Terminal queue BITBUCKET, on MIS3::LTA130:, mounted form LASERDEF
Generic printer queue CLUSTERPRINT
Terminal queue DRAFTFIN, on SYBIL::LTA137:, mounted form DEFAULT
Terminal queue FIELD_ENG, on SYBIL::LTA145:, mounted form DEFAULT
Printer queue LN03, on MIS3::LTA133, mounted form LPS$LN03R$FORM
Generic printer queue LSRMIS
Terminal queue LSRMIS1, on SYBIL::LTA131:, mounted form LASERDEF
Terminal queue LSRSMG, on SYBIL::LTA159:, mounted form LASERDEF
Terminal queue LTA139, on SYBIL::LTA139:, mounted form DEFAULT
Printer queue MIS3_LCA0, stalled, on MIS3::LCA0:, mounted form DEFAULT
Printer queue MIS3_LCB0, on MIS3::LCB0:, mounted form DEFAULT
Terminal queue PARTS, on MIS3::LTA142:, mounted form DEFAULT
Terminal queue SHIPPING, on MIS3::LTA141:, mounted form DEFAULT
Printer queue SPECIAL$PRINT, stopped, on SYBIL::, mounted form DEFAULT
Printer queue SYBIL_LIC0, on SYBIL::LIC0:, mounted form DEFAULT
```

Figure 13-2. SHOW QUEUE/DEVICE Command

Use SHOW QUEUE/ALL to examine all jobs waiting to be printed. If you do not provide a queue name with the command, the system displays all print jobs in all print queues. You may want to use this command to determine which queues are the least busy, rather than sending your print request to a queue in which a large number of jobs are already waiting to print.

The command in Figure 13-3 asks for a list of all jobs queued on BITBUCKET. Notice that the last two entries have "no privilege" instead of a Jobname. Because of file protection, you are only allowed to see your own print jobs and print jobs from other users in your group. Notice that BITBUCKET is stalled, which indicates a problem with the output device. The printer may be powered off, offline or out of paper. The first job has a status of printing which is really temporarily stopped because of the stalled status and there are three more jobs pending (*i.e.*, waiting to print).

```
$ SHOW QUEUE/ALL BITBUCKET
Printer queue BITBUCKET stalled, on MIS3::LTA130:, mounted form LASERDEF

   Jobname        Username      Entry  Blocks  Status
   -------        --------      -----  ------  ------
   APO512         APACCT         408       6   Printing
   APO563         APACCT         409      34   Pending
   no privilege                  410      19   Pending
   no privilege                  411      86   Pending
```

Figure 13-3. SHOW QUEUE/ALL Command

UNDERSTANDING QUEUE STATUS

Print queues can be in one of several states. A normal working queue has no status in the SHOW QUEUE display. If a status does appear on the first line, it may indicate maintenance activity or some kind of problem. Figure 13-4 explains most queue status conditions. When you have trouble printing, contact the operations staff or the system manager.

```
   Pausing             Temporary queue stop for paper change,
   Paused              form alignment, new ribbon

   Stopping            Queue stop in progress or complete
   Stop Pending        Jobs may complete
   Stopped             No jobs can start

   Stalled             Device related problem

   Resuming            Queue start in progress
   Starting            Queue start in progress
```

Figure 13-4. Print Queue Status Conditions

PRINTING A FILE

At this point, you have learned how to examine the print queues on your system, how to list the jobs waiting in each queue, and how to interpret queue status. Next we learn about the PRINT command, which places your print job in a print queue, and the various qualifiers used to modify print operations.

PRINT accepts one or more file specifications and understands nearly 40 different qualifiers. Some of the most commonly used qualifiers are listed in Figure 13-5.

You can use qualifiers on the command and on the individual files. Qualifiers on the command modify the way PRINT manages all files, and qualifiers on a file specification modify the way that file is printed.

```
$ PRINT file-spec[,...]        Command Format

  /AFTER=date-time             Print after specified date and time
  /COPIES=n                    Print n copies
  /DELETE                      Delete file after it is printed
  /FORM=form                   Use specified form name or number
  /NOFLAG                      Omit flag page (separator page)
  /NOTE=message                Print message on flag page
  /NOTIFY                      Send message when job is printed
  /PAGES=(start,stop)          Print pages start-stop
  /QUEUE=queue-name            Use specified queue for output
  /SPACE                       Double space output
```

Figure 13-5. PRINT Command and Qualifiers

Print Qualifiers

Like many file manipulation commands, PRINT can select files based on creation, modification, and backup date and time criteria using /CREATED, /MODIFIED, /BACKUP, /EXPIRED, /BEFORE, and /SINCE. Use /COPIES for multiple copies and /NOTIFY to receive a message when your job completes. To print on a specific device, use the /QUEUE qualifier and to delete your file when it is done printing add /DELETE to the command.

You can print your file after hours with the /AFTER qualifier and a date and time value. To print after midnight, use /AFTER=TOMORROW. Other qualifiers allow you to suppress the flag page (/NOFLAG), use a special form (/FORM), print a note on the separator page (/NOTE), and print only selected pages of your file (/PAGE). There are many qualifiers not included in this list. For more information, consult the HELP utility. Several example print commands are shown in Figure 13-6. These commands illustrate the use of the /COPIES, /QUEUE, /AFTER, and /PAGES qualifiers with one file, two files, and a wildcard file specification.

When you PRINT a file, the file is not actually copied into the queue. Instead, the entry points to the file to be printed when it comes to the front of the queue. If you delete a file before it is actually printed, an error will occur because your print job is now pointing to a non-existent file. To avoid this problem, use PRINT/DELETE, which deletes the file after it is successfully printed.

```
$ PRINT REPORT.DAT                 Print one file
$ PRINT/COPIES=3 REPORT.DAT        Print three copies

$ PRINT NAME.DAT, ZIPCODE.DAT      Print two files
$ PRINT/QUEUE=BITBUCKET *.DAT      Print .DAT files on BITBUCKET

$ PRINT/AFTER=20:00 MASTER.DAT     Print one file after 8 p.m.

$ PRINT/PAGES=(10,30) DEPT.DAT     Print pages 10-30 of DEPT.DAT

$ PRINT/AFTER=18:00/COPIES=3 -     Print three copies of
_$ INVENTORY.DAT                   INVENTORY.DAT after 6 p.m.
```

Figure 13-6. PRINT Command Examples

Print Information Messages

After processing your PRINT request, the system displays an information message containing the print job name, the queue to be used, the entry number, and a status. PRINT sends jobs to the systemwide print queue by default. When your job comes to the front of the queue, it is printed, even if you are no longer logged in.

In Figure 13-7, the first command displays an information message with a job name of MONITOR, a queue name of CLUSTERPRINT, an entry number of 915 and a status of started. This message indicates the file is printing on the device SYBIL_LIC0 which is a printer device name. The second command requests three copies of the same file to be printed after 6 p.m. The information message displays the same job and queue name, an entry number of 917, and a status of holding until 6 p.m. Each print job has a unique entry number, so you can always identify the job you want to stop or delete. Deleting a print job is covered later in this chapter.

```
$ PRINT MONITOR.COM
Job MONITOR (queue CLUSTERPRINT, entry 915) started on SYBIL_LICO

$ PRINT/COPIES=3/AFTER=18:00/NOTIFY MONITOR.COM
Job MONITOR (queue CLUSTERPRINT, entry 917) holding until 29-DEC-1989 18:00
```

Figure 13-7. PRINT Information Messages

FINDING YOUR PRINT JOB

Where SHOW QUEUE/DEVICE/ALL lists all jobs in one or all print queues, SHOW ENTRY lists only the jobs you have submitted for printing (Fig. 13-8). The standard command displays a two-line message for each one of your jobs in a print queue. SHOW ENTRY optionally accepts an entry number, which means you can also check the status of a specific print job.

```
$ SHOW ENTRY [entry-number]        Command Format

 /BY_JOB_STATUS                    List status of each print job
 /DEVICE[=(keyword,...)]           Display jobs by queue type
                                   (PRINTER, SERVER, or TERMINAL)
 /FULL                             Display complete description
```

Figure 13-8. SHOW ENTRY Command

Figure 13-9 illustrates both forms of SHOW ENTRY, with and without an entry number. You can check only print job status with the /BY_JOB_STATUS qualifier and display all the characteristics of your print job, including the full file specification, with the /FULL qualifier. With the /DEVICE qualifier, you can check print jobs on line printers, terminal queues, or sever queues. There are several other qualifiers that can be used with the SHOW ENTRY command. Consult HELP for more information.

```
$ SHOW ENTRY 917
Jobname          Username     Entry  Blocks  Status
-------          --------     -----  ------  ------
MONITOR          VMSWIZ        917       8   Pending
On generic printer queue CLUSTERPRINT

$ SHOW ENTRY
Jobname          Username     Entry  Blocks  Status
-------          --------     -----  ------  ------
MONITOR          VMSWIZ        917       8   Pending
On generic printer queue CLUSTERPRINT

EVESYSBUFS       VMSWIZ        186       3   Printing
On terminal queue BITBUCKET
```

Figure 13-9. SHOW ENTRY Display

If you have no print jobs (maybe they are all finished), SHOW ENTRY issues the "%JBC-E-NOSUCHENT, no such entry" message. JBC is an abbreviation for the job controller, the VMS module that manages queues.

USING PRINT FORMS

There are many reasons for using special forms with printed output: labels, invoices, payroll checks, FAX cover sheets, and thank you notes, to name a few. SHOW QUEUE/FORM display all available forms on your system. It also accepts a form name parameter, and displays information about that form only (Fig. 13-10). A form may control margins, font, and paper orientation, and may also be associated with a specific size or type of paper (e.g. checks, labels, envelopes).

```
$ SHOW QUEUE/FORM   [form-name]      Command Format
$ SHOW QUEUE/FORM                    List all predefined forms
$ SHOW QUEUE/FORM form-name          Brief description of this form
$ SHOW QUEUE/FORM/FULL form-name     Full description of this form
```

Figure 13-10. SHOW QUEUE/FORM Commands

Identifying Print Forms

In Figure 13-11, SHOW QUEUE/FORM displays a list of form names. Each print form has a name, number, and short description. The PRT forms select one of three different type sizes for normal portrait mode using standard 8.5x11-inch paper. The LND forms select one of three different type sizes for landscape printing which is done using 11x8.5-inch paper. When you select a form with the PRINT command (/FORM qualifier), you can enter either the form name or form number from the equivalent display on your system.

```
$ SHOW QUEUE/FORM
Form name                             Number   Description
---------                             ------   -----------
2_PART (stock=2_PART_PAPER)                2   2 Part Paper
CCALC_SPREADSHEETS (stock=1_PART)          8   C-Calc Spreadsheets
DEFAULT                                    0   System-defined default
FAX (stock=DEFAULT)                       31   FAX
LABELS                                     7   Labels
LASERDEF (stock=DEFAULT)                  20   Laser Default
LND (stock=DEFAULT)                       23   Laser landscape 10 pitch
LND12 (stock=DEFAULT)                     28   Laser landscape 12 pitch
LND14 (stock=DEFAULT)                     29   Laser landscape 14 pitch
PRT (stock=DEFAULT)                       21   Laser Portrait Default 10 Pitch
PRT12 (stock=DEFAULT)                     26   Laser portrait 12 pitch
PRT15 (stock=DEFAULT)                     27   Laser portrait 15 pitch
THANK_YOU_CARDS                            3   Thank You Cards
```

Figure 13-11. SHOW QUEUE/FORM Display

Several of the form names in this figure are designated "stock=DEFAULT," which means print jobs using these forms do not require a physical paper change. Otherwise, the paper stock in the output device must be physically changed to match that required by the form.

Selecting a Print Form

Once you identify the form you need, use PRINT/FORM= and provide either the form name or the form number as illustrated in Figure 13-12. In the first SHOW QUEUE/FORM command, the form LABELS appears after the /STOCK qualifier. This means that the LABELS form cannot be printed on the paper normally loaded in the printer — if LABELS were the standard form, you would see /STOCK=DEFAULT. To actually print labels, the operator must stop the printer and physically change the paper in the printer.

```
$ SHOW QUEUE/FORM/FULL LABELS
Form name                              Number     Description
---------                              ------     -----------
LABELS                                    7       Labels
/LENGTH=66 /MARGIN=(BOTTOM=6)/STOCK=LABELS/TRUNCATE/WIDTH=132

$ PRINT/FORM=LABELS/QUEUE=BITBUCKET CUSTOMER.LIS
```

Figure 13-12. Using a Print Form

If the form you request manipulates margins, font, or paper orientation, but does not require special paper, your print job is processed immediately. However, if your form is associated with a specific paper stock that is not normally loaded on the printer, the printer pauses until the correct paper is loaded. A message is automatically sent to the operator requesting the stock be loaded. The queue has a pending status until the paper is changed and the operator responds affirmatively to the paper change message. When the queue is started, your job begins printing.

STOPPING A PRINT JOB

DELETE/ENTRY deletes your print job from a queue. You can delete a print job whether it is pending or actually printing. DELETE/ENTRY requires an entry number, specified as a value on the /ENTRY qualifier, and optionally accepts a queue name (Fig. 13-13). You can delete several print jobs by providing a list of entry numbers, separated by commas.

If you have forgotten your entry number, you can look it up with SHOW ENTRY which displays your print jobs and associated entry numbers. You can optionally identify the queue from which your job is to be deleted, although this is not necessary — the system can figure it out for you. With normal user privileges, you can only remove your own jobs from the print queue.

```
$ DELETE/ENTRY=(entry-number[,....]) [queue-name]   Command Format

$ DELETE/ENTRY=915                            Delete entry 915
$ DELETE/ENTRY=130  BITBUCKET                 Delete entry 130 from
                                              the BITBUCKET queue
```

Figure 13-13. DELETE/ENTRY Command

Figure 13-14 illustrates the use of three commands to print, examine, and then delete a print job. A print job is submitted to start printing at noon, the queue is checked for the print job entry number, and the entry is deleted before it can print.

```
$ PRINT/AFTER=12:00/QUEUE=BITBUCKET DAILY.RPT
Job DAILY (queue BITBUCKET, entry 271) holding until 2-DEC-1989 12:00

$ SHOW ENTRY
Terminal queue BITBUCKET,on MIS3::LTA130:, mounted form LASERDEF
(stock=DEFAULT)
Jobname   Username    Entry Blocks  Status
-------   --------    ----- ------  ------
DAILY     VMSWIZ      271   1       Holding until 2-DEC-1989 12:00

$ DELETE/ENTRY=271
```

Figure 13-14. Deleting a Print Job

PRINT EXERCISES

1. How many print queues are on your system? What are their queue names?

```
In this display, we see eleven print queues. Two of the queues are generic
queues that may send output to one of several devices. Three of the queues
are printer queues that send output to a printer connected directly to the
system, and the remaining five are terminal queues that send output to ter-
minal server based printers. If you have a standalone system, terminal
queues refer to printers connected to one or more terminal ports.
```

```
$ SHOW QUEUE/DEVICE

Terminal queue BITBUCKET, on MIS3::LTA130:, mounted form LASERDEF
Generic printer queue CLUSTERPRINT
Printer queue LN03, on MIS3::LTA133, mounted form LPS$LN03R$FORM
Terminal queue LSRENG, on SYBIL::LTA149:, mounted form LASERDEF
Generic printer queue LSRMIS
Printer queue MIS3_LCB0, on MIS3::LCB0:, mounted form DEFAULT
Terminal queue LSRMIS1, on SYBIL::LTA131:, mounted form LASERDEF
Terminal queue LSRSMG, on SYBIL::LTA159:, mounted form LASERDEF
Terminal queue PARTS, on MIS3::LTA142:, mounted form DEFAULT
Terminal queue SHIPPING, on MIS3::LTA141:, mounted form DEFAULT
Printer queue SYBIL_LICO, on SYBIL::LICO:, mounted form DEFAULT
```

2. What is the difference between a generic queue, a printer queue, and a terminal queue?

```
Nearly every VAX system has one systemwide generic queue that routes print
jobs to one or more devices and the PRINT command sends print jobs to the
systemwide generic queue (which is frequently called SYS$PRINT). The
generic queue may send print jobs to one of several different printers. A
print request to a printer or terminal queue is output to that specific
device only. You select a specific queue (and thus a specific device) with
the /QUEUE=queue-name qualifier on the PRINT command.
```

3. Print out GLOSSARY.TXT from the EVE lesson using /NOTIFY. What message does the PRINT command return? Which queue does the PRINT command use?

```
PRINT uses the standard system print queue by default. In this example, the
systemwide generic queue is CLUSTERPRINT which routes the job to the
printer SYBIL_LICO.
```

```
$ PRINT/NOTIFY GLOSSARY.TXT
Job GLOSSARY (queue CLUSTERPRINT, entry 915) started on SYBIL_LICO
```

4. Print GLOSSARY.TXT after 6 p.m. today.

```
$ PRINT/NOTIFY/AFTER=18:00 GLOSSARY.DAT
Job GLOSSARY (queue CLUSTERPRINT, entry 917) holding until 19-JAN-1990 18:00
```

5. How can you look up your print jobs?

```
$ SHOW ENTRY

Jobname         Username      Entry  Blocks  Status
-------         --------      -----  ------  ------
GLOSSARY        VMSWIZ        915      8     Holding until 29-DEC-1989 18:00
On generic printer queue CLUSTERPRINT
```

6. Delete the job you submitted to print after 6 p.m.

```
$ DELETE/ENTRY=915
```

7. Make a copy of the GLOSSARY.TXT file, PRINT the copy, and have PRINT delete the file when the job is finished.

```
$ COPY GLOSSARY.TXT *
$ PRINT/DELETE/NOTIFY GLOSSARY.TXT
```

8. Are there any predefined forms on your system?

This system has eleven predefined forms. The second command displays a full description of the STATIONERY form, which handles 66 lines per page, has a bottom margin of six lines, and a line length of 132 characters.

```
$ SHOW QUEUE/FORM

Form name                        Number   Description
---------                        ------   -----------
DEFAULT                              0     System-defined default
LASERDEF (stock=DEFAULT)            20     Laser default
LND (stock=DEFAULT)                 23     Laser landscape 10 pitch
LND12 (stock=DEFAULT)               28     Laser landscape 12 pitch
LND14 (stock=DEFAULT)               29     Laser landscape 14 pitch
LND15 (stock=DEFAULT)               30     Laser landscape 14 pitch
PRT (stock=DEFAULT)                 21     Laser portrait 10 pitch
PRT12 (stock=DEFAULT)               26     Laser portrait 12 pitch
PRT15 (stock=DEFAULT)               27     Laser portrait 15 pitch
PRT8 (stock=DEFAULT)                25     Laser portrait 8 point
STATIONERY                           1     STATIONERY

$ SHOW QUEUE/FORM/FULL STATIONERY
Form name                        Number   Description
---------                        ------   -----------
STATIONERY                           1     STATIONERY
   /LENGTH=66 /MARGIN=(BOTTOM=6) /STOCK=STATIONERY /TRUNCATE /WIDTH=132
```

9. How would you get your output on one of the forms listed above?

```
$ PRINT/FORM=STATIONERY/QUEUE=LSRMIS1   GETWELL.DOC
    Job GETWELL (queue LSRMIS1, entry 423) started on LSRENG
```

10. How do you print five copies of the first ten pages of a file? How about pages 10 through 30 on a laser printer?

Use /COPIES and /PAGES qualifiers with the appropriate values.

```
$ PRINT/COPIES=5/PAGES=10   CHAPTER13.TXT
Job CHAPTER13 (queue CLUSTERPRINT, entry 633) started on SYBIL_LICO
$ PRINT/COPIES=5/PAGES=(10,30)/QUEUE=LSRMIS1 CHAPTER13.TXT
Job CHAPTER13 (queue LSRMIS1, entry 47) started on LSRMIS1
```

The MAIL Utility

INTRODUCTION

MAIL is probably the most popular VMS utility. MAIL allows you to exchange messages with any authorized user on a standalone system, cluster, or network. You can send messages composed online and text files created with an editor, spreadsheet, or other application. In fact, MAIL is the easiest way to exchange files with another user — it avoids all the hassle of protection keys and file ownership.

You can send messages to a single user or a distribution list, forward messages to another user, or edit and return a message back to the sender. You can also print messages on the printer of your choice and extract a message from your mail file and store it in a regular VMS file. Once messages begin to accumulate, you can create folders and file messages in folders. MAIL commands allow you to select and manipulate messages in any folder.

The first time you receive a message, a file called MAIL.MAI is created in your home directory. Never delete this file and never change the protection code. Mail files are only accessible by the owner of the file. Nobody else can read your mail or add or delete messages (unless you have shared your username and password).

MAIL HELP

Start this utility with the MAIL command. MAIL HELP works exactly like VMS HELP with respect to information organization (parameters, qualifiers, examples) and the Topic? and Subtopic? prompts. Figure 14-1 is a duplicate of the main Help screen. Not all MAIL commands are explained in this chapter, but you can easily gather the missing information by entering the appropriate HELP command.

```
$ MAIL
MAIL> HELP
HELP

Allows you to obtain information about the Mail Utility.
to obtain information about all of the MAIL commands, enter
the following command:

MAIL> HELP *

 To obtain information about individual  commands  or  topics,
 enter HELP followed by the command or topic name.

Format:

  HELP [topic]


Additional information available:

/EDIT   /PERSONAL_NAME   /SELF    /SUBJECT  ANSWER   ATTACH
BACK    COMPRESS  COPY    CURRENT  DEFINE   DELETE   DIRECTORY
EDIT    ERASE     EXIT    EXTRACT  FILE     FIRST    Folders
FORWARD GETTING_STARTED   HELP     KEYPAD   LAST     MAIL
MARK    MOVE      NEXT    PRINT    PURGE    QUIT     READ
REMOVE  REPLY     SEARCH  SELECT   SEND     SET-SHOW SPAWN
V5_CHANGES

Topic?

MAIL> Exit
```

Figure 14-1. MAIL Help Display

MAIL COMMANDS

All the commands in Figure 14-2 are issued at the MAIL> prompt and most of them assume the message you just read is the one to be operated on. If you use DELETE, EXTRACT, PRINT, MOVE, or REPLY without a current message, the error message "You aren't reading a message" appears. Read or select a mail message, and then reissue the command.

```
HELP             Full documentation on all MAIL commands

SEND             Send a message or document to one or more users
REPLY            Respond to a message you just read
FORWARD          Send a message you just read to someone else

READ             Read a message (current or by number)
READ/NEW         Read a message that just arrived

DELETE           Delete a message (current or by number)
EXTRACT          File a message in a VMS file
PRINT            Print the message

DIRECTORY        Directory of all messages in current folder
DIR/FOLDER       Directory of folders

MOVE             Move a message to a folder
SELECT           Change folders

SET              Define MAIL defaults
SHOW             Examine MAIL defaults

EXIT             Leave the MAIL utility
CTRL/Z           Leave the MAIL utility
```

Figure 14-2. Frequently Used MAIL Commands

SELECTING A MAIL EDITOR

After creating a few messages online, you will notice the standard MAIL editor is not very smart. Among other things, you must end each line with an explicit carriage return which is very inconvenient if you are used to a sophisticated editor or word processor. With the default editor, you are only allowed to correct mistakes on the same line you are typing. If you go to a new line you cannot back up.

There are two other options available: the EDT editor or the TPU editor. You can select and activate a default editor in two ways: SET EDITOR EDT selects EDT as the default editor and SET EDITOR TPU selects the site default TPU interface which is usually EVE. Once you define an editor, MAIL remembers the choice from session to session. You can check your selection with the SHOW EDITOR command. Then you have to request that the editor be invoked whenever editing is involved by starting MAIL with the /EDIT qualifier as shown in Figure 14-3.

```
$ MAIL

MAIL> SET EDITOR TPU                    Select EVE Editor
MAIL> SHOW EDITOR                       Display editor
Your editor is TPU
MAIL> EXIT                              Leave MAIL

$ MAIL/EDIT=(SEND,REPLY,FORWARD)        Start MAIL with EVE for
                                        SEND/REPLY/FORWARD commands
```

Figure 14-3. Using the EVE Editor in MAIL

If you start MAIL with the last command in Figure 14-3, your editor is automatically loaded each time you SEND, REPLY, or FORWARD a message — all the functions in the editor are available for use. It can be annoying to enter this long command each time you start MAIL. See Chapter 16 for instructions on how to create a symbol in your login file that permanently redefines the MAIL command.

Canceling a Message

Once in the editor, you may decide you do not want to SEND or REPLY to a message. You discard the response in one of three ways, depending upon the active editor (Fig. 14-4). If you are using the default MAIL editor, press CTRL/C. If you are using EDT, enter CTRL/Z. EDT responds with an asterisk (*) prompt at the beginning of the next line. At the asterisk, type QUIT, followed by RETURN, and EDT will quit without saving your file.

In EVE, press the DO key and look for the Command: prompt at the bottom of the screen. Type QUIT, followed by RETURN, and EVE will exit without saving the buffer contents. When you terminate the edit operation this way, MAIL notifies you that no message has been sent.

```
Editor                     Action
------------------------------------------------------------
MAIL default editor        CTRL/C
EDT                        CTRL/Z for the * prompt
                           QUIT to discard your reply
EVE                        DO key for the Command: prompt
                           QUIT to discard your reply
```

Figure 14-4. Canceling a SEND or REPLY

SENDING MESSAGES

To send a message, enter SEND at the MAIL> prompt. You are prompted with To: and Subj: fields. Fill in the To: field with the username of the person who will receive the message (Fig. 14-5). If you want the message to go to several users, enter all the usernames, separated by commas, on one line. To send a message to a user on another node, preface the username with the node name followed by a double colon (*e.g.*, SYBIL::GINABO). Before you can continue, MAIL verifies that the username is valid by checking it against the system authorization file. If the username is not valid, the system informs you of that fact and asks you to select another username.

Next, you are instructed to type in a message and terminate your message with CTRL/Z. When CTRL/Z is detected, the message is automatically sent to the username(s) in the To: field. MAIL also broadcasts a message to username(s) indicating a new message has arrived.

```
MAIL> SEND
To:     SYSTEM, OPERATOR
Subj:   File Restore Request
Enter message below. Press CTRL/Z when complete, or CTRL/C to quit:
Please restore the file ACCOUNTNG.DAT to my home directory.
Thank you.
CTRL/Z

MAIL>
```

Figure 14-5. Sending a Message

To send a file, place the file name immediately after the SEND command on the same line. You are prompted for To: and Subj:, and the file is sent without a message. In Figure 14-6, the file SCHEDULE.LIS is sent to username OPERATOR.

```
MAIL> SEND SCHEDULE.LIS
To:     OPERATOR
Subj:   Maintenance Schedule for May

MAIL>
```

Figure 14-6. Sending a File

USING A DISTRIBUTION LIST

MAIL allows you to send messages to users on a distribution list. To use a distribution list, you must first create it as text file using either the CREATE command or the editor of your choice. A distribution list contains one username per line. Pick a meaningful name for the file and use a file type of .DIS. If some of the users on your distribution list are on a different node, include the node name as shown in Figure 14-7.

```
$ CREATE MANAGERS.DIS        Make a distribution list
BBLOCKLEY                    Local node or cluster
SYBIL::GBOICE                Node SYBIL
KMCCARVILLE                  Local node or cluster
JECKYL::LMILLER              Node JECKYL
CTRL/Z                       Save the file
```

Figure 14-7. Creating a MAIL Distribution List

At the To: prompt, type in an at sign (@) followed by the name of the file containing the distribution list. In Figure 14-8, the file SCHEDULE.LIS is sent to all the users on the MANAGERS distribution list. You can create and use many distribution lists, as long as each has a file type of .DIS. You can also combine usernames and distribution lists in the To: field of the message.

Your message will be sent to all usernames on the list. MAIL validates all usernames on the list before the message is sent. If you have an incorrect username in the list, MAIL issues the message %MAIL-E-NOSUCHUSER and asks you if you want to send the message anyway. If you respond yes to the prompt, the message is delivered to all the valid users.

```
MAIL> SEND SCHEDULE.LIS          Send a file
To:    @MANAGERS                 To a distribution list
Subj:  Meeting Schedule for May
```

Figure 14-8. Using a MAIL Distribution List

READING MESSAGES

When you log in, MAIL will inform you if new messages have arrived since the previous login. Once you start MAIL, you can read new messages by pressing RETURN at the MAIL> prompt. MAIL displays your new messages in the order in which they were received. If new messages arrive while you are in MAIL, you have to use the READ/NEW command to see them. Use any of the commands in Figure 14-9 to move through your messages. The MAIL keypad diagram at the end of this chapter has predefined keys that perform these commands.

READ	Display next message
READ/NEW	Display next new message
FIRST	Display first message in folder
LAST	Display last message in folder
NEXT	Display next message
BACK	Display previous message

Figure 14-9. MAIL Read Commands

LISTING MESSAGES

Sometimes you want to read a specific message that you have already read or to read only one or two of the new messages that have arrived. The MAIL DIRECTORY command lists messages in the current folder by message number, sender, date and subject, and displays the current folder name in the upper right corner of the screen (Fig. 14-10). DIR/NEW lists all the unread messages (if any).

From this display, identify the number of the message you want to read, write, print, delete, move, or extract. Instead of manipulating the message you just read, you can operate on a specific message by entering the message number with most MAIL commands (*e.g.*, READ 5, EXTRACT 2, or DELETE 3).

```
MAIL> DIR
                                                    MAIL
# From               Date          Subject
1 (Deleted)
2 MIS4::SYSTEM        8-AUG-1989    RE: tomorrow
3 MIS1::PAUMCG       11-NOV-1989    RE: idea
4 MIS2::PAUMCG       17-NOV-1989    SEVERAL THINGS

MAIL> DIR/NEW
                                                 NEWMAIL
# From               Date          Subject
1 JIMGRE             24-JAN-1990    RE: Meeting
2 GINABO             24-JAN-1990    New Operator
3 KATMCC             24-JAN-1990    Page Format
```

Figure 14-10. MAIL DIRECTORY Command

By default, MAIL lists all messages in the current folder. If you have selected messages by time or date or a search string, DIRECTORY will only display the ones that matched the select criteria (see SELECT below).

ANSWERING MESSAGES

ANSWER and REPLY are equivalent commands. Both automatically fill in the To: field with the name of the user that sent the message, and the Subj: field with RE: followed by original message subject. Then MAIL places you in an editor, at which point you enter the text of your reply (Fig. 14-11). You may see the "Enter your message below" prompt or, if you have used the SET EDITOR command, you may be placed in either the EDT or EVE editor.

```
/EDIT              Edit message text before sending
/EXTRACT           Edit complete message before sending
/SELF              Send yourself a copy of the message
/CC_PROMPT         Issue a CC: prompt before sending
```

Figure 14-11. ANSWER and REPLY Qualifiers

When answering a message you have several options. You may just wish to type in a quick response and send it off. Or you may want to edit either the full message including the To, From, and Subject fields (/EXTRACT) or edit only the message text (/EDIT) before sending it back. You may want to send a copy of your response to yourself, which is done with the /SELF qualifier, and you can copy another user with /CC_PROMPT (can be abbreviated /CC) on either command.

FORWARDING MESSAGES

Occasionally, you will receive a message that really should be passed on to someone else. There are two ways to accomplish this: SEND/LAST and FORWARD. Both commands prompt with To: and Subj:, but not for a message, because the current message is treated as the message text (Fig. 14-12).

You have several options when forwarding a message. You can pass on the message without the header (To:, Subj:) with the /NOHEADER qualifier, edit the message before it is sent (/EDIT), add a CC: to the message (/CC_PROMPT), and send a copy to yourself with /SELF. FORWARD/NOHEADER and FORWARD/EDIT are the most commonly used options.

```
MAIL> SEND/LAST
To:   DJONES
Subj: FYI

MAIL> FORWARD
To:   JSTATZ
Subj: This is Yours!
```

Figure 14-12. Forwarding a MAIL Message

PRINTING MESSAGES

The MAIL PRINT command queues a copy of the current message for printing, but the print command is not actually issued until you exit MAIL. When you exit, you will see the normal information message from PRINT with your job name, queue name, and entry number (Fig. 14-13). Many of the standard print qualifiers are available, including /COPIES, /NOTIFY, /FORM, and /QUEUE.

```
MAIL> PRINT
MAIL> EXIT
Job MAIL (queue SYS$PRINT, entry 696) printing on SYBIL_LICO
```

Figure 14-13. Printing a MAIL Message

COPYING A MESSAGE TO A VMS FILE

The EXTRACT command moves the current message to a VMS file (Fig. 14-14). It prompts for a VMS file name in which to store the message. If you do not use a file type, it defaults to .TXT. Once extracted, you can copy this file, rename it, edit it, and treat it like any other text file.

```
MAIL> EXTRACT
File: TRAINING
%MAIL-I-CREATED, MISDSK:[VMSWIZ]TRAINING.TXT;1 created

MAIL>
```

Figure 14-14. Copying a Message to a VMS File

If you send or extract a message created with a word processor, the message may lose some of its formatting controls. There are two ways to avoid this problem. If available, use the VMS MAIL interface in the application. Otherwise, generate your document in generic text form in your word processor before manipulating it with MAIL or DCL commands.

SEARCHING MESSAGES

You can search all messages for a specific string with the SEARCH command (Fig. 14-15). If the search string is a phrase or contains blanks, enclose it in double quotes ("). MAIL responds with the first message containing the search string. To continue searching for the next occurrence of the same string, use the SEARCH command alone.

```
MAIL> SEARCH installation

From: MANAGER
To:   MARS
Subj: Delivery Date
Decserver installation is scheduled for Dec 19.

MAIL>
```

Figure 14-15. Searching Messages

DELETING A MESSAGE

DELETE moves the message you just read to the WASTEBASKET folder, where it stays until you leave MAIL. DELETE can operate on messages by message number (*i.e.*, DELETE n moves message number "n" to the WASTEBASKET) or you can delete all messages in a folder with the DELETE/ALL command (Fig. 14-16). DIRECTORY WASTEBASKET lists messages you have deleted by number, title, date, and subject.

```
MAIL> DEL
MAIL> DEL 7

MAIL> DIR WASTEBASKET

# From                Date             Subject
1 SYBIL::STEKIB        8-AUG-1989       Regional Conference
2 MIS4::SYSTEM         23-SEP-1989      RE: multiple sessions
```

Figure 14-16. Deleting a MAIL message

If you accidentally delete the wrong message, you can SELECT the WASTE-BASKET folder and MOVE the message back to a permanent folder. When you leave MAIL or use the PURGE command, the messages in the WASTEBASKET are deleted and you can no longer retrieve them.

USING MAIL FOLDERS

MAIL uses folders to keep track of messages the same way we use directories to keep our files in order. DIRECTORY/FOLDER lists folders, MOVE and FILE create folders, and you delete folders by removing all the messages. When there are no more messages in a folder, it is automatically deleted.

There are three folders used by MAIL all the time — NEWMAIL, MAIL, and WASTEBASKET. Messages you have already read are stored in the MAIL folder, unread messages reside in the NEWMAIL folder, and WASTEBASKET holds deleted messages. MAIL commands and qualifiers work in any folder, which means you can manipulate messages in one of the standard folders or in a folder you have created. However, the qualifier /NEW, which can be used with many commands, specifically selects the NEWMAIL folder and is an exception to this rule.

Listing Folders

DIRECTORY/FOLDER lists the standard MAIL folders and all folders you have defined in any MAIL session (Fig. 14-17). WASTEBASKET does not show up unless you have deleted a message during the current MAIL session.

```
MAIL> DIR/FOLDER
Listing of folders in USERD:[MIS.VMSWIZ]MAIL.MAI;1
     Press CTRL/C to cancel listing
MAIL            MAINTENANCE              WASTEBASKET
MAIL>
```

Figure 14-17. DIRECTORY/FOLDER Command

Creating a Folder

MOVE and FILE place the current message into the specified folder (Fig. 14-18). Use either to create a new folder or to file a message in an existing folder. If folder you request does not exist, answer yes to the prompt and MAIL will create it for you. Press RETURN at the "_File:" prompt unless you want to create another physically separate mail file in your directory (i.e., another .MAI file). Some users require multiple mail files, but the new user is best served with only one.

```
MAIL> MOVE
_Folder: MAINTENANCE
_File:
Folder MAINTENANCE does not exist.
Do you want to create it (Y/N, default is N)? y
%MAIL-I-NEWFOLDER, folder MAINTENANCE created

MAIL> DIR MAINTENANCE
                                              MAINTENANCE

# From               Date          Subject

1 SYSTEM             7-AUG-1989    RE: mis1 uic's
```

Figure 14-18. MAIL MOVE Command

Selecting a Folder

The SELECT command moves you from one folder to another (Fig. 14-19). You can verify the folder name by checking the upper right corner of your screen or by entering the SHOW FOLDER command. SELECT without a folder name places you in NEWMAIL if there are unread messages.

```
MAIL> SELECT MAINTENANCE
MAIL> DIR
                                              MAINTENANCE

# From               Date          Subject
1 (Deleted)
2 MIS4::SYSTEM        8-AUG-1989    RE: tomorrow
3 MIS1::PAUMCG       11-NOV-1989    RE: idea
4 MIS2::PAUMCG       17-NOV-1989    SEVERAL THINGS
```

Figure 14-19. Selecting a MAIL Folder

SELECT and SET FOLDER are equivalent commands. You use either command to change folders and to select messages based on the contents of any of the message header fields. The qualifiers you can use to select messages are listed in Figure 14-20. The /CC, /FROM, and /TO qualifiers expect a username or partial username to compare against and /SUBJ accepts either a single word or phrase enclosed in quotes. Subject matching is case independent and ignores the RE: portion of the subject field.

```
    /CC =    string          Match string in CC: field
    /FROM = string           Match string in From: field
    /TO =    string          Match string in To: field
    /SUBJ = string           Match string in Subj: field (RE: ignored)


    /BEFORE = date_time       Select messages before date and time
    /SINCE  = date_time       Select messages since date and time
```

Figure 14-20. MAIL SELECT and SET FOLDER Qualifiers

The /BEFORE and /SINCE qualifiers expect a date and time value and operate the same way in MAIL as they do with other commands. If you do not provide a date or time, it defaults to the current date and time. You can combine these qualifiers to retrieve messages by several matching criteria. For example, you might want to find all messages received from a specific username last month or all messages referring to the same subject. These commands are illustrated in Figure 14-21.

```
MAIL> SELECT/FROM=KATMCC/BEFORE=26-JAN/SINCE=1-JAN
%MAIL-I-SELECTED, 4 messages selected
MAIL> DIR

# From                    Date              Subject

1 KATMCC                   8-JAN-1990       Font Selection
2 KATMCC                  15-JAN-1990       RE: Schedule
3 KATMCC                  22-JAN-1990       Headers
4 KATMCC                  25-JAN-1990       Copy Edit

MAIL> SELECT/FROM=GINABO/SINCE=1-JAN/SUBJ=TRAINING
%MAIL-I-SELECTED, 2 messages selected
MAIL> DIR

# From                    Date              Subject

1 GINABO                  8-JAN-1990        VMS Training
2 GINABO                  9-JAN-1990        RE: Training
3 JOHBRO                  2-FEB-1990        SUN Training
```

Figure 14-21. Selecting MAIL Messages

MAIL FILE MAINTENANCE

MAIL does not physically remove deleted messages from your mail file, but only marks them as deleted. When you delete many messages, this deleted space can consume a large amount of your mail file space. Use the SHOW DELETED command to find out how much space deleted messages are using. If the number is over several hundred bytes, use the COMPRESS command to return deleted message space to your mail file. You should also perform this maintenance if files with very long names starting with MAIL$ appear in your directory.

COMPRESS creates a temporary file and copies all non-deleted messages to the temporary file. Then the original MAIL.MAI file is renamed to MAIL.OLD. If COMPRESS is successful, you can safely delete the MAIL.OLD copy because it is no longer needed. COMPRESS sends several information messages to you while the operation is in progress (Fig. 14-22). For the best possible response time from MAIL, use COMPRESS at least once a quarter, and more often if you receive and delete hundreds of messages.

```
MAIL> SHOW DELETED
Mail file USERD:[MIS.VMSWIZ]MAIL.MAI;1
        contains 10232 deleted message bytes.


MAIL> COMPRESS
%MAIL-S-CREATED,USERD:[MIS.VMSWIZ]MAIL_3535_COMPRESS.TMP;1 created
%MAIL-S-COPIED, USERD:[MIS.VMSWIZ]MAIL.MAI;1 copied to
USERD:[MIS.VMSWIZ]MAIL_3535_COMPRESS.TMP;1 (93 records)
%MAIL-S-RENAMED, USERD:[MIS.VMSWIZ]MAIL.MAI;1 renamed to
USERD:[MIS.VMSWIZ]MAIL.OLD;1
%MAIL-S-RENAMED,USERD:[MIS.VMSWIZ]MAIL_3535_COMPRESS.TMP;1
renamed to USERD:[MIS.VMSWIZ]MAIL.MAI;1


MAIL> SHOW DELETED
Mail file USERD:[MIS.VMSWIZ]MAIL.MAI;1
        contains 0 deleted message bytes.
```

Figure 14-22. Compressing a MAIL File

MAIL SET AND SHOW COMMANDS

In MAIL, SET and SHOW commands come in pairs. If you can SET something, you can also SHOW it.

- **SET/SHOW CC_PROMPT**
  SET CC_PROMPT instructs MAIL to generate a CC: prompt at the beginning of each message you send. SHOW CC_PROMPT displays the setting.

- **SET/SHOW COPY_SELF**
  If COPY_SELF is set, you receive a copy of all messages you send to other people. SHOW COPY_SELF displays the current setting.

- **SET/SHOW FOLDER**
  SET FOLDER selects a folder and SHOW FOLDER displays the current folder. SET FOLDER is equivalent to the SELECT command.

- **SET/SHOW FORM**
  SET FORM selects a default form to be used when printing messages. SHOW FORM displays the current selection.

- **SET/SHOW QUEUE**
  SET QUEUE selects the default queue where messages are to be printed. SHOW QUEUE displays the current selection.

- **SET/SHOW PERSONAL NAME**
  SET PERSONAL_NAME "string" appends the string to the end of your username where it appears in the To: field of messages you send. For example, you might want to set your personal name to your telephone extension or nickname. SHOW PERSONAL_NAME displays the current string.

- **SHOW ALL**
  SHOW ALL displays all the defaults currently in place for items you can modify with the SET command.

ACCESSING VMS FROM MAIL

The MAIL SPAWN command illustrated in Figure 14-23 creates a VMS subprocess from within MAIL that responds with the system prompt ($). You enter DCL commands as you normally would and logout when you are finished. Then you return to the MAIL> prompt. Spawned processes are explained in Chapter 10, File Manipulation, under the heading Using a Subprocess.

Use SPAWN to check the name of a file you want to send, to modify a distribution list, to read a memo before responding to a message, or to perform any other DCL command. Remember to log out afterwards and do not start the MAIL utility a second time from the spawned process.

```
MAIL> SPAWN
$ TYPE MANAGERS.DIS
SYBIL::GBOICE          Node SYBIL
KMCCARVILLE           Local node or cluster
JECKYL::LMILLER       Node JECKYL

$ LO
Process VMSWIZ_1 logged out at 9-Nov-1989 13:58:39.39
You have 0 new messages

MAIL>
```

Figure 14-23. MAIL SPAWN Command

MAIL KEYPAD FUNCTIONS

MAIL automatically defines the numeric keypad on the standard DEC keyboard with the most frequently used commands as shown in the diagram in Figure 14-24. As with editing functions, PF1 is the GOLD key. The upper function is activated by pressing the key. The lower function, in boldface, is activated by pressing the GOLD key, followed by the key.

PF1 GOLD KEY	PF2 HELP **DIR/FOLD**	PF3 EXT/MAIL **EXTRACT**	PF4 ERASE **SEL MAIL**
7 SEND **SEND/EDI**	8 REPLY **RP/ED/EX**	9 FORWARD **FRWD/EDI**	- READ/NEW **SHOW NEW**
4 CURRENT **CURR/EDI**	5 FIRST **FIRS/EDI**	6 LAST **LAST/EDI**	, DIR/NEW **DIR/MAIL**
1 BACK **BACK/EDI**	2 PRINT **P/P/NOTI**	3 DIR **DIR/9999**	ENTER
0 NEXT **NEXT/EDIT**		. FILE **DELETE**	ENTER **SELECT**

Figure 14-24. MAIL Keypad Diagram

MAIL EXERCISES

If you are practicing by yourself, you can learn MAIL by sending and replying to
to yourself. If you have friend to practice with, exchange messages with each other.

1. Start MAIL and ask for HELP.

```
$ MAIL
MAIL> HELP
```

2. Send a message to a friend.

```
MAIL> SEND
To:    ROBINS
Subj:  Meeting
Enter your message below. Press CTRL/Z when complete, or CTRL/C to quit:
Our meeting has been rescheduled for Wednesday at 9:00. See you then.
CTRL/Z
```

3. Send a message to yourself and CC: someone else.

```
MAIL> SEND/CC
To:    VMSWIZ
CC:    GINABO
Subj:  Lunch
Enter your message below. Press CTRL/Z when complete, or CTRL/C to quit:
We are meeting in the lobby at 11:30 for lunch today.
CTRL/Z
```

4. READ a message and REPLY to it. Watch how MAIL fills in the To: and Subj: fields.

```
MAIL>

    #1              29-JAN-1990 08:49:04.11         NEWMAIL
From:  DENHUB::ROBINS
To:    VMSWIZ
Subj:  Meeting

We are meeting in the lobby at 11:30 for lunch today.

MAIL> REPLY
To:   DENHUB::ROBINS
Subj: RE: Meeting
Enter your message below. Press CTRL/Z when complete, or CTRL/C to quit:
Ok, see you then.
CTRL/Z
MAIL>
```

5. Enter the SPAWN command. What happens?

> MAIL creates a subprocess that attaches to your terminal and responds with the system prompt. If you enter the command SHOW PROCESS at the system prompt, you will see two processes. The asterisk next to the "_1" process indicates that the DCL subprocess is active.

```
MAIL> SPAWN
$
```

6. With the editor, create a file called FRIENDS.DIS that will be used as a MAIL distribution list. Put the usernames of four friends into the text buffer and save the file.

```
$ EDIT/TPU FRIENDS.DIS
ROBSTA
RICSTA
VMSWIZ
KATMAN
CTRL/Z
```

7. Start the editor a second time and create another text file that will be the message sent to your friends. Save the text in a file called GREETINGS.LIS and exit the editor.

```
$ EDIT/TPU GREETINGS.LIS
Greetings to all my friends on the distribution list.
CTRL/Z
$
```

8. Terminate the DCL process with the LOGOUT command. This returns you to the MAIL> prompt. Define a personal name to be added to the end of your username for all future messages.

```
$ LO
MAIL> SET PERSONAL_NAME   "Is it Friday Yet?"
```

9. Send the message file you just created to the distribution list. Wait until all your messages arrive.

```
MAIL> SEND GREETINGS.LIS
To:     @FRIENDS.DIS
Subj:   Using a Distribution List
```

10. Use DIRECTORY/NEW command to get a list of messages waiting to be read.

```
MAIL> DIRECTORY/NEW
```

11. Use DIRECTORY/FOLDER to list your folders.

```
MAIL> DIRECTORY/FOLDER
Listing of folders in USERD:[MIS.VMSWIZ]MAIL.MAI;1
      Press CTRL/C to cancel listing
MAIL    NEWMAIL
```

You see two folders, MAIL where previously read messages are stored, and NEWMAIL where unread messages are stored.

12. Read a message and DELETE it.

```
MAIL>
To:    VMSWIZ
From:  ROBSTA
Subj:  Greetings

Greetings to all my friends on the distribution list.
MAIL> DELETE
```

13. Use the DIRECTORY/FOLDER command again. Do you see WASTEBASKET this time? Why?

```
MAIL> DIRECTORY/FOLDER
Listing of folders in USERD:[MIS.VMSWIZ]MAIL.MAI;1
      Press CTRL/C to cancel listing

MAIL          NEWMAIL          WASTEBASKET
```

You see the WASTEBASKET because you have deleted one message.

14. File the next two messages in a folder called JUNKMAIL using either MOVE or FILE. The first time you reference a folder that does not exist, MAIL creates it for you when you respond Y to the prompt. Do not enter a file name at the _File: prompt unless you want to create a folder in a physically separate mail file.

```
MAIL> MOVE
_Folder: JUNKMAIL                        [Folder name]
_File:                                   [Press RETURN]
Folder JUNKMAIL does not exist.          [Create new folder]
Do you want to create it (Y/N, default is N)? y
%MAIL-I-NEWFOLDER, folder JUNKMAIL created
```

15. SELECT the WASTEBASKET folder and use the DIRECTORY command to list messages you have deleted but are not yet gone. What other command can you use to list messages in any folder?

```
MAIL> SELECT WASTEBASKET
%MAIL-I-SELECTED, 2 messages selected
```

```
MAIL> DIR                                    [List the messages]
                                                      WASTEBASKET
   # From               Date          Subject
   1 JECKYL::JIMGRE      28-JAN-1990   NCP
   2 HYDE::JOHBRO        16-JAN-1990   RE: Network Mail

MAIL> DIR WASTEBASKET                         [Equivalent command]
                                                      WASTEBASKET
   # From               Date          Subject
   1 JECKYL::JIMGRE      28-JAN-1990   NCP
   2 HYDE::JOHBRO        16-JAN-1990   RE: Network Mail
```

16. List the messages in the JUNKMAIL folder.

```
MAIL> DIR JUNKMAIL
                                                         JUNKMAIL
   # From               Date          Subject
   1 DENHUB::VMSWIZ      31-JAN-1990   Greetings
   2 DENHUB::SYSTEM      1-FEB-1990    RE: tomorrow
   3 SYBIL::GINABO       1-FEB-1990    RE: error messages
```

17. SELECT one folder and read a message by message number. Print a message
    from one of the folders.

```
MAIL> SELECT JUNKMAIL
%MAIL-I-SELECTED, 2 messages selected
MAIL> READ 2

To:     VMSWIZ
From:   ROBSTA
Subj:   Greetings

Greetings to all my friends on the distribution list.
```

18. Extract a message from one of the folders. If you do not provide a file type, it
    defaults to .TXT.

```
MAIL> EXTRACT
_File: HSC
%MAIL-I-CREATED, USERD:[MIS.VMSWIZ]HSC.TXT;1 created
```

19. Delete all the messages in JUNKMAIL. How many folders do you have?

```
MAIL> SELECT JUNKMAIL
%MAIL-I-SELECTED, 2 messages selected
MAIL> DELETE/ALL
MAIL> DIR/FOLDERS
   Listing of folders in USERD:[MIS.VMSWIZ]MAIL.MAI;1
       Press CTRL/C to cancel listing
   MAIL             WASTEBASKET
```

The JUNKMAIL folder is gone because all its messages have been deleted.

20. Remove the messages in the WASTEBASKET.

```
MAIL> PURGE
%MAIL-I-DELMSGS, 2 messages deleted
MAIL>
```

21. How much deleted space do you have in your mail file? Use SHOW DELETED, COMPRESS your mail file, and look at the deleted space again. Is there a difference?

```
MAIL> SHOW DELETED
Mail file USERD:[MIS.VMSWIZ]MAIL.MAI;1
          contains 5719 deleted message bytes.
MAIL> COMPRESS
%MAIL-S-CREATED, USERD:[MIS.VMSWIZ]MAIL_7D1C_COMPRESS.TMP;1 created
%MAIL-S-COPIED, USERD:[MIS.VMSWIZ]MAIL.MAI;1 copied to
USERD:[MIS.VMSWIZ]MAIL_7D1C_COMPRESS.TMP;1 (94 records)
%MAIL-S-RENAMED, USERD:[MIS.VMSWIZ]MAIL.MAI;1 renamed to
USERD:[MIS.VMSWIZ]MAIL.OLD;2
%MAIL-S-RENAMED, USERD:[MIS.VMSWIZ]MAIL_7D1C_COMPRESS.TMP;1 renamed to
USERD:[MIS.VMSWIZ]MAIL.MAI;1
MAIL> SHOW DELETED
Mail file USERD:[MIS.VMSWIZ]MAIL.MAI;1
          contains 0 deleted message bytes
```

22. Exit the MAIL utility.

```
MAIL> EXIT or CTRL/Z
```

VMS Utilities

INTRODUCTION

Chapter 15 reviews some of the more popular VMS utilities: PHONE, SEARCH, DIFFERENCES, and SORT/MERGE. PHONE is an excellent tool for communicating with any user logged in to the system, SEARCH locates a word, string, or phrase in one or more files and DIFFERENCES compares files and highlights lines that are different. SORT and MERGE are complementary utilities that order and combine files based on alphabetic or numeric fields in ascending or descending order. The exercises at the end of this chapter should make you comfortable with all these utilities.

PHONE

PHONE is a fun utility for quick communication with another user when you do not want to wait for MAIL messages to go back and forth. PHONE works like a regular telephone and has many of the same features. You can call any user on your system or a network node and carry on an interactive discussion. PHONE supports conference calls and has commands to put a user on HOLD, REJECT a call, HANGUP, and send one-line MAIL messages.

PHONE broadcasts a message to your screen when someone is calling you. If you are in the middle of a rush project or a heavy creative effort, these messages can be a real bother. To screen out phone calls, use SET BROADCAST=NOPHONE. If you are in an editor when someone calls, the phone message is written across the screen. Don't panic — the message is not in your text file, it is only on the screen. Use CTRL/W to repaint the screen.

Starting PHONE

Enter PHONE to start this utility. PHONE responds by splitting your screen into three parts: the top two lines are for PHONE commands and messages, the middle section echoes what you type and the bottom section echoes what the other person types (Fig. 15-1). At this point, you are ready to make a call. Notice that your username is displayed at the top of the second part of the screen.

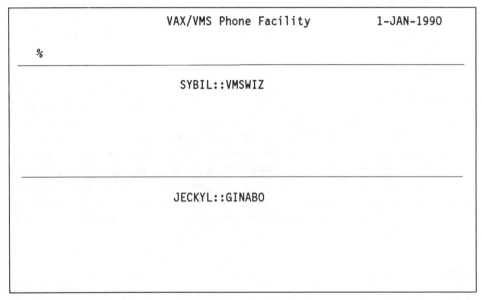

Figure 15-1. PHONE Screen

After the screen is formatted, the cursor appears on the top line next to the percent (%) prompt character where PHONE commands are entered. The percent character functions as an "escape" character that puts you on the command line. If you accidentally use the percent character during your conversation, you will find the cursor waiting on the top line. To continue the conversation, press RETURN.

PHONE Help

Like many other utilities, PHONE has an internal help function. However, PHONE displays information differently than HELP at the system prompt. When you ask for help on a PHONE command, the requested information is displayed until any character is typed at the keyboard. Then you are returned to the PHONE command line, instead of being prompted with a Topic? prompt. PHONE's main HELP screen is shown in Figure 15-2.

```
% HELP
The HELP command allows you to obtain information about the PHONE
facility. To obtain information about an individual command or
topic, type HELP followed by the command or topic name:

HELP topic

HELP also accepts all of the other standard VMS help argument
formats. The information you request is displayed at your
terminal until you type any character at your keyboard.

Additional information available:
ANSWER        Characters    DIAL      DIRECTORY    EXIT      FACSIMILE
HANGUP        HELP          HOLD      MAIL         REJECT
Switch_hook                 UNHOLD
```

Figure 15-2. PHONE HELP Screen

PHONE Commands

Figure 15-3 lists some of the most frequently used PHONE commands. If you compare this list with the one from the main HELP screen, you will notice that DIAL, FACSIMILE and MAIL have been omitted. DIAL is explained in the next section and people seldom use either of the other two commands.

```
ANSWER                     Answer an incoming call
DIRECTORY                  Provide a list of users you can call
HOLD                       Put everyone you are talking to on hold
UNHOLD                     Reverse the previous HOLD command
REJECT                     Reject a call
HANGUP                     Terminate this call
EXIT                       Leave the PHONE utility
CTRL/Z                     Leave the PHONE utility
```

Figure 15-3. PHONE Commands

PHONE Control Characters

There are three convenient control characters used during a PHONE conversation. CTRL/U erases the current line of text, CTRL/L erases all the text in your part of the screen, and CTRL/W repaints the entire screen.

Dialing a User

To call someone, enter the username of the person you want to call on the command line. If you have just started PHONE, the cursor will be resting on the top line of display next to the percent (%) prompt character. If you are in the middle of a conversation and want to call another user, enter the % in the middle of your conversation. PHONE returns the cursor to the command line where you can call another user or enter another command. When you call a user, you can optionally preface username with DIAL, but entering a username alone is sufficient. These two PHONE commands are equivalent:

% LMILLER
% DIAL LMILLER

If the person you called is not logged on, PHONE responds with the message "No one with that name is available right now." Otherwise, PHONE "rings" at username's terminal every ten seconds until one of three things happens.

- the person ANSWERs the phone

- the person REJECTs the call

- you type any character to terminate the call

If the person you called answers, the message "XXX has answered your call" appears on the PHONE command line and that person's node name and username appear at the top of the lower window. You are now ready to start the conversation.

Answering a Call

You know someone is calling you because PHONE broadcasts a message across your screen every ten seconds. To answer an incoming call, start PHONE and enter ANSWER at the % prompt. The node and username of the caller are displayed in the top window and your node and username appear in the lower portion of the screen.

The Conversation

When the conversation begins, the text you type is echoed in your window, which is the top part of the screen if you initiated the call and the lower part otherwise. When the other person types, text is echoed in the opposite window. If both parties type at the same time, the cursor alternates between windows which, with fast typists, can produce a dizzying effect.

Terminating a Call

If the person you called hangs up, the message "XXX just hung up the phone" appears on the message line. If you are finished with PHONE, enter the escape character (%) followed by EXIT or CTRL/Z — this exits PHONE and returns you to the system prompt. To terminate the conversation but remain in the PHONE utility, enter the escape character (%) and the HANGUP command. This leaves the cursor on the PHONE command line at which point you can call someone else or exit.

SEARCH

SEARCH is an incredibly useful tool for locating a word or phrase in a file or set of files. It is especially valuable when you forget which file holds the latest revision of a document or where you last stored an important file. SEARCH can scan one file, all files in a directory, or all files in a directory tree, depending upon the file specification used.

SEARCH requires two parameters, a file specification and a string (Fig. 15-4). The file specification is searched for all occurrences of the specified string. The file you enter may be a single file name, a wildcard, or a list of file names separated by commas. You specify the string to locate in two ways. If it contains only letters and numbers, enter the string by itself. If it contains special characters, punctuation or spaces, the string must be enclosed in double quotes ("). You may also specify more than one search string, as long as they are separated by commas.

When you use SEARCH interactively, each record that contains the search string appears on the screen and each instance of the string is highlighted. SEARCH can handle files with a maximum record length of 32,767 bytes, which means it can be used on production data files as well as normal text and source code files.

```
$ SEARCH file-spec[,...]  string[,...]   Command Format

$ SEARCH *.txt version                  Match upper and lowercase
$ SEARCH/EXACT *.txt "Version"          Match case exactly
$ SEARCH *.*   "annual report"          Match phrase, any case

$ SEARCH/OUT=REVS.LIS  *.C  revision    Send output to a file
```

Figure 15-4. SEARCH Command Examples

By default, string searching is case independent. In the first example in Figure 15-4, all occurrences of "version" will be displayed, regardless of whether the word is in upper, lower, or mixed case. If you want an exact match, you must enclose the search string in double quotes and use the /EXACT qualifier as shown in the second command.

SEARCH can also look through files for several strings, or locate files containing none of the strings. The /MATCH qualifier controls the type of comparison performed: /MATCH=AND selects records containing all of the strings and /MATCH=NAND returns a match if none of the strings are found.

To capture the output of the SEARCH command in a disk file, use the /OUTPUT qualifier. You can also select whether you want the search string in boldface or underlined in the output file with the /HIGHLIGHT qualifier (*i.e.*, /HIGHLIGHT=UNDERLINE or /HIGHLIGHT=OVERSTRIKE). The /FORMAT qualifier controls how SEARCH handles control characters.

You can use many other qualifiers to control how the SEARCH utility operates. SEARCH understands the normal date and time qualifiers and the /EXCLUDE qualifier which omits specified files from the search. For more details on these options and other examples, see HELP documentation for the SEARCH command.

DIFFERENCES

DIFFERENCES is a matching utility you use to compare files a line at a time. It has obvious use for programmers making changes to source code files, as each changed line can be tracked from one version to the next. You may find this tool useful for comparing differences in output files when updating documents and while testing new applications or troubleshooting software problems.

DIFFERENCES requires one parameter which is the file specification of the master file and accepts an optional second parameter which is the name of the revision file (Fig. 15-5). The revision file is compared against the master file. If you do not specify a revision file, DIFFERENCES uses the next lower version of the master file.

```
$ DIFFERENCES MASTER-FILE[.REVISION-FILE]      Command Format

$ DIFFERENCES LABELS.DAT                        Compare two highest
                                                versions of LABELS.DAT

$ DIFFERENCES LABELS.DAT, OLDLABELS.TXT         Compare LABELS.DAT
                                                with OLDLABELS.TXT
```

Figure 15-5. DIFFERENCES Command

The first command in Figure 15-5 compares the most recent version of LABELS.DAT against the previous version. If no previous version is available, DIFFERENCES issues an error message. If the text is not identical, the master file lines are displayed first, followed by the lines that differ in the previous version. In the second command, each line of LABELS.DAT is compared against each line of OLDLABELS.DAT. When the lines do not match, LABELS.DAT lines are displayed first, followed by lines from OLDLABELS.DAT.

DIFFERENCES can display lines that differ in each file in three ways:

- lines from the master file first, followed by those from the revision file

- a partial line of differences in each file can be displayed in parallel

- different records can be output to a text file in either the linear or parallel format. The parallel display is the easiest to use interactively.

By default, DIFFERENCES displays differences on the terminal, one section at a time in a linear listing, master file first and revision file second. You can get a side-by-side listing with the /PARALLEL qualifier and you can send the comparison to a disk file with the /OUTPUT qualifier (Fig. 15-6). The output file specification defaults to master-file.DIF unless you specify otherwise.

```
$ DIFF/PARALLEL LABELS.MASTER          Side by side display

$ DIFF/OUTPUT    LABELS.MASTER          Comparison stored in LABELS.DIF
```

Figure 15-6. DIFFERENCES Output

DIFFERENCES Qualifiers

There are many qualifiers that direct and control the matching operation — consult HELP DIFFERENCES for a complete description. Two commonly used qualifiers are /WIDTH and /IGNORE. /WIDTH specifies the width of lines in the output listing. By default, terminal output is the same as the terminal width and disk file output is 132 characters wide.

The /IGNORE=(option[,...]) qualifier tells DIFFERENCES to ignore blanks, special characters, strings, or records during the compare operation. /IGNORE = (TRAILING_SPACES, BLANK_LINES, SPACING) eliminates blanks from the matching algorithm. Several IGNORE options are listed in Figure 15-7, but this is not a complete list. Refer to HELP documentation for a more detailed explanation.

Option	Ignored Items
BLANK_LINES	Blank lines between data lines
FORM_FEED	Form feed characters
SPACING	Multiple spaces or tabs within lines of data
TRAILING_SPACE	Space and tab characters at the end of a line

Figure 15-7. DIFFERENCES/IGNORE Options

THE SORT AND MERGE UTILITIES

The SORT utility orders records in a file based on the first character in each record or the contents of one or more fields that appear in every record in the file. MERGE combines identically formatted files into one ordered file using one or more data fields that appear in every record. Any standard VMS file can be manipulated with these utilities, including text files and data files that contain text or binary information. You can use SORT and MERGE commands at the system prompt, in a command procedure, or access them from a program using the programming interface. SORT and MERGE have the same command format and use the same input and output qualifiers.

THE SORT UTILITY

SORT processes up to ten input files, accepts up to ten sort keys that identify the fields to use for ordering purposes, sorts the records according to the keys, and generates an output file containing the sorted records. If you omit a file type from either the input file or the output file, SORT assumes a default file type of .DAT.

SORT requires two parameters — an input file which is the file to be sorted and an output file where the sorted records will be stored (Fig. 15-8). If you specify the same file for both the input file and output file, the input file is overwritten by the records in the requested sort order. When sorting multiple input files, SORT requires that each file have the same organization, record type, and record layout.

```
$ SORT input-file[,...] output-file      Command Format

$ SORT CUSTOMER.DAT                       Reorder CUSTOMER.DAT
$ SORT CUSTOMER.DAT  MAY89.DAT            Store records in MAY89.DAT
```

Figure 15-8. SORT Command

The first command in Figure 15-8 sorts the records in CUSTOMER.DAT in alphabetical order and writes the records in that order to the same file (which destroys the original version). To keep the input file intact, you must specify a different output file as shown in the second example. In this case, the system sorts the records in CUSTOMER.DAT alphabetically and writes the sorted records to a new file called MAY89.DAT.

Both these examples use the simplest form of SORT which alphabetically orders the records using the first character in the record. Although the simplest form is handy, you will frequently need to sort data files based on a text string or numeric value at a certain location in the record. This string or value is called a sort key and is identified by a starting column position, length (*i.e.*, number of characters) and type (*e.g.*, text, decimal, binary).

Defining a Sort Key

You can sort records using a sort key that identifies a string or numeric value in any position in the record. Character keys can be up to 32,767 characters long, binary keys can be one, two, four, eight, or 16 bytes, and decimal keys can be a maximum of 31 digits. You can sort files in ascending or descending alphabetic or numeric order or a combination, using up to ten keys. You describe each key with a /KEY qualifier on the SORT command — the qualifier value specifies a starting position, size, data type, and ascending or descending order (Fig. 15-9). An ascending sort, from lowest to highest value, is the default.

```
$ SORT/KEY=(POSITION:n,SIZE:m[,DATA-TYPE[,SORT-ORDER]])

POSITION          Location within the record (1 is the first char)
SIZE              Length of the key (# of characters)
DATA-TYPE         Type of value to be sorted (default is CHARACTER)
SORT-ORDER        ASCENDING (default) or DESCENDING
```

Figure 15-9. SORT/KEY Usage

If there are identical values in the key field of several records, you may need to sort on a second field to properly order the data — use one /KEY qualifier for each text string or numeric value. When you use multiple keys, each record is sorted by the keys in the order in which they appear on the command line. For example, if you are sorting a file that contains a zip code and a last name in each record, you can specify the zip code as the first key and the last name as the second key. This sort will produce a file that is ordered in ascending sequence by zip code. For each duplicate zip code, the records will appear in alphabetical order by last name.

The data type of the sort field defaults to character. To sort binary or floating point numbers, specify a valid data type as part of the /KEY qualifier. Use HELP SORT/KEY for a list of data types and more information.

SORT Example

Assume you have a simple data file that contains three fields of information: mountain name, altitude, and number of trails. Mountain name starts in column one and is 16 characters long, altitude starts in column 17 and is five characters long, and number of trails starts in column 22 and is two characters long. The record format is shown in Figure 15-10. Four SORT commands in Figure 15-11 order this file by mountain name, by altitude in ascending and descending order, and by number of trails.

Mountain Name	Altitude	Trails
1 16	17 21	22 23

Figure 15-10. Example SORT Record

The first command alphabetizes the data file using the first character in each mountain name because it is the first field and overwrites the input file with the newly sorted data. The second command produces an output file with records organized by altitude, lowest to highest, because data is sorted in ascending order by default. Output is stored in the file LOHIGH.DAT.

```
$ SORT MOUNTAIN.DAT MOUNTAIN.DAT              Sort the same file

$ SORT/KEY=(POSITION:17,SIZE:5) -             By altitude ascending
_$ MOUNTAIN.DAT -                             Input file
_$ LOHIGH.DAT                                 Output file

$ SORT/KEY=(POSITION:17,SIZE:5,DESCENDING)    By altitude descending
_$ MOUNTAIN.DAT -                             Input File
_$ HIGHLO.DAT                                 Output File

$ SORT/KEY=(POSITION:22,SIZE:2) -             By trails ascending
_$ MOUNTAIN.DAT -                             Same Input File
_$ TRAILS.DAT                                 Output file
```

Figure 15-11. SORT Figure

The third command orders the records by altitude from highest to lowest because the keyword DESCENDING is included as part of the key description. Output is stored in the file HIGHLO.DAT. The fourth command sorts the file by number of trails and stores the output in TRAILS.DAT.

Sort Processing Algorithms

SORT can use four different processing algorithms — record, tag, address, or index. If you use SORT on a regular basis, you will notice that the default record algorithm takes a long time if you are sorting large files (*e.g.*, hundreds to thousands of records). As a novice user, you are likely to use the default record sort or the tag sort, as the other two versions create intermediate files that require a program to reconstruct the actual data records.

You select the algorithm to be used by specifying one of four keywords with the /PROCESS qualifier (Fig. 15-12): RECORD, TAG, ADDRESS, or INDEX. Each algorithm produces a different kind of output file, geared towards a specific use.

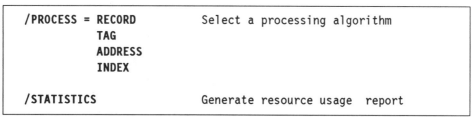

```
/PROCESS = RECORD            Select a processing algorithm
           TAG
           ADDRESS
           INDEX


/STATISTICS                  Generate resource usage   report
```

Figure 15-12. SORT Processing Qualifiers

To compare the speed of the different sort processing methods, use /STATISTICS on the SORT command. This qualifier directs SORT to provide a resource usage message that contains the number of records sorted, the elapsed time, and the CPU time used during the sort operation.

- RECORD Sort
  The record sort can handle multiple input files and reads each full record from the file for sorting purposes. The output file also contains each full record from the input file. This algorithm requires the most temporary workspace and requires the most CPU time because each record in the input file is read, processed, and written to the output file. If the file is sorted using multiple keys, each record may be read multiple times.

- TAG Sort
  The tag sort is faster but can only handle a single input file. This algorithm extracts and sorts the keys first and then reads input file records in the

order indicated by the sorted keys. The output file contains complete records just like the record sort. This sort is usually faster than the record sort for small keys and large records, because the system sorts only the key fields and processes each input record just once in creating the output file.

- ADDRESS Sort
  The address sort accepts one input file, sorts the keys only, and creates an output file that contains pointers to the records in sorted order. To physically create the output file, you need another program to read the input file records in the order specified by the address file. This algorithm has the fastest sort time, uses the smallest amount of workspace, and creates the smallest output file. Use this sort algorithm when the output file records will be processed sequentially.

- INDEX Sort
  The index sort is similar to the address sort, except that the output file contains key fields and pointers to records. Use this sort when the output file records will be processed by key.

SORT Output File

SORT expects the the output file organization to be identical with the first input file. If the input file is sequential with fixed length records, the output file will be sequential with fixed length records. You can override the default and select any type of VMS organization for the output file using an output file qualifier on the command line (Fig. 15-13).

```
$ SORT/KEY=(POS:1, SIZE:20) TEST.DAT     REPORT.DAT/SEQ
$ SORT/KEY=(POS:10,SIZE:4)  MASTER.DAT   PO.DAT/REL

   /SEQUENTIAL                          Create a sequential file
   /RELATIVE                            Create a relative file
   /INDEXED_SEQUENTIAL                  Create an ISAM file
```

Figure 15-13. SORT Output File Organization

If you want the output file to be an Indexed Sequential Access Method file, the output file must already exist and be empty. To add records to an empty file, you must use the /OVERLAY qualifier on the output file. You can use ANALYZE/RMS/FDL with an existing ISAM file to create an ISAM file description. Then use CREATE/FDL with the file description you just generated to create an empty file. Ask for help on FDL for more information.

SORT Workfiles

SORT workfiles are placed on the device and directory pointed to by the logical name SYS$SCRATCH, which is usually defined as a systemwide logical by the system manager. SORT normally uses two workfiles, referred to by the logical names SORTWORK0 and SORTWORK1. To use more workfiles, you can assign the logical names SORTWORK0 - SORTWORK9 to a specific device before you issue the sort command. Then start the operation with the command SORT/WORK_FILES=n. Using more than two workfiles can speed up SORT processing at the expense of disk space.

If all your workfiles are on the same disk, use /WORK_FILE= device-name to identify the disk to be used. The first qualifier is plural and the second is singular. When using multiple work files, if you place work files on different disks, SORT performance improves because disk read/write cycles overlap. Workfiles can consume up to twice the size of the input file, so make sure that there is adequate space on the disk where they are located.

SORT and MERGE Qualifiers

Many other qualifiers can be used with both utilities to direct the match and ordering algorithms and to control the format of the output file. See HELP on SORT/MERGE for more information. You can also create a specification file that contains the necessary qualifiers. Then, instead of entering a very long SORT or MERGE command interactively, you can direct either utility to read instructions from this file by adding /SPECIFICATION=file-spec to the command.

THE MERGE UTILITY

MERGE combines up to ten sorted input files into one ordered output file. All input files must have the same format and be sorted on the same key or keys. To combine records based on the value of one or more fields in each record, you must provide the same key definition for MERGE as the one used to SORT the file(s) originally (Fig. 15-14). MERGE understands the same qualifiers as the SORT utility and uses the same rules for handling input and output files.

```
$ MERGE input-file[,...] output-file        Command Format

$ MERGE/KEY=(POSITION=1,SIZE=16)            Field to merge with
_$ FEB89.DAT, MAR89.DAT -                    Input files
_$ TOTAL.DAT                                 Output file
```

Figure 15-14. MERGE Command

UTILITIES EXERCISES

PHONE exercises work best if you have one, and preferably two other users to practice with. If not, you can call yourself. These exercises are difficult to portray on paper because of the ir screen oriented nature, so only the PHONE commands are included.

PHONE Exercises

1. Start PHONE and ask for HELP on the DIRECTORY command (HELP DIR). Exit HELP by pressing any key and then ask for HELP on the DIAL command.

```
$ PHONE
% HELP DIR
% HELP DIAL
```

2. Dial a friend, carry on a conversation and place this person on hold.

```
% GINABO
% HOLD
```

3. If you do not have another person to practice with, skip to number 6. Otherwise, call a second person, UNHOLD the first person and see how well a three-way conversation works.

```
% DIAL KATMCC
% UNHOLD
```

4. Have the second person HANGUP and DIAL the second person again. If you are the second person called, REJECT this call.

```
% DIAL KATMCC
% REJECT
%PHONE-I-REJECT, that person has rejected your call
```

5. Terminate all conversations and exit PHONE.

```
% EXIT        or        % CTRL/Z
$
```

6. Set your terminal to ignore PHONE messages with SET BROADCAST=NOPHONE at the system prompt. Have another user call you and see what happens.

```
$ SET BROADCAST=NOPHONE
$ PHONE
%PHONE-I-UNPLUGGED, that person's phone is unplugged.
```

7. Exit PHONE and reset your terminal to accept PHONE messages.

```
% HANGUP
$ SET BROADCAST=PHONE
```

SEARCH and DIFFERENCES Exercises

These exercises assume you have created the GLOSSARY.TXT file from the EVE exercise.

1. Search GLOSSARY.TXT for the word walks.

```
$ SEARCH GLOSSARY.TXT WALKS
Walks on water
Walks on water if the sea is calm
Walks on water in an indoor swimming pool
Lifts buildings and walks under them
```

2. Search GLOSSARY.TXT for the phrase "walks on water".

```
$ SEARCH GLOSSARY.TXT "walks on water"
Walks on water
Walks on water if the sea is calm
Walks on water in an indoor swimming pool
```

3. Repeat the search from number 2 and save the output in a file called FOUND.LIS.

```
$ SEARCH/OUT=FOUND.LIS GLOSSARY.TXT "walks on water"
$ TYPE FOUND.LIS
Walks on water
Walks on water if the sea is calm
Walks on water in an indoor swimming pool
```

4. Edit GLOSSARY.TXT, delete the job titles DATA PROCESSING MANAGER and SENIOR PROGRAMMER and save a new version of the file. Compare these two versions of GLOSSARY.TXT with the standard DIFFERENCES command.

```
$ DIFFERENCES GLOSSARY.TXT
************
File SYS$UTIL:[SHARICK]GLOSSARY.TXT;2
1   Leaps tall buildings in a single bound
******
File SYS$UTIL:[SHARICK]GLOSSARY.TXT;1
    1    DATA PROCESSING MANAGER
    2    Leaps tall buildings in a single bound
************
************
File SYS$UTIL:[SHARICK]GLOSSARY.TXT;2
   35   Runs into buildings
******
File SYS$UTIL:[SHARICK]GLOSSARY.TXT;1
   36   SENIOR PROGRAMMER
   37   Runs into buildings
************

Number of difference sections found: 2
Number of difference records found: 2
```

```
DIFFERENCES /IGNORE=()/MERGED=1-
    SYS$UTIL:[SHARICK]GLOSSARY.TXT;2-
    SYS$UTIL:[SHARICK]GLOSSARY.TXT;1
```

5. Compare these two versions of GLOSSARY.TXT with a /PARALLEL display.

```
$ DIFFERENCES/PARALLEL GLOSSARY.TXT
-----------------------------------------------------------------------------
File SYS$UTIL:[MIS]GLOSSARY.TXT;2        | File SYS$UTIL:[MIS]GLOSSARY.TXT;1
------------------- 1 -----------------------------------------  1 ------------
                                         | DATA PROCESSING MANAGER
------------------- 35 -----------------------------------------  36 -----------
                                         | SENIOR PROGRAMMER
-----------------------------------------------------------------------------

Number of difference sections found: 2
Number of difference records found: 2

DIFFERENCES /IGNORE=()/PARALLEL-
    SYS$UTIL:[MIS]GLOSSARY.TXT;2-
    SYS$UTIL:[MISGLOSSARY.TXT;1
```

6. Repeat number 5 and save the output of the DIFFERENCES comparison in a file called CHANGES.DIF.

Add the qualifier /OUT=CHANGES to the previous DIFFERENCES command. DIF-FERENCES provides a file type default of .DIF if none is given.

```
$ DIFF/PARALLEL/OUT=CHANGES GLOSSARY.TXT
$ TYPE CHANGES.DIF
-----------------------------------------------------------------------------
File SYS$UTIL:[MIS]GLOSSARY.TXT;3        | File SYS$UTIL:[MIS]GLOSSARY.TXT;2
------------------- 1 -----------------------------------------  1 -----------
                                         | DATA PROCESSING MANAGER
------------------- 35 -----------------------------------------  36 ----------
                                         | SENIOR PROGRAMMER
-----------------------------------------------------------------------------

Number of difference sections found: 2
Number of difference records found: 2

DIFFERENCES /IGNORE=()/OUTPUT=SYS$UTIL:[SHARICK]CHANGES.DIF;2/PARALLEL-
    SYS$UTIL:[MIS]GLOSSARY.TXT;2-
    SYS$UTIL:[MIS]GLOSSARY.TXT;1
```

SORT and MERGE Exercises

1. Create a sort practice file with the editor that contains the first and last names and the ages of seven people in a file called FRIENDS.DAT in the format shown.

Field	Position	Size
First Name	1	10
Last Name	11	10
Age	22	2

```
$ EDIT/TPU FRIENDS.DAT
[End of file]
gina       boice        31
linda      miller       36
kata       mccarville 34
steve      kibby        33
tony       carrato      40
stan       yellott      36
dave       johnson      51
7 lines written to file SYS$UTIL:[MIS]FRIENDS.DAT;1
```

2. Sort the FRIENDS.DAT file by last name using LASTNAME1.DAT as the output file. Type out the file to make sure the sort worked. If it did not, check the column positions in the data file and on the sort key, correct any errors and sort the file again.

```
$ SORT/KEY=(SIZ:10,POS:11) FRIENDS.DAT LASTNAME1.DAT
$ TYPE LASTNAME1.DAT
gina       boice        31
tony       carrato      40
dave       johnson      51
steve      kibby        33
kata       mccarville 34
linda      miller       36
stan       yellott      36
```

3. Sort the file by age using AGE.DAT as the output file. Type out the file to verify the sort worked. Again, if it did not work, check that the age value appears in the correct column and that you use the same column position in the sort key.

```
$ SORT/KEY=(SIZ:2,POS:22) FRIENDS.DAT AGE.DAT
$ TYPE AGE.DAT
gina       boice        31
steve      kibby        33
kata       mccarville 34
linda      miller       36
stan       yellott      36
tony       carrato      40
dave       johnson      46
```

4. Create a second file called NEIGHBORS.DAT that contains five records using the same format as the FRIENDS.DAT file.

```
$ EDIT/TPU NEIGHBORS.DAT
[End of file]
sarah      larimer    10
christy    smith       6
```

```
amanda    smith      9
kathy     larimer   35
phil      smith     48
5 lines written to SYS$UTIL:[MIS]NEIGHBORS.DAT;1
```

5. Sort NEIGHBORS.DAT by last name and store the output in LASTNAME2.DAT.

```
$ SORT/KEY=(POS:11,SIZE:10) NEIGHBORS.DAT LASTNAME2.DAT
$ TYPE LASTNAME2.DAT
kathy     larimer   35
sarah     larimer   10
amanda    smith      9
christy   smith      6
phil      smith     48
```

6. MERGE the two last name files into a file called LASTNAME.DAT. Type out the file to verify data from both input files are there and in the correct sorted order. You should have three LASTNAME files, LASTNAME1.DAT, LASTNAME2.DAT, and LASTNAME.DAT. The first one has sorted records from FRIENDS.DAT, the second contains records from NEIGHBORS.DAT and the third is a merged list of both files.

```
$ MERGE/KEY=(POS:11,SIZE:10) LASTNAME1.DAT, LASTNAME2.DAT  LASTNAME.DAT
$ TYPE LASTNAME.DAT
gina      boice      31
tony      carrato    40
dave      johnson    51
steve     kibby      33
kathy     larimer    35
sarah     larimer    10
kata      mccarville 34
linda     miller     36
christy   smith       6
amanda    smith       9
phil      smith      48
stan      yellott    36
```

7. Sort the merged output file by age and store the results in the output file AGE.DAT.

```
$ SORT/KEY=(POS:22,SIZE:2) LASTNAME.DAT AGE.DAT
$ TYPE AGE.DAT
christy   smith       6
amanda    smith       9
sarah     larimer    10
gina      boice      31
steve     kibby      33
kata      mccarville 34
kathy     larimer    35
linda     miller     36
stan      yellott    36
tony      carrato    40
phil      smith      48
dave      johnson    51
```

Personalizing Your Environment

INTRODUCTION

Chapter 16 shows you how to personalize your VMS environment with SET commands, custom key definitions, command abbreviations and a shorthand notation for file specifications. You can change your process name, the system prompt, terminal characteristics, the current directory, and many other things with the SET command. DEFINE/KEY, SHOW KEY, and DELETE/KEY allow you to create, examine, and delete custom key definitions. DCL symbols create synonyms for often used commands and applications, and logical names shorten frequently used file names, directories, and device names.

You can tailor your environment at the system prompt for the current session. When you get things right, you can save your custom definitions in a login file. Then each time you log in, the system performs the commands in your login file and the definitions become a permanent part of your environment. You will find a brief introduction to command procedures and a review of the steps required to create, test, and use a login file at the end of this chapter.

TAILORING WITH SET COMMANDS

In Chapter 6, Looking at the System, we discussed the SHOW command and mentioned that for nearly every SHOW command there is a corresponding SET command. There are exceptions — although you can SHOW the number of users logged in or the device name for a particular disk, you cannot SET them. You have already seen several of the SET commands in Figure 16-1 in earlier chapters — they are included for review. You may wish to use three other SET options to tailor your environment: SET BROADCAST, SET CONTROL, and SET PROCESS/NAME.

```
$ SET BROADCAST         Enable/disable unsolicited messages
$ SET CONTROL           Enable/disable CTRL/Y and CTRL/T
$ SET DEFAULT           Change location
$ SET ENTRY             Change queue entry characteristics
$ SET FILE              Change file characteristics
$ SET PASSWORD          Change password
$ SET PROCESS/NAME      Change process name
$ SET PROMPT            Change system prompt
$ SET PROTECTION        Change file or default protection
$ SET TERMINAL          Change terminal characteristics
```

Figure 16-1. SET Commands

Controlling Message Delivery

SET BROADCAST enables or disables delivery of messages that are issued by MAIL, PHONE, operators, and the operating system. When you log in, the system enables message delivery for all classes of messages. You can screen out all messages with SET TERMINAL/NOBROADCAST, or use various options with the SET BROADCAST command to selectively enable and disable message delivery by message class. To turn message delivery back on, use SET TERMINAL/BROADCAST. The command format and message types are shown in Figure 16-2. If there is more than one type of message to enable or disable, string them together with commas and enclose the list in parentheses.

```
$ SET BROADCAST=(type[,...])    Command Format

  Message Type                  Message Purpose
  ALL                           All message classes enabled
  [NO]DCL                       CTRL/T and SPAWN/NOTIFY messages
  [NO]GENERAL                   All normal REPLY messages
  [NO]MAIL                      Notification of mail
  NONE                          All message classes disabled
  [NO]PHONE                     Messages from the Phone utility
  [NO]QUEUE                     Messages from by batch and print jobs
  [NO]SHUTDOWN                  Messages issued from REPLY/SHUTDOWN
  [NO]URGENT                    Messages issued from REPLY/URGENT
```

Figure 16-2. Broadcast Message Types

Never disable shutdown and urgent messages, because they are reserved for special situations. You want to know if the system will be shut down in five minutes so you can save your work. Figure 16-3 shows an example of disabling all messages, enabling all messages, and disabling PHONE and new MAIL messages.

```
$ SET BROADCAST= NONE                    Disable all messages
$ SET BROADCAST= ALL                     Enable all messages
$ SET BROADCAST=(ALL,NOMAIL,NOPHONE)     No MAIL or PHONE messages
```

Figure 16-3. SET BROADCAST Figure

Using CTRL/Y and CTRL/T

There are two control characters that you can enable or disable with SET CONTROL (Fig. 16-4). CTRL/Y aborts commands, utilities, command procedures and applications (unless specifically disabled within the command procedure or application), and should be left enabled at all times. Otherwise you cannot stop an operation that you start incorrectly. CTRL/T monitors CPU and other resource usage during the current session. It is normally enabled and there is no reason to disable it.

```
$ SET CONTROL=(Y,T)                      Enable both functions
$ SET NOCONTROL=(Y,T)                    Disable both functions
```

Figure 16-4. SET CONTROL Command

Changing Your Process Name

When you use SHOW PROCESS, you will see that your process name is normally the same as your username — process name is occasionally changed by application packages to indicate users active in that application. You can use SET PROCESS/NAME to change your process name as shown in Figure 16-5. Some sites allow users to change process name and at other sites it is strongly discouraged. The string you provide can be a maximum of 15 characters. If the string you choose contains blanks, enclose it in double quotes. You an see the result of this command by following it with either SHOW PROCESS or SHOW USERS/FULL, both of which display your process name.

```
$ SET PROCESS/NAME = string              Command Format

$ SET PROCESS/NAME = big-brother         Select one word
$ SET PROCESS/NAME = "rock and roll"     Select a phrase
```

Figure 16-5. SET PROCESS/NAME Command

DEFINING CUSTOM KEYS

If you use MAIL, the editor, DIRECTORY, and SET DEFAULT, and run the same applications on a daily basis, it is convenient to have each command activated by a key press. You use DEFINE/KEY to map commands to a single key or combination keystroke on the keyboard, SHOW KEY to examine one or all key definitions and DELETE/KEY to remove one or all key definitions. Most keys on the standard DEC keyboard are candidates for custom definitions, including the grey editing keys, numeric keypad keys, some of the function keys and many CTRL/typing key combinations.

Defining a Key

The DEFINE/KEY command and some examples are shown in Figure 16-6. You must provide a legal key name and specify the definition as a string. If the string contains more than one word, enclose it in double quotes. Once the definition is entered, the next time you press the key, that string is automatically inserted on the command line. The function of the /TERMINATE qualifier is explained below under the heading of DEFINE/KEY qualifiers.

The VMS documentation indicates that you have to enable numeric keypad keys and function keys F7-F14 before you can use the definitions. If you have trouble defining numeric keypad keys, enter the command SET TERMINAL/ APPLICATION, issue the define commands again, and see if the problem goes away. Likewise, the documentation indicates you must enable function keys with CTRL/V before you can define them.

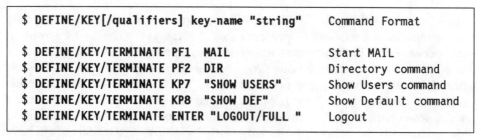

```
$ DEFINE/KEY[/qualifiers] key-name "string"        Command Format

$ DEFINE/KEY/TERMINATE PF1  MAIL                   Start MAIL
$ DEFINE/KEY/TERMINATE PF2  DIR                    Directory command
$ DEFINE/KEY/TERMINATE KP7  "SHOW USERS"           Show Users command
$ DEFINE/KEY/TERMINATE KP8  "SHOW DEF"             Show Default command
$ DEFINE/KEY/TERMINATE ENTER "LOGOUT/FULL "        Logout
```

Figure 16-6. DEFINE/KEY Examples

Key Names and Key Labels

The keys that you can define include function keys F7-F20, numeric keypad keys, and the grey editing keypad keys (with the exception of the UP and DOWN arrow keys). Key names are normally the same as the key labels on the keyboard. Figure 16-7 contains a list of most key names — mouse buttons have been omitted.

Key name	Key Label	Key name	Key Label
PF1	PF1	E1	Find
PF2	PF2	E2	Insert Here
PF3	PF3	E3	Remove
PF4	PF4	E4	Select
KP0-KP9	0-9	E5	Prev Screen
PERIOD	.	E6	Next Screen
COMMA	,	HELP	Help
MINUS	-	DO	Do
ENTER	Enter	F7-F20	F7-F20
LEFT	←		
RIGHT	→		

Figure 16-7. Key Names and Key Labels

DEFINE/KEY Qualifiers

Of the five qualifiers listed in Figure 16-8, /TERMINATE is the most important. You can create key definitions in two ways — the definition either terminates, which sends a RETURN after the key press, or the definition does not, in which case you are responsible for entering the RETURN. Simple definitions should always terminate. Sophisticated users may put part of a command on one key (*e.g.,* SHOW) and the rest of the command on another key (*e.g.,* DEFAULT or USERS), so that the first command does not terminate, but the second one does.

/TERMINATE	Terminate string with RETURN
/ECHO	Echo string on the command line
/ERASE	Erase command line before string is inserted
/LOG	Issue message that definition has been made
/NOLOG	Disable confirmation message

Figure 16-8. DEFINE/KEY Qualifiers

DEFINE/KEY normally sends a log message indicating that you have defined a key. If you are creating key definitions in a login file, you may want to disable the log messages with the /NOLOG qualifier. You can use several more elaborate qualifiers to make key definitions active only under certain conditions by associating a "state" with the definition. Novice users rarely need this level of sophistication. Use HELP DEFINE/KEY for more information on using these advanced features.

Examining Key Definitions

SHOW KEY accepts either a key name or the /ALL qualifier and displays one or all of the definitions currently mapped to the keyboard (Fig. 16-9). Remember that KEY is an option to the SHOW command and is separated from the command by a blank, in contrast to a qualifier separated by a slash. If you define a key to be the SHOW KEY command, you won't have to remember the difference.

```
$ SHOW KEY [key-name]          Command Format

$ SHOW KEY PF1                 Display PF1 definition
$ SHOW KEY/ALL                 Display all definitions
```

Figure 16-9. SHOW KEY Command

Deleting Key Definitions

DELETE/KEY accepts either a key name or the /ALL qualifier and removes a definition from one or all keys (Fig. 16-10). DEFINE and DELETE both accept /KEY as a qualifier.

```
$ DELETE/KEY  [key-name]       Command Format

$ DELETE/KEY PF1               Delete PF1 definition
$ DELETE/KEY/ALL               Delete all definitions
```

Figure 16-10. DELETE/KEY Command

DEFINING AND USING SYMBOLS

As you become familiar with VMS, you will find yourself using the same commands over and over again. The thought will cross your mind that command abbreviations are just the thing you need to keep typing to a minimum. If you are using a directory tree to manage files, typing in a full directory specification or relative path name with SET DEFAULT each time you change locations gets rather tedious.

VMS allows you to create command synonym by defining a symbol that represents a command. Symbols defined at the system prompt remain active until you redefine them, delete, them, or log off. Symbol names are composed of alphabetic and numeric characters, the dollar sign ($) and the underscore (_). A symbol can represent either a character string or numeric value and the value can be a maximum of 255 characters long. A symbol name can be entered in upper, lower, or mixed case because it is always converted to uppercase by the command interpreter.

Suppose you always use PRINT with the /NOTIFY qualifier. You might shorten the command by defining a symbol PN to represent the string PRINT/NOTIFY. Once defined, you type PN each time you want to use the PRINT/NOTIFY command. If the first word on the command line is not a valid command, the command interpreter assumes it must be a symbol. The interpreter searches your symbol table for the PN symbol and substitutes the replacement string PRINT/NOTIFY. The result is the same as if you had typed the whole command.

We can expand on this idea by creating two more symbols, one for EVE and one for MAIL. EVE is an abbreviation for the EDIT/TPU command and MAIL redefines the MAIL command to start your preferred editor each time you send, reply, or answer a message. Now there are three symbols defined for your process: PN, EVE, and MAIL (Fig. 16-11).

```
$ PN = "PRINT/NOTIFY"                      Define a PN command
$ PN := PRINT/NOTIFY

$ EVE = "EDIT/TPU"                         Define an EVE command
$ EVE := EDIT/TPU

$ MAIL = "MAIL/EDIT=(SEND,REPLY,ANSWER)"   Define a MAIL command
$ MAIL := MAIL/EDIT=(SENT,REPLY,ANSWER)
```

Figure 16-11. Symbol Definitions

Figure 16-11 illustrates two legal ways to define a symbol that represents a string value. In the first case, you use an equal sign (=) and the replacement text appears in double quotes on the right of the equal sign. In the second case, you use the colon-equal (:=) operator and omit the double quotes around the replacement text. The second form is more popular because it is easier to type.

However, there is one significant difference between these two forms of symbol definition — the first preserves the case of the text appearing inside the double quotes and the second always converts the replacement text to uppercase. If you want the case of the string value to be preserved, use the first form with the equal sign and double quotes. Use the second form to define a symbol that is a VMS command, when the value does not contain quotes, and whenever the case of the replacement string is not important.

In addition to creating command synonyms and defining a preferred mode of execution for VMS commands, symbols also facilitate moving around in a tree structure (Fig. 16-12). The first symbol, HOME, combines the device and directory specification SYS$LOGIN with SET DEFAULT and moves you to your home disk and directory. The second definition is the symbol UP, which moves you up one level from your current directory. SOURCE, the third symbol, moves you down one level from your current location to a directory called SOURCE and MILLER moves to a directory of the same name under ADMIN. The last symbol, CALC, starts a program called CCALC that is stored in a directory identified by the logical name UTILITIES.

```
$ HOME     := SET DEFAULT SYS$LOGIN         Move to home directory

$ UP       := SET DEFAULT [-]               Move up one level
$ SOURCE   := SET DEFAULT [.SOURCE]         Move down to SOURCE
$ MILLER   := SET DEFAULT [ADMIN.MILLER]    Move to MILLER directory

$ CALC     := RUN UTILITIES:CCALC           Run CCALC program
```

Figure 16-12. More Symbol Definitions

A few words of caution are in order here. The [.SOURCE] path name used with SET DEFAULT is a relative directory specification that moves you down one level from the current directory. If you are not already in SOURCE's parent directory, this command will not work. Why? Because there may not be a SOURCE directory immediately below your current location. When you create symbols that reference files or directories, you should use absolute specifications to avoid this problem. The CALC symbol does use an absolute file specification and will execute the program correctly, regardless of your current location.

Local and Global Symbols

You can define two types of symbols, local symbols and global symbols. Each user process has a two symbol tables — a local symbol table and a global symbol table — in which the definitions are stored. You create a local symbol at the system prompt with a single equal sign. The definitions in Figures 16-11 and 16-12 create local symbols. You create global symbols at the system prompt and in your login file and other command procedures by using a double equal sign (==) in the symbol definition. A global symbol is available at the system prompt and from within any command procedure until it is redefined, deleted, or you log off.

If you are working interactively at the system prompt, there is no practical difference between local and global symbols. If, however, you are working with command procedures, it is very important for you to understand the difference.

Each time you execute a command procedure, the system creates a symbol table where symbols local to that procedure are stored.

When the command procedure exits, the local symbol table is deleted. Symbols defined with a single equal sign inside a command procedure are not available to any outer command procedure or at the system prompt because they are deleted when the procedure that defines them exits. If you want your symbol definitions to remain until you log off, you must define them as global symbols in your login file or other command procedure.

When the command interpreter encounters a symbol reference, it searches the local symbol table first and the global symbol table second — this search order means that local definitions always take precedence over global definitions. This search order is a great convenience when you do not like the definitions created by the system manager or when global definitions conflict with normal VMS command usage. When conflicts occur, you can define a local symbol with the same name as a global symbol and, because of the search order, your definition is always used first.

Examining Symbol Definitions

SHOW SYMBOL accepts an optional symbol-name parameter and displays either local or global symbol definitions (Fig. 16-13). To examine all definitions in either category use the /ALL qualifier. You may encounter two definitions for the same symbol, one local and one global — the definitions may be the same or they may be different. Because of the symbol search order, local definitions always have precedence over global definitions.

At each site, the system manager defines a number of global symbols in the systemwide login file. When each user logs in, these definitions are processed and placed in that user's global symbol table. This technique is a convenient way to make the same symbols available to all users on the system. You can examine the predefined symbols on your system with SHOW SYMBOL/GLOBAL/ALL.

```
$ SHOW SYMBOL [symbol-name]        Command Format
      /ALL                         Display all definitions
      /GLOBAL                      Display global definition

$ SHOW SYMBOL EVE                  Display local EVE definition
$ SHOW SYMBOL/ALL                  Display all local symbols

$ SHOW SYMBOL/GLOBAL SD            Display global SD definition
$ SHOW SYMBOL/GLOBAL/ALL           Display all global symbols
```

Figure 16-13. SHOW SYMBOL Command

Deleting Symbols

DELETE/SYMBOL accepts an optional symbol-name parameter and deletes either a local or global symbol (Fig. 16-14). To remove a local definition, use DELETE/SYMBOL with the symbol you want to delete; to remove a global symbol, use DELETE/SYMBOL/GLOBAL with the appropriate symbol name. To delete all local or global symbols, use the /ALL qualifier. DELETE/SYMBOL only accepts one symbol name as a parameter. If there are many symbols to delete, issue the command once for each symbol.

```
$ DELETE/SYMBOL[ [symbol-name]         Command Format
        /ALL                           Delete all definitions
        /GLOBAL                        Delete global definition

$ DELETE/SYMBOL/ALL                    Delete all local symbols
$ DELETE/SYMBOL        SD              Delete local SD symbol

$ DELETE/SYMBOL/GLOBAL/ALL             Delete all global symbols
$ DELETE/SYMBOL/GLOBAL DEL             Delete global DEL symbol
```

Figure 16-14. DELETE/SYMBOL Command

Occasionally, global symbol definitions get in the way of using normal VMS commands. One good example of this is when a system manager defines DELETE to be the string DELETE/CONFIRM. When you use DELETE to remove a print job, you get a warning message because DELETE/ENTRY does not accept the /CONFIRM qualifier. When you remove the global DEL symbol, the problem goes away.

DEFINING AND USING LOGICAL NAMES

Logical names are a shorthand technique for device, directory, and file references. Logical names should not be confused with symbols which are used almost exclusively for command synonyms. A logical name takes the place of a device, directory, or file specification and provides both a shorthand form of a file specification and device independence for the various utilities and commands.

Logical names have a wide variety of uses. In Chapter 5, The User Environment, we discussed the SYS$INPUT, SYS$OUTPUT, and SYS$ERROR logical names VMS defines for your process. These reserved logicals are used as standard input, output, and error devices for utilities and commands. Logical names also identify all major components of the operating system (*e.g.*, HELP libraries, language dependent-object libraries, examples, system messages and so on).

You can use logical names to shorten file specifications, simplify complex directory structures, implement group-based names for software development projects, and to point to data files that vary in name and location from run to run. You create logical names with the DEFINE command, examine them with SHOW TRANSLATION or SHOW LOGICAL, and delete them with DEASSIGN.

Defining Logical Names

You can always define logical names for your process and your job (which includes all processes in your tree). You may be able to define logicals for a UIC group or systemwide, if you have the necessary privileges. You can collect a set of related logical names in a logical name table on a process or job basis, or into a group or system table if you have adequate privileges.

The DEFINE command requires two parameters — the logical name being defined and the equivalence string assigned to the logical name. The equivalence string can be a device, directory, file, or any form of a file specification. The equivalence string can also be a character string or another logical name. In the examples in Figure 16-15, the logical name "ADMIN" represents a directory and the logical name "DATA" represents a file. Each definition uses an absolute file specification to avoid reference problems.

When you define a logical name to represent a directory specification, you can use it with any VMS command that accepts a directory specification. In Figure 16-15, ADMIN is the target directory for SET DEFAULT and the DIRECTORY command. In the first case you establish a new default directory and in the second, you list the files in the ADMIN directory.

```
$ DEFINE logical-name equivalence-string      Command Format

$ DEFINE ADMIN   USERA:[MIS.ADMIN]            Define a location
$ DEFINE DATA    USERB:[PO]WEEKLY.DAT         Define a data file

$ SET DEFAULT ADMIN                           Use ADMIN logical name
$ DIR ADMIN                                   as a directory

$ DIR DATA                                    Use DATA logical name
$ TYPE DATA                                   as a file
```

Figure 16-15. DEFINE Command

When you define a logical name to represent a file specification, you can use it with any VMS command that accepts a file specification. You can use the logical name DATA with DIRECTORY to look up the file USERB:[PO]WEEKLY.DAT and with TYPE to display the file on your terminal. You can also use DATA with file manipulation commands (*e.g.*, COPY DATA), with utilities (*e.g.*, SEARCH DATA), or as a file name when you start the editor (*e.g.*, EDIT/TPU DATA).

Logical Name Categories

VMS understands four categories of logical names: process, job, group, and system. Process logical names are accessible to all commands and programs you activate at the system prompt. We have already discussed the standard SYS$ logicals defined for each process and the way they are used by utilities and commands to control input, output, and error messages (See Chapter 5, The User Environment). Job logical names are available to your main process and any child processes (*i.e.*, spawned processes) created during your interactive session. The standard VMS process and job logical names are listed in Figure 16-16.

```
   Process Logical Names      Description
   ---------------------------------------------------------------
   SYS$DISK                   The disk you are on
   SYS$INPUT                  The default input device
   SYS$OUTPUT                 The default output device
   SYS$ERROR                  The device where errors are posted
   SYS$COMMAND                Identifies your terminal as the
                              source of VMS commands
   Job Logical Names
   ---------------------------------------------------------------
   SYS$LOGIN_DEVICE           Your home disk
   SYS$LOGIN                  Your home disk and directory
```

Figure 16-16. Process and Job Logical Names

Group logical names are defined on a UIC basis. They are made available at login to each member of a specific UIC group and are popular for development projects and heavily used applications. The GRPNAM privilege is required to define and delete group logical names.

System logical names are available to all users and can only be created by someone with system privileges. The system manager defines many system logicals to locate and identify layered products and other applications. VMS also uses logical names to locate nearly all parts of the operating system — a list of typical operating system logical names can be found in the exercises at the end of this chapter.

DEFINE Qualifiers

There are four qualifiers used to create the four categories of logical names: /PROCESS, /JOB, /GROUP, and /SYSTEM. DEFINE creates a process logical name by default, so no qualifier is required. For anything other than a process logical name, you must use the appropriate qualifier (Fig. 16-17).

```
/PROCESS        Place definition in the process table
/GROUP          Place definition to the group table
                (requires GRPNAM priv)
/JOB            Place definition to the job table
/SYSTEM         Place definition to the system table
                (requires SYSNAM priv)
/USER_MODE      This definition is good only for the next
                executable command or program
/LOG            Confirm assignment with message
/NOLOG          Suppress confirmation message
```

Figure 16-17. DEFINE Qualifiers

/LOG Qualifier

DEFINE sends a message to the current output device indicating that a logical name has been defined or redefined. While these messages may be useful for testing, they can be a real bother when you have several definitions in your login file or in a frequently used command procedure. /NOLOG suppresses these messages.

/USER_MODE Qualifier

/USER_MODE creates a logical name definition that is active only until the next executable statement completes. While at first glance such a feature seems unnecessary, there are circumstances where it is useful. Many VMS commands have an /OUTPUT qualifier that redirects SYS$OUTPUT for a single use of the command. When /OUTPUT is not available, DEFINE/USER_MODE accomplishes the same task.

For example, SHOW SYMBOL always displays the results of a symbol definition on the terminal — there is no /OUTPUT qualifier available. The same is true for the SHOW PROTECTION command. In Figure 16-18 you see how the /USER_MODE qualifier captures the output of each command in a disk file. Although these examples illustrate the use of this qualifier, they are a bit artificial. /OUTPUT is available on so many commands that you seldom need to redirect output this way. You will find more uses for this qualifier in a command procedure and when you run programs than in normal interactive mode.

```
$ DEFINE/USER_MODE SYS$OUTPUT SYMBOLS.LIS      Redirect output
$ SHOW SYMBOL/GLOBAL/ALL                       Output in SYMBOLS.LIS
$ TYPE SYMBOLS.LIS                             Examine output file

$ DEFINE/USER_MODE SYS$OUTPUT PURGE.LOG        Redirect output
$ PURGE/LOG                                    Messages in PURGE.LOG
$ TYPE PURGE.LOG                               Examine output file
```

Figure 16-18. DEFINE/USER_MODE Examples

Examining Logical Names

You can use two commands to display the equivalence string for a logical name: SHOW LOGICAL and SHOW TRANSLATION. The first command is preferred, as it is much more sophisticated. SHOW LOGICAL optionally accepts a logical name parameter, which can be either a logical name or a partial name with a wildcard. If you do not provide a parameter, all process, job, group, and system defined logical names are displayed, usually in multiple screens. SHOW TRANSLATION requires a logical name parameter and does not accept wildcards.

In Figure 16-19, SHOW LOGICAL and SHOW TRANSLATION display the translation of the ADMIN logical name defined in Figure 16-15. Because ADMIN has only one equivalence string, output from these commands is the same. The third command uses a wildcard to look up all logical names that start with the string "manman" followed by anything. There are no matching definitions in the process, job or group tables, but there are three definitions that match in the system logical name table.

Look carefully at the output from the last command in Figure 16-15. You see a set of four long names enclosed in parentheses. These are the names VMS uses to identify each logical name table in which the various categories of names are stored. When you examine a logical name, you can tell what kind of logical name it is by the name of the table included with the translation.

SHOW LOGICAL performs an iterative translation on the logical name and SHOW TRANSLATION displays only the first definition. Why is this important? In many cases, there is more than one translation associated with the same logical name. This happens when a logical name is defined with an equivalence string that is another logical name.

```
$ SHOW LOGICAL [logical-name]          Command Format
$ SHOW TRANSLATION logical-name        Command Format

$ SHOW LOGICAL ADMIN
  "ADMIN" = "USERA:[MIS.ADMIN]"    (LNM$PROCESS_TABLE)
$ SHOW TRANSLATION ADMIN
  "ADMIN" = "USERA:[MIS.ADMIN]"    (LNM$PROCESS_TABLE)

$ SHOW LOG MANMAN*                      Using a wildcard
  (LNM$PROCESS_TABLE)                  No process definitions
  (LNM$JOB_8147A6E0)                   No job definitions
  (LNM$GROUP_000010)                   No group definitions
  (LNM$SYSTEM_TABLE)                   Three manman definitions
                                       in the system table

  "MANMAN1" = "$1$DUA20:"
  "MANMAN2" = "$1$DUA30:"
  "MANMAN3" = "$1$DUA40:"
```

Figure 16-19. Examining Logical Names

For example, inside an application, an input file might be referred to as INPUT. Before you start the program, you define INPUT as a logical name that points to a generic input file PO_JOURNAL, which in turn is assigned to the file of the day or week (Fig. 16-20). If you use SHOW TRANSLATION for the name INPUT, you only see the equivalence string PO_JOURNAL. SHOW LOGICAL displays all translations and uniquely identifies the file as PRODB:[PO]DAILY.DAT.

```
$ DEFINE INPUT  PO_JOURNAL
$ DEFINE PO_JOURNAL  PRODB:[PO]DAILY233.DAT

$ SHOW TRANSLATION INPUT
   "INPUT" = "PO_JOURNAL"  (LNM$PROCESS_TABLE)

$ SHOW LOGICAL INPUT
   "INPUT" = "PO_JOURNAL"  (LNM$PROCESS_TABLE)
1  "PO_JOURNAL" = "PRODB:[PO]DAILY.DAT"  (LNM$PROCESS_TABLE)
```

Figure 16-20. SHOW LOGICAL and SHOW TRANSLATION

Logical Name Tables

As mentioned earlier, VMS provides a table for each category of logical name in which the logical names and their equivalence strings are stored. SHOW LOGICAL accepts the four qualifiers, /PROCESS, /JOB, /GROUP, /SYSTEM, and responds with the logical name and equivalence string stored in the requested table (Fig. 16-21). You can use /ALL to list all names and /FULL to see the complete definition, in combination with any of the other qualifiers.

/PROCESS	Process definition
/JOB	Job definition
/GROUP	Group definition
/SYSTEM	System definition
/ALL	All definitions
/FULL	Complete definition

Figure 16-21. SHOW LOGICAL Qualifiers

The process and job tables are user specific. When a group table is defined, it is associated with a particular UIC group and a single copy of the table is shared by all members of that UIC group. If a group table exists, it is linked into each user process when a member of the group logs in. All users share the systemwide logical name table which contains logical names defined by the operating system, system manager, layered products, and other application packages.

Figure 16-22 displays the process level logical names defined for the current session. Notice the name LNM$PROCESS_TABLE in the display, which is the system name for the process logical name table. Each logical name appears to the left of the equal sign and the equivalence string to the right of the equal sign.

```
$ SHOW LOGICAL/PROCESS/ALL
 (LNM$PROCESS_TABLE)

 "SYS$COMMAND" = "_SYBIL$VTA577:"
 "SYS$DISK" = "USERD:"
 "SYS$ERROR" = "_SYBIL$VTA577:"
 "SYS$INPUT" = "_SYBIL$VTA577:"
 "SYS$OUTPUT" [super] = "_SYBIL$VTA577:"
 "SYS$OUTPUT" [exec] = "_SYBIL$VTA577:"
 "TT" = "VTA577:"
```

Figure 16-22. SHOW LOGICAL Display

Logical Name Translation

Logical name tables are important when resolving a logical name definition. In normal circumstances, SHOW LOGICAL and SHOW TRANSLATION search the process, job, group, and system tables in that order. This allows you to redefine job, group, or system logical names by placing your own definition in the process table. Because the first match is returned and the process table is searched first (unless the standard search order has been redefined), the process definition takes precedence over definitions in other tables.

Deleting Logical Names

DEASSIGN requires one parameter which is the logical name to be deleted (Fig. 16-23). DEASSIGN alone removes a process level logical name. Use the /JOB qualifier to remove a job logical name. Although /GROUP and /SYSTEM qualifiers are included in this figure, you probably do not have the privileges required to define or remove either category of logical names. To remove all definitions from any of the tables, add /ALL to the command.

```
$ DEASSIGN logical-name        Command Format

   /USER_MODE                  Remove user mode definition
   /PROCESS                    Remove process table definition
   /GROUP                      Remove group table definition
   /SYSTEM                     Remove system table definition
   /ALL                        Remove all definitions
```

Figure 16-23. DEASSIGN Command

There can be multiple definitions of the same logical name. To find out how a logical name is defined, use SHOW LOGICAL to display the equivalent string and table in which the definition is stored. If there are multiple definitions, identify the logical name you want to delete and use DEASSIGN with qualifiers that match those in the display.

In Figure 16-24, the first three commands illustrate how you delete a process logical name called DIAL. You examine the definition, remove it, and check to see that it is gone. In the second set of commands, there are multiple definitions for ATC$FORMS — one in the process table and one in the system table. You might use the process definition for testing and the system definition for normal production mode. You remove the process definition with DEASSIGN. The second SHOW LOGICAL displays the remaining system definition for ATC$FORMS.

```
$ SHOW LOGICAL DIAL
"DIAL" [super] = SYS$LOGIN:DIAL.COM
$ DEASSIGN DIAL
$ SHOW LOGICAL DIAL
%SHOW-S-NOTRAN, no translation for logical name DIAL

$ SHOW LOG/FULL ATC$FORMS
"ATC$FORMS" [super] = "ATC$ROOT:[TEST.FORMS]" (LNM$PROCESS_TABLE)
"ATC$FORMS" [exec] = "ATC$ROOT:[FORMS]" (LNM$SYSTEM_TABLE)
$ DEASSIGN ATC$FORMS
$ SHOW LOG/FULL ATC$FORMS
"ATC$FORMS" [exec] = "ATC$ATCROOT:[FORMS]" (LNM$SYSTEM_TABLE)
```

Figure 16-24. Deleting a Logical Name

User-Defined Logical Name Tables

Users and programmers can create custom logical name tables by referencing a logical name table on the DEFINE, SHOW LOGICAL, and DEASSIGN commands using the /TABLE=table-name qualifier. Although a full discussion of custom tables is beyond this book, you use this qualifier with each of the four logical name commands to create and manipulate names in a specific table.

- CREATE/NAME_TABLE creates a new logical name table. When you create a process logical name table, the new table is catalogued in the master process logical name table called the LNM$PROCESS_DIRECTORY.

- DEFINE/TABLE=table-name places a definition in your table, instead of in a system-defined table.

- SHOW LOGICAL/TABLE=table-name displays one or all the definitions in the table.

- DEASSIGN/TABLE=table-name deletes a logical name from your table.

- DEASSIGN/TABLE=LNM$PROCESS_DIRECTORY table-name deletes the logical name table from the master process logical name table.

DO I USE A SYMBOL OR A LOGICAL NAME?

This is one of the most commonly asked questions by both new and experienced VMS users. In general, symbols create command synonyms and logical names represent device, directory, and file specifications. Symbol definitions may include a logical name, as when a logical name represents a file. When a symbol definition incorporates a logical name as part of the replacement text, the logical name functions as a device, directory, or file specification. Normally, the symbol invokes the command and the logical name in the definition functions as the target of the command action (*e.g.,* HOME :=SET DEFAULT SYS$LOGIN).

You cannot reverse the function of the symbols and logicals — a logical name does not start a command or utility and a symbol seldom represents a device, directory, or file specification without a command. This usage is determined, in part, by the way commands are recognized by the command interpreter.

The command interpreter expects the first item in a command line to be a command, a symbol, a reserved word, or an at sign (@). If the first item is not a command, the interpreter checks to see if it is a symbol. If so, it is either a symbol definition or a reference. If it is a definition, the command interpreter processes the definition and stores it in the appropriate symbol table. If it is a reference and the symbol is defined, the replacement text is substituted. Because the replacement text appears immediately following the system prompt, it must contain a valid command, or at least a valid command verb. If your input is not a command or a symbol, an error occurs.

A logical name cannot appear as the first item in the command line because it is not translated when it appears in this position — this restriction prevents a logical name from representing a command. A logical name can appear anywhere else — the system substitutes the equivalent text in any other location. Figure 16-25 suggests a use for both a symbol and logical name to support the same operation. In all cases, you use symbols to start VMS commands and utilities and logical names to identify files and directories.

```
Symbol Usage                      Logical Name Usage
-------------------------------------------------------------------
DEFINE/KEY Command                Not Applicable
DEFINE/KEY/TERM KP1 MAIL


DIRECTORY  Command                Target Directory Specification
DP ="DIR/OWN/PROT"                DEFINE WORK USERA:[MIS.WORK]
DP WORK


SET DEFAULT Command               Target Directory Specification
SDF = "SET DEFAULT"               DEFINE WORK USERA:[MIS.WORK]
SDF WORK


Start a program                   Program File Specification
PO = "RUN POTEST"                 DEFINE POTEST PROD1:[PO.TEST]PO.EXE
```

Figure 16-25. Symbol and Logical Name Usage

DEFINE/KEY has no use for logical names because no file specification is needed. The DIRECTORY example defines the symbol DP for DIR/OWN/PROT, and the logical name "work" as a directory location. SET DEFAULT is shortened to SDF and the same logical name "work" used as the target directory. The symbol PO starts a program pointed to by the logical name POTEST which is the full file specification of the program to run.

USING A LOGIN.COM FILE

We have reviewed several ways of customizing the VMS environment for your own requirements and needs. Once you are familiar with SET and DEFINE/KEY commands and with using symbols and logical names, you soon tire of creating the definitions each time you log in. If you place these same definitions in a LOGIN.COM file, they will be automatically processed each time you start a new interactive or batch session.

A login file is a text file that contains one or more VMS commands, has a file name of LOGIN, and a file type of .COM. When a file with the name LOGIN.COM appears in your home directory, it is automatically executed by VMS when you log in. Thus, if you define the symbols and logicals you use all the time in a login file, they are always part of your environment.

Creating a Login File

A login file is an example of a DCL command procedure. Each line in a command procedure begins with a $, which is the standard system prompt, and there is one VMS command per line. You can continue commands from one line to the next by placing a hyphen (-) as the last character on the command line and you can include comments by placing an exclamation point after the command. Any VMS command can appear in your login file, along with symbol and logical name definitions. The last line in every command procedure should be $ EXIT, which signals the end of the procedure.

There is one small catch to placing symbol definitions in a login file. If you use a single equal sign, the symbols are defined only for the duration of the command procedure and are deleted when the procedure terminates. To ensure that the definitions remain after the procedure exits, create global definitions with a double equal sign (==). Because the global symbol table remains part of your environment until you log off, the definitions created this way are available after the login file terminates.

A login file typically contains symbols for frequently used commands, commands to define keys, commands to activate applications and utilities, a command to purge files back to one or two versions and perhaps logical name definitions. The example LOGIN.COM file in Figure 16-26 performs several of these functions.

When you look at this example, you will notice that commands and symbols appear in both uppercase and lowercase. Because they are always translated to uppercase, you can use the form that you are most comfortable with. The only time case is preserved is when a string is enclosed in double quotes, as with the SET PROMPT command which selects a process name of "fire fighter."

```
$ IF F$MODE() .EQS. "BATCH" THEN EXIT          ! Exit if Batch Mode
$ SET TERM/DEVICE=VT300                        ! VT300 Terminal
$ !        Comment Line
$ home     :== SET DEFAULT SYS$LOGIN           ! Symbol Definitions
$ up       :== SET DEFAULT [-]                 ! for VMS commands
$ sd       :== SET DEFAULT
$ shd      :== SHOW DEFAULT
$ mail     :== MAIL/EDIT=(SEND,REPLY)
$ pg       :== PURGE/LOG
$ w80      :== SET TERM/WIDTH=80
$ w132     :== SET TERM/WIDTH=132
$ eve      :== EDIT/TPU
$ miller   :== SET DEFAULT [ADMIN.MILLER]
$ !
$ calc     :== RUN UTILITIES:CCALC             ! Symbol definitions
$ cookie   :== RUN UTILITIES:COOKIE            ! for programs
$ !
$ SET PROCESS/NAME = "fire fighter"            ! Set process name
$ COOKIE                                       ! Get today's fortune
$ EXIT                                         ! Terminate procedure
```

Figure 16-26. A Sample LOGIN.COM File

The first line in this login file is an executable statement that uses the lexical function F$MODE to interrogate the mode of the process (*i.e.*, interactive, batch, network) and exit if it is running in batch mode. Because you create most symbols to facilitate interactive use, you usually need the symbols only in interactive mode. When you develop more sophisticated command procedures that compile, link, and run development or production programs as batch jobs, you may need symbol definitions for the batch jobs to execute properly — in this situation, omit this line from your command procedure.

The next line defines your terminal as a VT300 device. The exclamation point (!) signals a comment and instructs the system to ignore the rest of the line. Next are symbol definitions for DCL commands and definitions for running the CALC and COOKIE programs stored in the UTILITIES directory. UTILITIES is a system logical name that points to an area where public domain programs are stored.

The next two lines execute VMS commands and the EXIT command tells the login procedure to terminate.

Executing LOGIN.COM

These definitions have been typed into a text file, but have not yet been processed by VMS. To activate the definitions, you must execute the command procedure using the at sign (@). When you enter @LOGIN at the system prompt, the command procedure is processed one line at a time (Fig. 16-27). You can execute any other command procedure by preceding it with an at sign. If your command procedure does not have a file type of .COM, you must enter the file type explicitly.

```
$ @LOGIN                        Execute the LOGIN.COM file
$
```

Figure 16-27. Executing a Login File

The system opens the LOGIN.COM file and performs each command. When $ EXIT is encountered, the file is closed and control returns to the system prompt. Assuming no errors occurred, the symbol definitions are now stored in the global symbol table. To use one of the new symbols, simply type it on the command line as shown in Figure 16-28.

```
$ MILLER                        Use the MILLER symbol
$ SHD                           Use the SHD synonym
  USERA:[ADMIN.MILLER]          Correct location
$ UP                            Use the UP symbol
$ SHD                           Look again
  USERA:[ADMIN]                 In the group area
```

Figure 16-28. Using Symbols Defined by LOGIN.COM

Testing LOGIN.COM

If errors occur when the login file is processed, you will see familiar %DCL messages on your screen. It can be difficult to associate an error message with the line that has the problem. Enter SET VERIFY at the system prompt and execute your login file again. SET VERIFY helps you locate the line causing the error because it echoes every line of the command procedure on your terminal and the error message appears right after the line with problems. SET VERIFY will also echo every line of any other command procedure you use. The only time SET VERIFY does not work is when the command procedure itself has turned verify off internally.

After verify is turned on, when you execute your login file each line is echoed on the terminal as it is executed, as shown in Figure 16-29. This makes it easy to see which lines are causing the errors and why. When you finish making corrections and are sure the procedure works, use SET NOVERIFY to turn off the echo feature. To protect your login file or other command procedure from prying eyes, make SET NOVERIFY the first statement in the procedure. Even though verify may be enabled at the system prompt, the SET NOVERIFY in the procedure disables command line echo until it is explicitly turned back on.

```
$ SET VERIFY                              Turn on command line echo

$ @LOGIN                                  Execute LOGIN.COM

$ IF F$MODE() .EQS. "BATCH" THEN EXIT     ! Exit if batch mode
$ SET TERM/DEVICE= VT300                  ! VT300 terminal
  ......
$ EXIT                                    ! End of login file

$ SET NOVERIFY                            Turn off command line echo
$ @LOGIN                                  Execute LOGIN.COM again
$                                         No line echo
```

Figure 16-29. SET VERIFY/NOVERIFY Command

SUMMARY

Command procedures can evolve into sophisticated operations. There are many DCL statements available for processing input and output to a terminal (INQUIRE or READ) or a disk file (OPEN/CLOSE/READ/WRITE). There is a statement that evaluates numeric and string expressions (IF/THEN/ELSE/ENDIF) and performs different clauses based on the result of the expression. There are several methods used to transfer control to and from statements in a command procedure (GOTO, GOSUB, CALL, RETURN, EXIT) and several techniques used to trap and handle error conditions (ON WARNING, ON ERROR). The HELP utility contains information on all these control statements (*i.e.*, HELP IF or HELP OPEN).

Lexical functions — F$ functions like F$MODE— provide easy access to system services for date and time functions, string manipulation, locating files and parsing file names, and querying the personal or system environment. See HELP for a complete description of the lexical functions and examples of how they are used. A full discussion of the features available in command procedures is beyond the scope of this book. For additional information see Volume 3 of the VMS General User documentation, specifically the section titled *Guide to Writing Command Procedures*.

PERSONALIZING EXERCISES

1. Enter the DEFINE/KEY commands for PF1 through PF4 shown in Figure 16-6.

```
$ DEFINE/KEY/TERM KP1  MAIL
%DCL-I-DEFKEY, DEFAULT key KP1 has been defined
$ DEFINE/KEY/TERM KP2  DIR
%DCL-I-DEFKEY, DEFAULT key KP2 has been defined
$ DEFINE/KEY/TERM KP3  "SHOW USERS"
%DCL-I-DEFKEY, DEFAULT key KP3 has been defined
$ DEFINE/KEY/TERM KP4  "SHOW DEF"
%DCL-I-DEFKEY, DEFAULT key KP4 has been defined
```

2. Use SHOW KEY to examine the definitions and try each key to make sure it works. Delete all the definitions when you are done. SHOW KEY accepts a key name as a parameter or the /ALL qualifier. Try it both ways.

```
$ SHOW KEY KP1
DEFAULT keypad definitions:
  KP1 = "MAIL"
$ SHOW KEY/ALL
DEFAULT keypad definitions:
  KP1 = "MAIL"
  KP2 = "DIR"
  KP3 = "SHOW USERS"
  KP4 = "SHOW DEF"
```

3. Delete key definitions KP1 through KP4. DELETE/KEY accepts a key name as a parameter or the /ALL qualifier. Try it both ways.

```
$ DELETE/KEY KP1
%DCL-I-DELKEY, DEFAULT key KP1 has been deleted
$ DELETE/KEY/ALL
%DCL-I-DELKEY, DEFAULT key KP2 has been deleted
%DCL-I-DELKEY, DEFAULT key KP3 has been deleted
%DCL-I-DELKEY, DEFAULT key KP4 has been deleted
```

4. Look at all the global symbols defined for you by the system login file with the command SHOW SYMBOL/GLOBAL/ALL. Which symbols are used for VMS command abbreviations?   Which symbols start a command procedure and which run programs? How can you tell?

```
Symbols that are command abbreviations equate to complete VMS commands. Sym-
bols that start command procedures have an at sign (@) as the first charac-
ter after the equal sign. Symbols that run programs have either a dollar
sign ($) or the RUN command immediately after the equal sign.

$ SHOW SYMBOL/GLOBAL/ALL
$RESTART == "FALSE"                         [Process specific symbols]
$SEVERITY == "0"
$STATUS == "%X00000001"
```

```
DTR == "@USERD:[UTILITIES.COMMANDS]DTR.COM"   [Command procedure]
GETMAIL == "@LIBRARY:[MIS_UTILS.MISC.COMS]GETMAIL"
GO == "@LIBRARY:[MIS_UTILS.WHO.COMS]GO.COM"
HOME == "SET DEF SYS$LOGIN"                   [Command synonym]
LOCH*AR == "SET TERM/LOWERCASE"               [Command synonym]
MAIL == "MAIL/EDIT=(SEND,REPLY)"
REMIND*ER == "$USERD:[UTILS.REMIND]REMINDER" [Start a program]
RESET == "@USERD:[UTILS.COMMANDS]RESET.COM"  [Command procedure]
ROT == "@USERD:[UTILS.COMMANDS]ROTATE.COM"
WHERE == "SHO LOG SYS$NODE"                   [Command synonym]
WHO == "@LIBRARY:[MIS_UTILS.WHO.COMS]WHO"    [Command procedure]
```

5. Delete one of the global symbols and examine the definition to make sure it is gone. Pick a symbol that you are unlikely to use during the current session.

```
$ DELETE/SYMBOL/GLOBAL ROT
$ SHOW SYMBOL ROT
%DCL-W-UNDSYM, undefined symbol - check validity and spelling
```

6. Create symbols at the system prompt to move to the different directories in the music tree created in the exercises in Chapter 9. Have the BACH symbol set your default to BACH, HAYDN to HAYDN and so on. Should you use a single or double equal sign and why? Then try one or two of the symbols. Do they work?

```
At the system prompt, it doesn't make any difference. The double equal sign
is necessary only when you define symbols from within a command procedure
and you want to use the symbols after the command procedure terminates.
```

```
$ MUSIC   = "SET DEFAULT USERD:[VMSWIZ.MUSIC]"
$ BACH    = "SET DEFAULT USERD:[VMSWIZ.MUSIC.BACH]"
$ HAYDN   = "SET DEFAULT USERD:[VMSWIZ.MUSIC.HAYDN]"
$ MOZART  = "SET DEFAULT USERD:[VMSWIZ.MUSIC.MOZART]"
$ MUSIC
$ SHOW DEF
  USERD:[VMSWIZ.MUSIC]
$ BACH
$ SHOW DEF
  USERD:[MIS.VMSWIZ.MUSIC.BACH]
```

7. When you create the symbol definitions, you can use either an absolute or relative directory specification. How is a symbol you create with an absolute directory spec different from one you create with a relative directory spec?

```
The absolute form moves you to the target directory regardless of your cur-
rent location. The relative form only works if you are in a directory imme-
diately above the target directory. Likewise, if you create a symbol to run
a program, you should use an absolute file specification. The  you can
start the program regardless of your current location.
```

```
$ MUSIC = "SET DEFAULT USERD:[VMSWIZ.MUSIC]"    Absolute directory spec
$ MUSIC = "SET DEFAULT [.MUSIC]"                Relative directory spec
```

8. Look at your process logical names. Does the display on your system look similar to the one in Figure 16-6? What are the equivalence names for SYS$INPUT, SYS$OUTPUT, and SYS$ERROR? Have you used a command that redirects any of these logical names?

Each time you use a VMS command with the /OUTPUT= qualifier you are redirecting SYS$OUTPUT to the file spec you include with this qualifier.

```
$ SHOW LOGICAL/PROCESS
(LNM$PROCESS_TABLE)

"SYS$COMMAND" = "_SYBIL$VTA5917:"
"SYS$DISK" = "USERD:"
"SYS$ERROR" = "_SYBIL$VTA5917:"
"SYS$INPUT" = "_SYBIL$VTA5917:"
"SYS$OUTPUT" [super] = "_SYBIL$VTA5917:"
"SYS$OUTPUT" [exec] = "_SYBIL$VTA5917:"
"TT" = "VTA5917:"
```

9. Look at your job logical names. What are the equivalence names for SYS$LOGIN, SYS$LOGIN_DIRECTORY, and SYS$DISK? How might you use one or more of these logical names?

```
$ SHOW LOGICAL/JOB

(LNM$JOB_8149D100)

"SYS$LOGIN" = "USERD:[VMSWIZ]"
"SYS$LOGIN_DEVICE" = "USERD:"
"SYS$SCRATCH" = "USERD:[VMSWIZ]"
```

You can use SYS$LOGIN as part of a symbol definition to return to your home directory from any location. You might use SYS$SCRATCH as a directory specification for temporary files created by either a command procedure or a program.

10. How many systemwide logical names that start with SYS$ are defined? These logicals locate various parts of VMS.

Notice the SHOW LOGICAL command uses the asterisk wildcard to examine all names that start with the string SYS$. Many of the intervening names have been omitted to reduce the size of this list.

```
$ SHO LOG/SYS SYS$*
(LNM$SYSTEM_TABLE)

"SYS$ANNOUNCE" = "@utilitiesroot:[news]SYBILann.txt"    [Login message]
"SYS$BATCH" = "SYBILBATCH"                               [System batch queue]
"SYS$COMMON" = "$1$DUS72:[SYS0.SYSCOMMON.]"             [Common system files]
"SYS$DISK" = "$1$DUS72:"                                 [System disk]
...
```

```
"SYS$EXAMPLES" = "SYS$SYSROOT:[SYSHLP.EXAMPLES]"        [VMS example files]
"SYS$HELP" = "SYS$SYSROOT:[SYSHLP]"                     [VMS HELP files]
"SYS$INSTRUCTION" = "SYS$SYSROOT:[SYSCBI]"              [Course instruction]
"SYS$LANGUAGE" = "ENGLISH"                              [Language spoken]
"SYS$LIBRARY" = "SYS$SYSROOT:[SYSLIB]"                  [VMS library files]
...
"SYS$MANAGER" = "SYS$SYSROOT:[SYSMGR]"                  [System manager dir]
"SYS$MESSAGE" = "SYS$SYSROOT:[SYSMSG]"                  [System message dir]
"SYS$MONITOR" = "$1$DUA11:[SITEMGR.MONITOR]"            [System monitor files]
"SYS$NODE" = "SYBIL::"                                  [Network node name]
"SYS$PRINT" = "CLUSTERPRINT"                            [System print queue]
"SYS$SHARE" = "SYS$SYSROOT:[SYSLIB]"                    [Shared images]
"SYS$STARTUP" = "SYS$SYSROOT:[SYS$STARTUP]"             [System startup dir]
        = "SYS$MANAGER"
"SYS$SYLOGIN" = "SYS$MANAGER:SYLOGIN.COM"               [System login file]
...
"SYS$SYSROOT" = "$1$DUS72:[SYS0.]"                      [Top of VMS tree]
        = "SYS$COMMON:"
"SYS$SYSTEM" = "SYS$SYSROOT:[SYSEXE]"                   [VMS images]
        = "SYS$SYSROOT:[001054]"
"SYS$TEST" = "SYS$SYSROOT:[SYSTEST]"                    [Field service dir]
"SYS$TOPSYS" = "SYS0"                                   [Top of VMS tree]
"SYS$UPDATE" = "SYS$SYSROOT:[SYSUPD]"                   [System update dir]
```

11. Define one logical name for each directory path in the MUSIC tree. Use two or three of these logicals with SET DEFAULT and check your location afterwards with SHOW DEFAULT. In these definitions, you have a choice between an absolute and relative directory specification and, as before, the absolute form is best.

```
Each logical name now equates to a specific directory location that can be
used as a target for many VMS commands. You can also use these logical
names as part of a file specification. For example, to create a file in the
music directory, you might use the file specification MUSIC:COMPOSERS.LIS
```

```
$ DEFINE MUSIC USERD:[VMSWIZ.MUSIC]
$ SHO LOG MUSIC
  "MUSIC" = "USERD:[VMSWIZ.MUSIC]" (LNM$PROCESS_TABLE)
$ DEFINE BACH USERD:[VMSWIZ.MUSIC.BACH]
$ DEFINE HAYDN USERD:[VMSWIZ.MUSIC.HAYDN]
$ DEFINE MOZART USERD:[VMSWIZ.MUSIC.MOZART]
$ SET DEFAULT BACH
$ SHO DEF
  USERD:[VMSWIZ.MUSIC.BACH]
```

12. What is the difference between using MUSIC as a symbol and as a logical name?

```
You have defined a symbol called music and a logical name called music. You
can examine the definition of each using SHOW SYMBOL and SHOW LOGICAL
respectively. The symbol is a complete VMS command that moves you to the
MUSIC directory and has no other use. Because the logical name music is a
shorthand name for the music directory itself, it can be used as a direc-
```

tory specification or as part of a file specification with many different
VMS commands. The logical name is much more versatile and can be used in
many different ways whenever a directory specification is required.

```
$ SHOW SYMBOL MUSIC                               [Display definition]
  "MUSIC" == "SET DEFAULT USERD:[VMSWIZ.MUSIC]"
$ MUSIC                                           [Use the symbol]
$ SHOW DEFAULT                                    [Examine default dir]
  USERD:[VMSWIZ.MUSIC]                            [Music directory]

$ SHOW LOGICAL MUSIC                              [Display definition]
  "MUSIC" = "USERD:[VMSWIZ.MUSIC]" (LNM$PROCESS_TABLE)
$ SET DEFAULT MUSIC                               [Use the logical name]
$ SHOW DEFAULT                                    [Examine default dir]
  USERD:[VMSWIZ.MUSIC]
$ CREATE MUSIC:TEST                               [Logical as a directory]
12345                                             [Create file called TEST]
CTRL/Z                                            [Terminate file input]
$ DIR MUSIC:TEST                                  [Logical as a directory]

USERD:[VMSWIZ.MUSIC]                              [To find the new file]

TEST.;1

Total of 1 file
```

13. Create a LOGIN.COM file using the EVE editor. Enter all but the last two lines
    in the example LOGIN.COM file in Figure 16-25. If you are not using a VT300,
    change the SET TERMINAL/DEVICE command to use your terminal type.

```
$ EDIT/TPU LOGIN.COM
[End of File]

$ IF F$MODE() .EQS. "BATCH" THEN EXIT      ! Exit if Batch Mode
$ SET TERM/DEVICE=VT300                     ! VT300 Terminal
$ SET PROCESS/NAME = "fire fighter"         ! Set process name
$ !
$ home      == "SET DEFAULT SYS$LOGIN"      ! Symbol Definitions
$ up        == "SET DEFAULT [-]"            ! for VMS commands
$ sd        == "SET DEFAULT"
$ shd       == "SHOW DEFAULT"
$ mail      == "MAIL/EDIT=(SEND,REPLY)"
$ pg        == "PURGE/LOG"
$ w80       == "SET TERM/WIDTH=80"
$ w132      == "SET TERM/WIDTH=132"
$ eve       == "EDIT/TPU"
$ exit

14 lines written to SYS$UTIL:[SHARICK]LOGIN.COM;1
```

14. Execute the LOGIN file to activate the definitions. If you didn't get any error
    messages, skip to number 11.

```
$ @LOGIN                                    [Perform the login file]
$                                           [No error messages]
```

15. If you did see one or more messages, identify your mistakes by turning on verify, and executing the procedure again. Correct the mistakes with an editor and try it again. Continue this cycle until you have no more messages. Then turn off verify.

```
$ SET VERIFY
$ @LOGIN
$ IF F$MODE().EQS. "BATCH" THEN EXIT
$ ....
$ SET NOVERIFY
```

16. Look at the symbols defined in this procedure. Are they all there? If not, check to see that you used == in each definition. No error messages is not a guarantee that every line in your login file worked. Check each symbol explicitly.

```
$ SHOW SYMBOL HOME
  "HOME" = "SET DEFAULT SYS$LOGIN"
$ SHOW SYMBOL SD
  "SD" = "SET DEFAULT"
$ SHOW SYMBOL UP
  "UP" = "SET DEFAULT [-]"
$ SHOW SYMBOL MAIL
  "MAIL" = "MAIL/EDIT=(SEND,REPLY)"
$ SHOW SYMBOL W80
  "W80" = "SET TERM/WIDTH = 80"
$ SHOW SYMBOL W132
  "W132" = "SET TERM/WIDTH = 132"
$ SHOW SYMBOL EVE
  "EVE" = "EDIT/TPU"
```

17. Add the key definitions created in the first exercise to your login file. Use the EVE symbol to start the editor this time, enter the key definitions, and save a new version of the file. Execute the login file again to activate the new commands and examine the key definitions to make sure they are correct.

```
$ EVE LOGIN.COM
$ DEFINE/KEY/TERM KP1  MAIL                 [Add to the login file]
$ DEFINE/KEY/TERM KP2  DIR
$ DEFINE/KEY/TERM KP3  "SHOW USERS"
$ DEFINE/KEY/TERM KP4  "SHOW DEF"
18 lines written to SYS$UTIL:[SHARICK]LOGIN.COM;2

$ @LOGIN                                    [Perform the login file]
$ SHOW KEY/ALL                              [Check key definitions]
DEFAULT keypad definitions:
  KP1 = "MAIL"
  KP2 = "DIR"
  KP3 = "SHOW USERS"
  KP4 = "SHOW DEF"
```

Appendix A: Command Summary Tables

Commonly used commands are collected in these summary tables. There are many more sophisticated commands available in each category. As you acquire skills, you will expand your repertoire. Use the HELP utility to obtain information on the more advanced commands.

```
Server Command              Function
-----------------------------------------------------------
HELP                        List all server commands

SHOW Server                 List server name and characteristics
SHOW Nodes                  List all reachable nodes
SHOW Services               List available applications and nodes
SHOW Sessions               List all sessions for this user
SHOW Users                  List all users on this server
SHOW Port                   List port characteristics

Connect                     Start a session to requested service
Disconnect Session n        Abort session number n

Resume                      Resume current session
Forward                     Resume next session
Backward                    Resume previous session

Lock                        Secure your terminal
Logout                      Terminate server activity
```

Table A-1. DECserver 200 Commands

SHOW Option	Function
Broadcast	Message types enabled
Cluster	All cluster nodes
Default	Current device and directory
Device	One or all system devices
Entry	Print or batch jobs queued
Key	One or all key definitions
Logical	Equivalence name
Memory	Physical memory and usage information
Network	All network nodes
Process	Process characteristics
Protection	Default protection mask
Queue	Queue names and characteristics
Queue/Form	List predefined print forms
Symbol	Equivalent string
System	System processes
Terminal	Terminal characteristics
Time	Current date and time
Users	All system users

Table A-2. SHOW Commands

SET Option	Function
Broadcast	Enable/disable message types
Control	Enable/disable CTRL/Y and CTRL/T
Default	Change device and/or directory
Directory	Modify directory attributes
Entry	Modify print/batch job characteristics
File	Modify file attributes
Host	Initiate a remote login
Password	Change password
Process/name	Change process name
Prompt	Change system prompt
Protection	Change file protection
Terminal	Control terminal characteristics
Verify	Enable/disable command procedure echo

Table A-3. SET Commands

```
File specification:
Node::Device:[Directory]Name.Type;Version
Network file specification:
Node"username password"::Device:[Directory]Name.Type;Version


Command                    Function
-----------------------------------------------------------------
@                          Execute a command procedure
Append                     Add to the end of an existing file
Copy                       Duplicate a file
Create                     Make a file at the system prompt
Create/DIR                 Make a directory file
Delete                     Delete a file
Edit/TPU                   Create/modify a file using EVE editor
Print                      Print a file
Purge                      Remove lower versions of a file
Rename                     Change file name
Run                        Start a  program interactively
Spawn                      Create a subprocess
Submit                     Start a  batch program
Type                       Display a file
```

Table A-4. File Manipulation Commands

```
Command                    Function
-----------------------------------------------------------------
Create/Name_Table          Create a logical name table
Deassign                   Delete a logical name
Define                     Create a logical name
Delete/entry               Delete a print/batch job from a queue
Delete/key                 Delete a key definition
Delete/symbol              Delete a symbol definition
Differences                Compare one file to another
Help                       Access online documentation
Logout                     Terminate a VAX session
Mail                       Start electronic MAIL
Merge                      Start the MERGE utility
Phone                      Start electronic PHONE
Recall                     Retrieve a previous command
Search                     Search a file for a string of text
Sort                       Start the SORT utility
```

Table A-5. Additional Utilities and Commands

```
$ MAIL/EDIT=(SEND,REPLY,FORWARD)        Start MAIL with editor selected
                                        by SET EDITOR command


  HELP                          Full documentation on MAIL commands

  READ                          Read the next message
  READ nn                       Read message number nn
    /NEW                        Read a message that just arrived
  FIRST                         Read first message in folder
  LAST                          Read last message in folder
  NEXT                          Read next message in folder
  BACK                          Read previous message in folder

  SEND                          Send a message
  SEND file-spec                Send a file
  SEND/LAST                     Send last message to someone else

  FORWARD                       Send current message to someone else

  ANSWER                        Respond to a message
  REPLY                         Equivalent command
    /CC                         Send a copy to another user
    /EDIT                       Edit message text before sending
    /SELF                       Copy yourself on the reply
    /EXTRACT                    Edit message with header

  DELETE                        Delete the current message
  DELETE nn                     Delete message number nn
    /ALL                        Delete all messages in folder

  PRINT                         Print current message
  EXTRACT                       Place current message in a VMS file
  SEARCH string                 Search message text for string
  COMPRESS                      Reorganize mail file

  PURGE                         Remove deleted messages
  SPAWN                         Start a DCL subprocess
  EXIT or CTRL/Z                Leave the MAIL utility
```

Table A-6. MAIL Commands

```
DIRECTORY                    List messages in current folder
DIR/NEW                      List new (unread) messages

DIR/FOLDER                   List all Mail folders
DIR folder-name              List messages in this folder

MOVE                         Create new folder or move a message
FILE                         to a folder

SELECT folder                Change folders
  /BEFORE = date/time        Select messages before date/time
  /CC = string               Select messages by /CC field
  /FROM = string             Select messages by /FROM field
  /NEW                       Select NEWMAIL folder
  /SINCE = date/time         Select messages since date/time
  /SUBJ = string             Select messages by /SUBJ field
  /TO = string               Select messages by /TO field

SET                          Define MAIL defaults
  CC_PROMPT                  Enable CC_PROMPT for all messages
  COPY_SELF                  Send yourself a copy of everything
  EDITOR EDT                 Use EDT for editing
  EDITOR TPU                 Use EVE for editing
  FOLDER                     Change to this folder
  FORM                       Select a print form
  NOEDITOR                   Use EDT default editor
  PERSONAL_NAME              Select a personal name
  QUEUE                      Select a print queue

SHOW                         Examine MAIL defaults
  ALL                        Look at everything
  CC_PROMPT                  CC_PROMPT status
  COPY_SELF                  COPY_SELF status
  DELETED                    Space used by deleted messages
  EDITOR                     Active MAIL editor
  FOLDER                     Current folder
  FORM                       Selected form
  PERSONAL_NAME              Personal name string
  QUEUE                      Selected queue
```

Table A-6. MAIL Commands *(continued)*

List Of Topics (Commands)

For help on EVE topics, type the name of a topic and press RETURN.

   o   For a keypad diagram, press HELP.
   o   For help on VAXTPU builtins, type TPU and press RETURN.
   o   To exit from help and resume editing, press RETURN.

EDITING TEXT

Change Mode	Erase Word	Restore Character
Copy	Insert Here	Restore Line
Cut	Insert Mode	Restore Selection
Delete	Overstrike Mode	Restore Sentence
Erase Character	Paste	Restore Word
Erase Line	Quote	Select
Erase Previous Word	Remove	Select All
Erase Start Of Line	Restore	Store Text

SEARCHES

Find	Set Find Case Noexact	Set Wildcard VMS
Find Next	Set Find Nowhitespace	Show Wildcards
Find Selected	Set Find Whitespace	Spell
Replace	Set Wildcard Ultrix	Wildcard Find
Set Find Case Exact		

CURSOR MOVEMENT AND SCROLLING

Bottom	Mark	Move Right	Set Cursor Free
Change Direction	Move By Line	Move Up	Set Scroll Margins
End Of Line	Move By Page	Next Screen	Start Of Line
Forward	Move By Word	Previous Screen	Top
Go To	Move Down	Reverse	What Line
Line	Move Left	Set Cursor Bound	

GENERAL-PURPOSE COMMANDS

Attach	Do	Help	Recall	Reset	Show	Tab
DCL	Exit	Quit	Repeat	Return	Spawn	

FILES AND BUFFERS

Buffer	Open Selected	Set Journaling
Delete Buffer	Previous Buffer	Set Journaling All
Get File	Recover Buffer	Set Nojournaling
Include File	Recover Buffer All	Set Nojournaling All
New	Save File	Show Buffers
Next Buffer	Save File As	Show System Buffers
Open	Set Buffer	Write File

Table A-7. EVE Commands

WINDOWS AND DISPLAY

Delete Window	One Window	Set Width	Shrink Window
Enlarge Window	Previous Window	Shift Left	Split Window
Next Window	Refresh	Shift Right	Two Windows

FORMATTING AND CASE CHANGES

Capitalize Word	Insert Page Break	Set Paragraph Indent
Center Line	Lowercase Word	Set Right Margin
Fill	Paginate	Set Tabs
Fill Paragraph	Set Left Margin	Set Wrap
Fill Range	Set Nowrap	Uppercase Word

KEY DEFINITIONS

Define Key	Set Gold Key	Set Keypad VT100
Learn	Set Keypad EDT	Set Keypad WPS
Remember	Set Keypad NoEDT	Set Nogold Key
Set Func Key DECwindows	Set Keypad NoWPS	Show Key
Set Func Key NoDECwindows	Set Keypad Numeric	Undefine Key

CUSTOMIZING

@	Set Noclipboard
Define Menu Entry	Set Nodefault Command File
Extend All	Set Nodefault Section File
Extend EVE	Set Noexit Attribute Check
Extend This	Set Nopending Delete
Save Attributes	Set Nosection File Prompting
Save Extended EVE	Set Pending Delete
Save System Attributes	Set Section File Prompting
Set Clipboard	Show Defaults Buffer
Set Default Command File	Show Summary
Set Default Section File	TPU
Set Exit Attribute Check	Undefine Menu Entry

INFORMATIONAL TOPICS

Abbreviating	EDT Differences	New Features
About	Gold Keys	New User
Attributes	Initialization Files	Position Cursor
Canceling Commands	Journal Files	Prompts And Responses
Choices Buffer	Keypad (diagram)	Quick Copy
Command Files	Keys (list)	Ruler Keys
Control Keys	List Of Topics	Scroll Bars
DECwindows Differences	Mail Editing	Section Files
Defaults	Menus	Status Line
Dialog Boxes	Message Buffer	Typing Keys
Editing Command Lines	Mouse	Windows
EDT Conversion	Names For Keys	WPS Differences

Table A-7. EVE Commands *(continued)*

Appendix B: Common Error Messages

Command, Parameter, and Qualifier Messages

Command: $ DOR
Message: %DCL-W-IVVERB, unrecognized command verb - check validity and spelling
        \DOR\
Reason: You misspelled a DCL command or did not put a space between the command and the parameter. Check the text between the backslashes to see what you typed incorrectly.

Command: $ SHOW USRRS
Message: %DCL-W-IVKEYW, unrecognized keyword - check validity and spelling
        \USRRS\
Reason: You misspelled a SHOW option or other command keyword.

Command: $ REN TEST.DAT TEMP.DAT
Message: %DCL-W-ABVERB, ambiguous command verb - supply more characters
        \REN\
Reason: You did not enter enough characters to uniquely identify a command or qualifier.

Command: $ DIR/TEMP.DAT
Message: %DCL-W-IVQUAL, unrecognized qualifier - check validity, spelling, and placement
        \TEMP.DAT\
Reason: You put a slash in the wrong place, misspelled a qualifier or put a command qualifier on a parameter or vice versa.

Command: $ SET PROCESS/NAME
Message: %DCL-W-VALREQ, missing qualifier or keyword value - supply all required values
        \NAME\
Reason: You did not specify a process name as a value with the /NAME qualifier. This message appears whenever you forget to enter a qualifier value and there is no default provided by the command.

Command: $ DIR/MODIFIED
Message: %CLI-F-QUALMISS,/BEFORE or /SINCE missing from command line.
Reason: You need to add /BEFORE or /SINCE when you select a file using any of the dates in the file header.

Command: $ DELETE LOGIN.COM
Message: %DELETE-E-DELVER, explicit version number or wild card required
Reason: You must provide a file version number when deleting a file. Add a semicolon alone (;) selects the most recent version. Use the semincolon and a version number to delete a specific file (;3).

Problems with Spaces

Command: $ RENAME TEST .DAT TEMP.DAT
Message: %DCL-W-MAXPARM, too many parameters - reenter command with fewer parameters
         \TEMP.DAT\
Reason: You have extra spaces in a file name or other parameter, which turns one parameter into two, two parameters into three, and so on.Here, TEST is one parameter, .DAT is the second, and TEMP.DAT is the third. RENAME accepts only two parameters.

Command: $ DIR[ADMIN]
Message: %DCL-W-UNDSYM, undefined symbol - check validity and spelling
Reason: You are missing a space between the command and parameter. Because NAME[M:N] is a legitimate symbol notation, the command interpreter thinks ADMIN is a symbol and expects it to have a numeric value.

Command: $ DIR[.ADMIN]
Message: %DCL-W-IVOPER, unrecognized operator in expression - check spelling and syntax
         \.ADMIN\
Reason: You are missing a space between the command and parameter. Here again the CLI is interpreting the string as a symbol. Because of the period, the CLI expects an expression. This message is not straightforward.

Command: $ DIR {ADMIN]
Message: %DCL-W-PARMDEL, invalid parameter delimiter, check use of special characters
         \]\
Reason: You must enclose a directory name in square brackets.

File Not Found Messages

Command: $ TYPE MESSAGE.TXT
Message: %TYPE-W-SEARCHFAIL, error searching for SYS$UTIL:[PAUSHA]MESSAGE.TXT;
         -RMS-E-FNF, file not found
Reason: The file you asked for does not exist or you misspelled the file name. The first message is sent by TYPE, the second by RMS

Command: $ DIR [.ADMIN]
Message: %DIRECT-E-OPENIN, error opening SYS$UTIL:[PAUSHA.ADMIN]*.*;* as input
         -RMS-E-DNF, directory not found
         -SYSTEM-W-NOSUCHFILE, no such file

Reason: You specified a directory that does not exist or you misspelled the directory name. This error rates three messages from the system. The first comes from the command that encountered the error, the second from RMS for the directory error, and the third from the system for the file error (which the DIRECTORY command defaults to *.*;*).

File Protection Violation and Privilege Messages

Command: $ CREATE/DIR [FARM]
Message: %CREATE-E-DIRNOTCRE, [FARM] directory file not created
              -SYSTEM-F-NOPRIV, no privilege for attempted operation
Reason: You are trying to create a directory at the same level as your home directory. Most users do not have the privileges for this operation. If you want to create a directory below your home directory, place a period in front of the directory name.

Command: $ DIR [MILLER]
Message: %DIRECT-E-OPENIN, error opening USERB:[MILLER]*.*;* as input
              -RMS-E-PRV, insufficient privilege or file protection violation
Reason: The protection on this directory prohibits access for your UIC. The owner of the directory must change the protection before you can access the files stored there.

Command: $ DELETE ADMIN.DIR;
Message: %DELETE-W-FILNOTDEL, error deleting USERB:[PAUSHA]ADMIN.DIR:1
              -RMS-E-PRV, insufficient privilege or file protection violation
Reason: The directory protection code does not permit owner delete access. You are not allowed to delete directories that do not belong to you.

Symbol and Logical Name Messages

Command: $ SHOW LOGICAL ADMIN
Message: %SHOW-S-NOTRAN, no translation for logical name ADMIN
Reason: ADMIN is misspelled, not defined or is not defined as a process logical name. Perhaps it is a job or group logical name, so add /JOB or /GROUP to the command.

Command: $ DEASSIGN ADMIN
Message: %SYSTEM-F-LOGNAM, no logical name match
Reason: ADMIN is misspelled, not defined ,or is not defined as a process logical. You may need to add /JOB or /GROUP to the command.

Command: $ SHOW SYMBOL MUSIC
Message: %DCL-W-UNDSYM, undefined symbol, check validity and spelling
Reason: MUSIC is misspelled, not defined, or is defined as a global symbol. Both SHOW SYMBOL and DELETE SYMBOL expect a local symbol. You may need to add /GLOBAL to the command.

Index